"As a hospitality and culinary educator, it's great to see a book that is focused on the specific needs of our industry, rather than one that uses generic scenarios. The vignette approach allows for the discussion of relevant cases, rather than just stating theory. A welcome addition to the limited body of knowledge related to human resources in the hospitality industry."

Samuel Glass M.Ed., CEC, CCE, AAC,
School of Hospitality, Tourism and Culinary Arts, Canada

"A timely book that focused on applied skills needed to address today's complex issues within the hospitality and tourism industry. The "Think Point" sections highlight authentic hospitality and tourism examples and/or cases to challenge students to think critically and creatively. Students will be motivated to use complex leadership behaviors to demonstrate a mastery of knowledge and key concepts. Future hospitality leaders will be made from the exposure of this textbook."

James Arthur Williams PhD,
University of Tennessee, USA

"Hospitality leaders know the greatest challenge the industry faces is in human resources, including talent acquisition, management, and retention. The need to ensure Hospitality Management graduates attain the skills and knowledge required to manage human resources is high. This is an overdue teaching resource that will improve instruction – providing real-life cases students need to solidify understanding and strengthen management skills."

James Griffin Ed.D.,
College of Hospitality Management, Johnson & Wales University, USA

Human Resource Management in Hospitality Cases

Human Resource Management in Hospitality Cases adopts a practical case-based approach to develop critical thinking and problem-solving skills in future hospitality managers. Using tried-and-tested real-life scenarios, this book thoroughly prepares hospitality students for a career in the field.

Chapters are comprised of 75 short vignettes, split into nine sections that reflect and cover the primary challenges facing hospitality managers on a daily basis, including leadership credibility, building and managing employee performance, managing a diverse workforce, dealing with problem behaviors, and many others, all contextualized within the hospitality industry. With a main "think point" and series of questions for each case, the book is a highly insightful and engaging read. Suggested answers and solutions to the questions can be found within the extensive online resources that complement the book. Each section is also contextualized and theorized with an additional reading section, organized by key concept.

This book will be essential for all students of hospitality and an invaluable resource for current practitioners in the field as well.

Peter Szende has over 25 years of management experience in the hospitality industry in both Europe and North America. He joined Boston University's School of Hospitality Administration as a faculty member in 2003. Between 2016–2019, he served as the associate dean of academic affairs at Boston University. Currently, Peter is programme lead in hospitality management at Oxford Brookes Business School in the UK. Dr. Szende received a Fulbright U.S. Scholar Grant in 2014.

Suzanne Markham Bagnera has over 20 years of hospitality management experience followed by over 15 years of higher education experience. She joined the faculty at Boston University, School of Hospitality Administration in 2015. In 2019, she was promoted to chair of undergraduate programs and is presently ranked as a clinical assistant professor. Dr. Bagnera received the Lamp of Knowledge Award for being an Outstanding US Educator in 2016 from the American Hotel Lodging Educational Institute.

Danielle Clark Cole is the director of human resources at Trillium Brewing Company in Boston. She is a graduate of the Boston University School of Hospitality Administration and has human resources leadership experience in both Massachusetts and Hawaii at both union and non-union properties.

Human Resource Management in Hospitality Cases

Peter Szende
Suzanne Markham Bagnera
Danielle Clark Cole

Routledge
Taylor & Francis Group

LONDON AND NEW YORK

First published 2020
by Routledge
2 Park Square, Milton Park, Abingdon, Oxon OX14 4RN

and by Routledge
52 Vanderbilt Avenue, New York, NY 10017

Routledge is an imprint of the Taylor & Francis Group, an informa business

British Library Cataloguing-in-Publication Data
A catalogue record for this book is available from the British Library

Library of Congress Cataloging-in-Publication Data
Names: Szende, Peter, author. | Bagnera, Suzanne Markham, author. | Cole,
    Danielle Clark, author.
Title: Human resource management in hospitality cases / Peter Szende,
    Suzanne Markham Bagnera, and Danielle Clark Cole.
Description: New York : Routledge, 2020. | Includes bibliographical
    references and index.
Identifiers: LCCN 2020005139 (print) | LCCN 2020005140 (ebook) |
    ISBN 9780815378013 (hardback) | ISBN 9780815378020 (paperback) |
    ISBN 9781351233316 (ebook)
Subjects: LCSH: Hospitality industry—Management—Case studies. | Critical
    thinking—Case studies. | Personnel management—Case studies.
Classification: LCC TX911.3.M27 S954 2020 (print) | LCC TX911.3.M27 (ebook) |
    DDC 338.4/791068—dc23
LC record available at https://lccn.loc.gov/2020005139
LC ebook record available at https://lccn.loc.gov/2020005140

ISBN: 978-0-8153-7801-3 (hbk)
ISBN: 978-0-8153-7802-0 (pbk)
ISBN: 978-1-351-23331-6 (ebk)

Typeset in Frutiger
by Apex CoVantage, LLC

Visit the eResources: www.routledge.com/9781351233316

Contents

Contents

Contents

Acknowledgements

The authors would like to acknowledge the supportive research services provided by several undergraduate student assistants. Beighley Berger and Jane Hwang are students in the undergraduate program in the School of Hospitality Administration at Boston University. Beighley and Jane are both scheduled to graduate in May 2021. The immense value and technical support to update the manuscript with additional resources is most appreciated.

Introduction

The case method is proving itself to be a very effective tool in hospitality programs. Case studies give students the opportunity to develop problem-solving skills and to think critically. They will allow students to explore contrary points of view relative to a variety of questions.

In 2010, Peter Szende published a book that included cases depicting real-life managerial dilemmas, titled *Case Scenarios in Hospitality Supervision* by Delmar-Cengage Learning. Given the constant changes in the field of human resources management and to ensure that the book content would be relevant and include the most updated information, Peter Szende teamed up with Suzanne Markham Bagnera and Danielle Clark Cole to carefully revise and modernize the cases.

In this case collection, we present scenarios, most requiring management decisions or actions. Although most of the cases are very short, they are challenging without being overwhelming. Many of the cases are based on actual business situations we personally encountered throughout our hospitality career. The cases have been tested in the classroom at Boston University School of Hospitality Administration.

The 75 vignettes are organized into nine sections that reflect human resources-related challenges that are pertinent for hospitality managers. A correlation table shows the connection between cases and covered subjects. Topics include many of the issues a supervisor is confronted with on a daily basis. The skills and competencies necessary to deal with these problems are discussed throughout this book.

The cases may be used to stimulate class discussion or introduce students to HR management topics. Each case concludes with a list of questions for the students to answer concerning the scenarios they are given. The book can complement any hospitality management curriculum (including human resources management, supervision, leadership, and organizational behavior) and will reinforce theories and concepts that students study throughout the course.

This text is accompanied by a robust instructor's manual containing detailed exploration of each case with suggested answers and solutions to the questions.

Case presentation styles

The book is structured using specific case presentation styles. A variety of case types that differ according to format and/or intended learning outcomes exist (Lundberg, Rainsford, Shay, & Young, 2001). Thus, these cases are written in a variety of presentation styles. This range in case presentation makes the cases more appealing for the students and illustrates that the daily challenges of hotel life can be reflected in a number of forms. The five case presentation styles used are as follows:

1 Incident cases

The case often describes a single incident in somewhat specific detail, circumscribed by time and place. The student's task is to compare the incident with either generally accepted practices or his or her own experience. Issues of problem identification are addressed. Students may be asked to determine what additional information is necessary or helpful and to surmise how the organizational context of the incident would impact the situation.

2 Head cases

In this type of case, one or more principal actors' interactions, activities, thoughts, and feelings are described. The student's task is to surface the assumptions, reasoning, attitudes, or needs to basically get inside the principal's head and see how these are manifested in patterned action and interaction.

3 Application cases

This type of case describes the application of a management technique or describes a situation in which the student can apply some known technique. Such cases typically provide much information, but it may be highly unstructured. The student's task is to state how the manager performs the task and what the manager must consider to be more effective.

4 Data cases

The student's usual task is to find ideas in descriptions or to organize these data in some meaningful way. By doing this, students also learn to be better consumers of information.

5 Issue cases

In an issue case, a matter or point is in question (e.g., is the manager's behavior appropriate?). The student's task is to understand and appreciate the antecedents, contexts, and dynamics of the salient issue.

Note: The preceding classification is not exclusive; many of the cases embrace the characteristics of more than one case type.

Source: Journal of Management Education (1991) by Craig C. Lundberg, Peter Rainsford, Jeff P. Shay, Cheri A. Young, Copyright 2001 by Sage Publications Inc. Journals. Reproduced with permission of Sage Publications Inc. Journals in the format Textbook via Copyright Clearance Center.

Reference

Lundberg, C. C., Rainsford, P., Shay, J. P., & Young, C. A. (2001). Case writing reconsidered. *Journal of Management Education, 25*(4), 450–463.

How to use the cases

In the chapters that follow, various employee-related challenges will be presented as a case. Each case is designed to examine the various employee-related work issues that may arise in a hospitality operation. Each case will have a THINK POINT, where the various management challenges will be highlighted prior to the case example. This information will help to give the reader insight into a challenge from a management perspective. Then the small case scenario will be presented followed by a list of some potential questions to answer. At the conclusion of this part is an ADDITIONAL READING section, where context for each topical reference is provided with a citation and reference.

Key terms

Term	Defined	Found in part
Accepting criticism	The ability to be capable of receiving critical comments which may include severe judgment or faultfinding.	8
ADA	Americans with Disabilities Act of 1990, a form of legislation that prohibits discrimination against persons with disabilities; the law requires that reasonable accommodations are made to remove barriers to persons with disabilities in the workplace.	1, 3
Analytical	An individual skilled in or habitually using analysis.	5
Anger	Strong feeling of displeasure.	2, 6
Assertiveness	A sense of being self-assured or confidently aggressive by nature.	2, 7, 8
Authority	The individual who is the accepted source of information by possessing the rights and powers required to make decisions and be action oriented to get the job done.	1, 2, 3, 5, 7, 8

Term	Defined	Found in part
Bias	A tendency, inclination, feeling, or opinion, which is preconceived, unreasoned, or unsupported by evidence.	9
Big picture	A broad overall view or perspective of an issue or problem.	2, 5, 8
Bullying	To act in a manner that is loud, arrogant, and overbearing of others.	5
Buy-in	The act or instance of buying in or agreeing to a matter.	2, 7
Chain of command	A series of lines along which responsibility and authority are delegated, depicting who has direct and indirect authority over the person immediately below.	1, 3, 5, 7, 8
Change	To transform or redirect to the future course of (something) different from what is happening or what would happen if left alone.	2, 5, 7
Coaching	Instruction or advice that is presented to an individual in the form of corrective, on-the-job training that is focused on improving performance.	2, 3, 4, 5, 6, 8, 9
Controlling costs	A management function concerned with monitoring, measuring, and evaluating results to goals and standards previously agreed upon and taking corrective action when necessary to stay on course.	1, 7
Credibility	The quality of an individual to be believable or worthy of trust.	2, 7, 8
Decision-making	The skill that requires an act or logical process of making choices or decisions after identifying the causes and solutions to problems.	2, 5
Defensiveness	Being protective or appearing to act in a purposeful manner to resist an attack.	2, 6, 7
Delegation	Passing a portion of one's responsibilities and authority to a subordinate.	2, 8
Discipline	The system of rules and procedures for how and when punishment is administered and how severe the punishment should be.	6, 7
Discrimination	The act of making a distinction or providing special treatment or consideration in favor of or against a specific group, class, or category of individuals. Most commonly, it is connected with the Civil Rights Act of 1964, Title VII, an act that makes it unlawful to discriminate against applicants or employees on the basis of protected classes (i.e., race, color, religion, gender, or national origin).	1, 3, 9
Diversity	When the members in an organization differ from one another along one or more important dimensions.	1, 3, 9
Feedback	The process of providing evaluative information in response to a process or the performance of an individual or group back to them during or after the performance of a task or job.	2, 3, 4, 5, 6, 8, 9

Continued

Term	Defined	Found in part
Flexibility	Willingness to accept modification or adaptation, capable of being bent without breaking.	1, 2, 5, 7
Gossip	Idle talk, chatter, or rumor, especially about the personal or private affairs of others; can also be considered tattling.	5, 7
Hands-on	An individual who has active participation in an activity; requiring manual operation, control, or adjustment.	2
Harassment	Intimidating, hostile, offensive, or unwelcome behaviors toward someone or the creation of an offensive environment for someone based on gender, race, religion, national origin, age, and other protected characteristics by harassing, disturbing, pestering, or troubling repeatedly.	2, 5, 9
Humor/sarcasm	Humor: An instance of being or attempting to be comical or amusing in order to soothe or make content more agreeable. Sarcasm: Harsh or bitter comment that can be sharply ironic, sneering or a cutting remark.	2, 5
Incivility	Discourteous behavior or treatment.	2, 5
Influence	The capacity or power of a person or things to serve as a compelling force to produce certain actions, behaviors, opinions, and so on, of others.	2
Insubordination	Being disobedient to authority; defiance.	7, 9
Job description	A documented statement which indicates what the job entails. It includes the title and purpose of the job and a general overview of the tasks, duties, and responsibilities that a particular job entails, as well as the reporting relationship for an individual in the position.	1, 3, 4, 7, 9
Job design	The process of identifying how a job's characteristics (i.e., task organization, how and when tasks are done, factors that affect the work, the order of tasks to be completed, and the conditions under which tasks are completed) are experienced from the employee's perspective in order to enhance the individual's well-being and performance.	1, 3, 4, 7, 9
Leadership styles	The style of interaction a manager uses when directing subordinates.	2
Managing up	The pattern of interaction a lower-level manager or employee utilizes to manage or facilitate working most appropriately with the direct line supervisor above.	7, 8
Meetings	The act of coming together for a specific purpose.	2, 5
Micromanagement	The act of managing or controlling with excessive attention to minor details.	8

Term	Defined	Found in part
Motivation	An underlying reason that causes people to behave in certain ways. It can be at the heart of what causes an employee to choose to expend the effort that will support an organizational activity.	4, 8
Open-door policy	A policy whereby unrestricted admission or access to individuals in the organization is allowed and encouraged.	2, 7, 8
Organizational politics	The political methods, maneuvers, principles, or practice that is customarily found as unique ways of conducting business in an organization.	4, 5, 7, 8
Organizational structure	Often referred to as the organization chart; the diagram or structure of a company's organization depicting levels of management and lines by which authority and responsibility are exchanged.	1, 2, 4, 5, 7
Overtime	Hours worked above the normal 40-hour workweek, for which there is usually a pay premium, typically, time and a half.	7
Perfectionism	A personal standard, attitude, or philosophy which demands perfection and rejects anything less.	5, 8
Performance appraisal	The specific and formal evaluation of an employee to determine the degree to which the employee is performing his or her job effectively.	3, 5
Prejudice	A preconceived favorable or unfavorable opinion or feeling formed beforehand without knowledge, thought, or reason.	9
Productivity	An economic measure of efficiency that summarizes and reflects the value of the outputs created by an individual, organization, industry, or economic system relative to the value of the inputs used to create them.	3, 7
Promotion	The advancement of rank or position.	4, 8, 9
Rapport	A relation or connection that can be harmonious or sympathetic in nature.	2, 5, 6
Recruiting	The process of developing a pool of qualified applicants who are interested in working for the organization and from which the organization might reasonably select the best individual(s) to hire.	1, 5, 9
Religion	A specific fundamental set of beliefs and practices one believes in and follows devotedly, a point or matter of ethics or conscience.	3, 9
Respect	Esteem or a sense of worth or excellence of a person.	4, 5, 7, 9
Rewards	Something given or received in return for service, merit, or hardship.	4
Selection	Identifying the best candidate(s) for the job from among a pool of qualified applicants developed during the recruiting process.	1, 5, 9

Continued

Term	Defined	Found in part
Self-confidence	A realistic confidence in one's own judgment, ability, and power. Can also include an excessive or inflated confidence.	2, 3
Stereotype	A simplified and standardized conception, image, assumption, or belief generally attributed to members of a particular racial or social group simply because they appear to be a member of that group.	9
Team building	The cooperative actions that a team performs to build or construct an effective business.	2
Training	A planned attempt by an organization to facilitate employee learning of job-related knowledge, skills, and behaviors.	2
Trust	To rely upon or place confidence in someone or something; hope.	2, 5, 7, 8
Unpopular decisions	In disfavor with particular acts, processes, or judgment.	2
Workaholism	The act of working compulsively at the expense of other pursuits.	5
Work systems	A collection of processes; a series of repeatable steps.	3, 4, 5

Matrix of cases and subjects

Main subjects	Incident case	Head case	Application case	Data case	Issue case
Accepting criticism		62			
ADA	22	9	3		
Analytical					39
Anger			16, 44		
Assertiveness	13	54, 62	16, 17		15
Authority	13, 48, 50, 51, 55, 56	1, 7, 20, 49, 53, 54, 61	18		38, 52,58, 59
Bias			64		
Big picture		57			15, 39, 40
Bullying	46				37
Buy-in	48		16, 18		12, 15
Chain of command		1, 61			37, 52, 58, 59
Change	36, 55		16, 18		12, 15, 36
Coaching	13, 22	32, 45, 61, 67	18, 24, 43, 44		21, 25, 31, 33, 36, 37, 38, 39, 40, 41, 72
Controlling costs	48			8, 30	15
Credibility	55, 56	7, 20, 54, 61	18, 47		12, 52, 58
Decision-making			18		15, 32
Delegation		57			
Defensiveness	55	45, 54, 62	17		
Discrimination	19	5, 6, 65, 66, 67, 68	3, 64		63, 72, 75
Discipline	46, 48, 50, 51, 55, 74	45, 49, 53, 54	43, 44, 47		
Diversity	19, 71, 74	5, 65, 66, 67, 68, 70	3, 64		63, 72, 73, 75
Feedback	13, 35	7, 32, 34, 36, 45, 61, 62, 70	17, 24, 29, 44		31, 33, 36, 37, 39
Flexibility	48		9		41
Generations					4

Continued

Main subjects	Incident case	Head case	Application case	Data case	Issue case
Gossip	35, 56	20			
Harassment	14, 69, 71	11, 70			37
Hands-on		37			
Humor / sarcasm	14	34			
Incivility	13, 46	34			37
Influence		60	18		12, 59
Insubordination	48, 50, 51, 74	53, 54			
Job design / Job description	50, 74	1, 9			23, 28
Leadership styles			18		
Managing up	56	57, 61, 62			58, 59
Meetings		34			36
Micromanagement		57			
Motivation		26, 60	29	30	25, 27, 28
Open-door policy		11, 53, 61			52, 58
Organizational politics	56	60	29		58
Organizational structure		1			27, 42, 52
Perfectionism		57			40
Performance appraisal	19		24		37
Prejudice			64		
Productivity	48	9		8	21, 23
Promotion		60			27, 72
Rapport		32, 45	16, 17		
Recruiting / selection		5, 6, 10, 65	2, 3		4
Religion	19				73
Respect	55	34, 54, 70	29		15
Rewards		26		30	25, 27
Self-confidence		10, 32			31, 37, 38
Stereotypes		70	64		75
Unions			47		
Unpopular decisions			16		12, 15
Team building			16		42
Trust	55	11, 57	18		15, 31, 52
Workaholism					41
Work systems					23, 25, 42

The Royal Hotel

To make the cases more accessible and to keep them consistent, all scenarios unfold in the same fictitious hotel. The organizational chart of the Royal Hotel will provide students with the names and job titles of the main characters. Many of the characters are lower-level supervisors, exactly the types of roles most of our students expect to assume shortly after graduation. This will add to the real-life feeling and will help students to bridge the gap between classroom and industry.

ROYAL HOTEL

Overlooking the scenic Bedford River, the Royal Hotel is in the center of the city and just a short drive from the airport. Built a century ago, this landmark hotel features a stone façade flanked by two golden lions. The Royal Hotel radiates Victorian splendor less than two blocks from shopping on Commercial Street. The grandeur of the Royal Hotel, coupled with its reputation for impeccable service, promises a truly memorable experience.

The Royal's lobby retains many original features and is warmed by an open fireplace. The 400 guestrooms feature views of either Bedford River or the city park. Separate seating areas offer comfortable reading chairs and Italian leather desks. Bathrooms feature marble countertops and floors, terry-cloth bathrobes, and complimentary toiletries. The hotel's health club features an indoor lap pool with palm trees, a fitness room, saunas, and treatment rooms. The hotel maintains its Victorian ambiance with intimate meeting rooms and a spectacular ballroom showcasing antique mahogany furnishings, oil paintings, and wood paneling. The Harvest Room restaurant offers an extensive à la carte menu composed of international selections and regional favorites. The Riverside Lounge and Bar serves light meals and cocktails and offers a specialty martini menu. Room service is available 24 hours a day.

The Royal Hotel is currently a non-unionized environment.

Exhibit A The Royal Hotel's organizational chart

Robert Kunz
General Manager

Jane Peterson
Hotel Manager

David Steele
Security Manager

Katherine Norton
Director of Human Resources

Betty Chu
Human Resources Manager

Dan Mazur
Director of Rooms

Judith Grace
Front Office Manager

Marina Wright
Revenue Manager

Carlos Diaz
Guest Services Manager

Shakia Andrews
Executive Housekeeper

Lori Canelle
Spa Manager

Kalinda Stenton
PBX Manager

Yvonne Clark
Director of Sales & Marketing

Fiona O'Brien
Public Relations Manager

Debbie Murphy
Sales Manager

Rhiannon Palmer
Convention Services Manager

Kelly Woodstock
Catering Manager

Matthew Knorr
Director of Food & Beverage

Pascal Gateau
Executive Chef

Thomas Waxer
Banquet Manager

Jennifer Ortiz
Restaurant Manager

Wesley Edwards
Room Service Manager

Emily Perkins
Lounge and Bar Manager

John Ferreira
Chief Steward

Louise Rausch
Director of Finance

Yuan Yao
Assistant Director of Finance

Mike Lee
Accounting Manager

Alison Finley
Credit Manager

Paul Bello
Purchasing Manager

William Ming
IT Manager

Charlie Jones
Director of Engineering

Brian White
Assistant Director of Engineering

The Royal Hotel's organizational structure [key positions]

The executive committee

Robert Kunz, General Manager

Directs hotel operations by developing and implementing strategies and services which meet or exceed the needs of owners, employees, and guests.

Jane Peterson, Hotel Manager

Oversees the day-to-day operations and assignments of the hotel staff and assists the general manager in the development and communication of departmental strategies and goals.

Katherine Norton, Director of Human Resources

Develops HR strategies, directs all areas of human resource administration within the hotel, including employment, salary administration, benefits, and training.

Dan Mazur, Director of Rooms

Provides guidance and leadership to the Rooms Division, ensuring consistent compliance of hotel policies and maximizing department profits.

Yvonne Clark, Director of Sales and Marketing

Leads the development and execution of strategic sales and marketing plans and is responsible for developing initiatives in order to achieve budget and revenue goals.

Matthew Knorr, Director of Food and Beverage

Responsible for the overall operation of the food and beverage division, ensuring revenues are met and high standards are upheld, and mentors the F&B managers.

Louise Rausch, Director of Finance

Supervises and directs the financial activities of the hotel, safeguards the assets, and prepares all financial reports.

Charlie Jones, Director of Engineering

Maintains the entire hotel facility, including physical building structure and all mechanical, electrical, HVAC systems and related equipment.

The Royal Hotel

Managers (listed in alphabetical order)

Shakia Andrews, Executive Housekeeper

Provides supervision and direction for all housekeeping activities of the hotel; ensures the highest level of cleanliness.

Paul Bello, Purchasing Manager

Oversees the purchasing function of the hotel, including food, beverage, and property operation supplies.

Lori Canelle, Spa Manager

Responsible for all aspects of the Health Club operation.

Betty Chu, Human Resources Manager

Assists in the day-to-day management of human resources, including recruiting, benefits, employee relations, and training.

Carlos Diaz, Guest Services Manager

Oversees the door attendants, valet parkers, bell staff, gift shop, and concierge employees.

Wesley Edwards, Room Service Manager

Responsible for managing the food and beverage service of in-room dining; ensures that private bars are replenished.

John Ferreira, Chief Steward

Responsible for the setups of china, glassware, and silverware items for all banquet functions; ensures that the kitchen and back-of-the-house area are clean.

Alison Finely, Credit Manager

Responsible for ensuring that all outstanding balances due to the hotel are paid on a timely basis.

Pascal Gateau, Executive Chef

Responsible for all menu planning, preparation, production, and control for all F&B outlets and banquet facilities.

Judith Grace, Front Office Manager

Oversees all front desk operations, including guest registrations and check-outs.

Mike Lee, Accounting Manager

Oversees the hotel's day audit, accounts payable, accounts receivable, and payroll functions.

William Ming, IT Manager

Responsible for the overall operation of the information technology infrastructure.

Debbie Murphy, Sales Manager

Directs the day-to-day activities of the sales team and promotes group and individual hotel business.

Fiona O'Brien, Public Relations Manager

Develops and implements innovative public relations strategies to support the hotel's objectives.

Jennifer Ortiz, Restaurant Manager (The Harvest Room)

Responsible for the daily operations of the restaurant; ensures that staff provides quality service.

Rhiannon Palmer, Convention Services Manager

Coordinates all details pertaining to groups; serves as the primary liaison between groups and hotel departments.

Emily Perkins, Lounge and Bar Manager (The Riverside)

Responsible for the daily operations of the lounge and bar; ensures that staff provides quality service.

David Steele, Security Manager

Supervises the activities of the security staff; responsibilities include incident reporting, safety inspections, and loss prevention inspections. The security manager reports directly to the hotel manager.

Kalinda Stenton, PBX Manager

Oversees the communications center of the hotel; connects incoming calls, takes messages, and executes wake-up calls.

Thomas Waxer, Banquet Manager

Ensures the proper execution of all banquet functions.

Brian White, Assistant Director of Engineering

Runs the day-to-day, routine operations of engineering.

Marina Wright, Revenue Manager

Responsible for maximizing rooms' revenue through management of the hotel's room inventory and for supervising the day-to-day activities of the reservations department.

The Royal Hotel

The revenue manager reports to the director of rooms but works closely with the director of sales and marketing.

Kelly Woodstock, Catering Manager

Responsible for the sales and planning of all catered functions; the catering manager reports to the director of food and beverage but works closely with the director of sales and marketing.

Yuan Yao, Assistant Director of Finance

Assists with the day-to-day accounting office operation; supports the director of finance.

Dealing with employee problems and problem employees – a general guideline

Everybody has a bad day once in a while. Problems are normal, natural, and human. An employee becomes a problem when the problem persists and a pattern is developing. Difficult employees come in varying degrees. Dealing with people simply means dealing with difficult behaviors.

In a large number of cases presented in this book, supervisors will encounter difficult behaviors. According to the references reviewed for this work, here is a general guideline to deal successfully with employee behavior-related problems.

1 Identify the problem behavior

- State the unsatisfactory behavior in factual terms.
- What is it about the person's behavior that has an adverse impact on the work being completed?
- Who is affected by the behavior, and how frequently does it occur?
- Offer specific instances of times that the problem behavior has occurred.

2 Recognize the reasons for the problem

- Acknowledge any underlying causes for the problem behavior.
- Clues to possible causes of problem behavior can be identified by examining how the employee interacts with others.

3 Discuss the behavior with the employees

- Engage the person in a private discussion that follows these steps:
    a State the meeting's purpose.
    b Describe the behavior's negative impact. Carefully separate the behavior from the person. (It's the behavior you object to, not the person.)
    c Seek to understand the cause of the behavior.
    d Clarify the expectations; model the behavior you want to see.
    e Explore solutions acceptable to both parties.
    f Agree on a solution; obtain a commitment on specific actions the person will take.
    g Set deadlines and progress review dates.

Dealing with employee problems and problem employees – a general guideline

4   Acknowledge improved behavior.

- Follow up with the person.
- Recognize and comment on any progress you've observed.
- Re-evaluate the action plan, and revise it as necessary.

Part 1

Meeting human resources requirements

How to use this part

This portion of the book looks at the design in which positions are organized to create an organizational chart. Cases will examine opportunities to be inclusive during the selection process when looking at possible discrimination. Cases will give the reader an opportunity to think critically about what details should be included or excluded from a job description.

Key terms

The key terms found in the cases in this section are listed in the following, their definition can be found on pages xiv–xviii.

ADA
Authority
Chain of command
Controlling costs
Discrimination
Diversity
Flexibility
Job design
Job description
Organizational structure
Recruiting
Selection

The organizational chart

Main subjects
Authority, chain of command, job design / job description, organizational structure

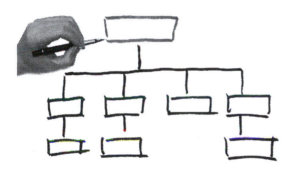

Who's who
- Yvonne Clark, Director of Sales and Marketing
- Matthew Knorr, Director of Food and Beverage
- Robert Kunz, General Manager
- Dan Mazur, Director of Rooms
- Kelly Woodstock, Catering Manager
- Marina Wright, Revenue Manager

Think point

The use of an organizational chart, where reporting lines are depicted, can assist the employees in understanding who reports to whom to better understand the chain of command. Despite having a chart, conflicts may arise among employees based on their perception and understanding of how the business operates.

This morning, the general manager presented the new organizational chart of the Royal Hotel. [See Exhibit A on page xxii)

"This chart depicts the hierarchical relationships between divisions, departments, and positions within the Royal Hotel," explained Kunz. "We have a pretty simple structure with direct vertical lines between the different levels of the organization. As you all know, Yvonne is responsible for developing initiatives in order to achieve our budget and revenue goals. As of today, Yvonne will support Marina and Kelly by providing them with her specialized expertise."

Executive committee members looked excited; only Dan and Matthew seemed somewhat puzzled.

1   Describe potential conflicts that may arise in line-staff relationships.

   a   From the viewpoint of Yvonne.
   b   From the viewpoint of Dan and Matthew.
   c   From the viewpoint of Marina and Kelly.

2   How can the Royal Hotel minimize the risk of potential conflicts?

3   Identify managers at the Royal Hotel with functional authority.

Exhibit 1.1 Royal Hotel – manager's handbook (excerpts)

The Royal Hotel organizational chart

At the Royal Hotel, three types of authority are present: line, staff, and functional.

1   The solid lines, referred to as **line authority**, indicate the direct authority a manager has over a subordinate. Line authority flows down the chain of command.
2   **Staff authority** is the right to advise or counsel other subordinates outside of a manager's direct line authority. This reporting relationship is depicted by dotted lines.
3   **Functional authority** covers specific task areas only. It is given to managers who, in order to meet responsibilities in their own areas, must be able to exercise some control over organizational members in other areas.

Red flags

Main subjects
Recruiting/selection

Who's who
• Betty Chu, Human Resources Manager
• Judith Grace, Front Office Manager
• Dan Mazur, Director of Rooms

Think point

Once a position has been posted, it is important to have a strategy to collect and screen the applications. The first attempt to narrow down the candidate pool is to screen applications for potential red flags or warning signals that the candidate might not be the best fit for the position. Up to 85% of individuals will lie about information recorded on their résumé (O'Donnell, 2017).

Meeting human resources requirements

Betty from HR left a voice mail to Dan. "Hi, Dan, I understand that Judith is going back to school soon, and you might be looking for another front office manager. I emailed you three applications. Just to let you know, I did not have a chance to look for red flags. I have some time next week and would like start with one interview. Could you let me know which one of the three candidates should be called in?"

1   Warning signs / red flags. Often, evidence indicating a bad apple is right on the application or the résumé. Review the applications for any items that don't make sense or leave you with an uneasy feeling.

2   Why do some managers believe that long-term, stable applicants may become bad hires?

3   For employers, fake education credentials pose significant problems. Please explain why.

4   What can employers do to prevent candidates from exaggerating or lying about their qualifications or inflating their job titles, job descriptions, or salary histories?

5   In states where this is legal, why do you think asking for a salary history can be helpful to HR professionals?

6   Careful reference checking is the best way to objectively evaluate an individual's job performance over time and from different points of view. Suggest questions to ask candidates who have changed jobs frequently.

Attachment: 3 application forms
Application form 1

 THE ROYAL HOTEL

Employment Application

Applicant Information					
Full Name:	Smith	Mary		W	Date: 1/3/2018
	Last	*First*		*M.I.*	

Education

College:	Baltimore College		Major:	Hospitality			
From: 2011	To: 2015		Did you graduate?	YES ☑	NO ☐	Degree:	B.S.
Other:			Major:				
From:	To:		Did you graduate?	YES ☐	NO ☐	Degree:	

Previous Employment

Company:	Hotel Empire, Baltimore		Phone:	(410) 111-1111
Job Title:	Assistant Front Office Manager	Starting Salary: $52,000	Ending Salary: $58,000	
Responsibilities:	Maximized financial performance of hotel			
From: 9/1/2017 To: 12/10/2017	Reason for Leaving:	My dream is to join the Royal Hotel		
Company:	Hotel Victoria, Baltimore		Phone:	(410) 222-2222
Job Title:	Front Office Supervisor	Starting Salary: $26,000	Ending Salary: $28,000	
Responsibilities:	Managed all aspects of the operation			
From: 4/1/2017 To: 8/15/2017	Reason for Leaving:	Opportunity to assist the opening of Hotel Empire		
Company:	Hotel Park, Philadelphia		Phone:	(215) 333-3333
Job Title:	Front Desk Agent	Starting Salary: $10/hour	Ending Salary: $11/hour	
Responsibilities:	Checked guests in and out of the hotel			
From: 2016 To: 3/10/2017	Reason for Leaving:	Personal		

References

Mr. Louis Herman, Restaurant Manager - Hotel Victoria
Ms. Angelica Bold, Executive Housekeeper - Hotel Park

Interests/Special Skills/ Clubs

Please list any interests, special skills, clubs or organization to which you belong which directly relate to the job for which you are applying

skiing, swimming, inline skating

Meeting human resources requirements

Application form 2

 THE ROYAL HOTEL

Employment Application

Applicant Information				
Full Name: Brown	John	B	Date:	1/3/2018
Last	First	M.I.		

Education

College: New Orleans University	Major: Anthropology			
From: 2011 To: 2015	Did you graduate? YES ☒ NO ☐	Degree: B.S.		
Other: New Orleans City College	Major: Geography			
From: 2009 To: 2011	Did you graduate? YES ☒ NO ☐	Degree: Associate Degree		

Previous Employment

Company: Hotel Astoria, New Orleans		Phone: (504) 555-5555	
Job Title: Asst. Front Office Mgr	Starting Salary: $33,000	Ending Salary: $34,000	
Responsibilities: Assisted the Front office manager in overseeing PBX, concierges and Front Desk, maintained high quality of standards			
From: 2/1/2017 To: 12/15/2017	Reason for Leaving:	No opportunity for promotion at Hotel Astoria	

Company: Hotel Astoria, New Orleans		Phone: (504) 555-5555	
Job Title: Front Desk Supervisor	Starting Salary: $29,000	Ending Salary: $29,500	
Responsibilities: Supervised Front Desk staff, Resolved guest concerns			
From: 2/10/2016 To: 1/31/2017	Reason for Leaving:		

Company: Hotel Astoria, New Orleans		Phone: (504) 555-5555	
Job Title: Front Desk Agent	Starting Salary: $10.50/hr	Ending Salary: $10.50/hr	
Responsibilities: Performed a variety of duties including guest registration and handling of guest inquiries			
From: 6/30/2015 To: 2/9/2016	Reason for Leaving:		

References

Mr. Bruce Gates, Director of Rooms, Hotel Astoria, New Orleans

Mrs. Esther LaValle, Human Resources Manager, Hotel Astoria, New Orleans

Interests/Special Skills/ Clubs

Please list any interests, special skills, clubs or organization to which you belong which directly relate to the job for which you are applying

Golf lover, Attends most PGA tournaments

Application form 3

 THE ROYAL HOTEL

Employment Application

Applicant Information					
Full Name:	Rogers	Leslie		Date:	1/3/2018
	Last	*First*	*M.I.*		

Education				
College:	Bellevue University	Major:	Business Administration	
From: 2016	To: 2017	Did you graduate? YES ☒ NO ☐	Degree:	Ph.D
Other:	Seattle University	Major:	Hospitality	
From: 2012	To: 2016	Did you graduate? YES ☒ NO ☐	Degree:	B.S.

Previous Employment			
Company:	Hotel Pacific, Seattle	Phone:	(206) 444-4444
Job Title:	Assistant Housekeeper	Starting Salary: $ 36,000	Ending Salary: $ 37,000
Responsibilities:	Managed day-to-day activities of the department. Scheduled employees to ensure proper coverage		
From: 7/1/2017	To: 12/10/2017	Reason for Leaving: —	
Company:	Hotel Pacific, Seattle	Phone:	(206) 444-4444
Job Title:	Assistant Front Office Manager	Starting Salary: $ 30,000	Ending Salary: $ 31,000
Responsibilities:	Effectively managed the daily operations of the front desk.		
From: 5/4/2017	To: 6/30/2011	Reason for Leaving:	
Company:	The Mansion, Portland	Phone:	(503) 999-9999
Job Title:	Assistant Front Office Manager	Starting Salary: $ 30,000	Ending Salary: $ 30,000
Responsibilities:	Established and maintained attentive and courteous hospitality		
From: 3/7/2010	To: 11/30/2011	Reason for Leaving: Disagreed with policies	

References
Mr. Greg Ebelin - Front Office Manager - Hotel Pacific, Seattle
Ms. Kate Williams - Executive Housekeeper - Hotel Pacific, Seattle

Interests/Special Skills/ Clubs
Please list any interests, special skills, clubs or organization to which you belong which directly relate to the job for which you are applying
Hiking, Surfing, playing piano and guitar with other musicians

Reference

O'Donnell, J. T. (2017, August 15). 85 Percent of job applicants lie on resumes. Here's how to spot a dishonest candidate. Retrieved November 10, 2019, from Inc.com website: www.inc.com/jt-odonnell/staggering-85-of-job-applicants-lying-on-resumes-.html

Candidate screening

Main subjects
ADA, discrimination, diversity, recruiting / selection

Who's who
• Shakia Andrews, Executive Housekeeper
• Betty Chu, Human Resources Manager
• Mary Kispesti, Candidate

Think point

It is considered to be good business practice that the people who are interviewing candidates and asking questions have been properly trained to ensure they are asking questions that are both legal and make sense to the position the candidate is applying for. In such instances that the manager has not been properly trained, it can lead to errors and open the operations to liability. In most cases, these questions are asked without intention of discrimination; however, the information collected could lead to a bias toward or against the candidate. Carefully consider what questions should be avoided in the interview process.

The phone was ringing when Shakia entered her office. It was Betty from HR.

"I hope you like it here at the Royal. I look forward to seeing you at the second orientation day next Tuesday," Betty told Shakia. Shakia did not have a chance to answer, as Betty continued by saying, "By the way, I've just received another application for the assistant manager position. Would you mind meeting with this individual?"

"Absolutely, I'm available to see the candidate tomorrow, first thing in the morning," Shakia answered.

The next morning, the following conversation occurred between the candidate and the executive housekeeper.

Shakia: So, what brings you to the Royal?

Candidate: I have heard so many great things about this hotel.

Shakia: (glances at the application) Do you wish to be addressed as Mrs.? Ms.? or Miss?

Candidate: It really doesn't matter; feel free to call me Mary.

Shakia: (still looking at the application form) What is your maiden name?

Candidate: My name is Mary Kispesti.

Shakia: You have a very unusual last name. What is its origin?

Candidate: (laughing) I am not sure. I know more about the origin of my first name.

Shakia: (trying to put the candidate at ease) What a gloomy day! It's almost 8:00 AM but still so dark. Nice dress, Mary. Is it matching the color of your eyes?

Candidate: (thinking) I am not sure. At home, everybody says that I have greenish-hazel eyes.

Shakia: (laughing) Are you sure about that? For me, they look brownish. What language is spoken at home?

Candidate: Mostly English.

Shakia: Where do you see yourself in five years?

Candidate: (becomes talkative) As you can see in my résumé, I have gained tremendous experience in the hotel industry, and I really would like to work my way up to become a department head. I know very well that your hotel has very high standards, and I really would like to live up your expectations on a long-term basis. I am a responsible woman and would be interested what your thoughts are on career versus marriage.

Shakia: (hesitating) Mary, I am not married.

Shakia: (after a brief pause) You know, it's a physically demanding job. **Do you have any disability that would prevent you from performing the job?**

Candidate: No, I can do this job.

Shakia: Reliability is a key requirement at the Royal. How many days were you absent from work last year because of illness?

Candidate: Two or three.

Shakia: Mary, we need someone who is fully flexible. Can you work during major holidays like Christmas?

Candidate: Sure, I am available anytime.

Shakia: How about on Saturdays and Sundays?

Candidate: No problem.

Shakia: As you know, at this point, we are only screening applicants. However, I may need to quickly get a hold of you. What is the name and address of the relative to be notified in case of an emergency?

Candidate: I can give you the name of a cousin.

Shakia: All right, Mary, we'll be in touch. Let me walk with you to your car.

Candidate: Actually, I took public transportation.

1. Outline the problems with this interview.

2. What advice might you give to the Royal Hotel?

Generations in the workplace

Main subjects
Generations, recruiting / selection

Who's who
• Matthew Knorr, Director of Food and Beverage
• Wesley Edwards, Room Service Manager
• Adam Clark, Assistant Restaurant Manager

Think point

The hospitality industry is a very diverse industry where people from multiple generations come together to work. There could be the possibility where multiple generations are all working together at the same time; this can inadvertently lead to communication failures. Understanding the expectations and communication preferences of each generation will help both manage and be more productive employees. Generations in the workplace include traditionalists, Baby Boomers, Generation X, Millennials, and Generation Z.

Last night, Wesley gave his notice, and there is now an opening at the Royal Hotel for a room service manager. Matthew (a Baby Boomer) is the hiring manager and posted the position as soon as he heard so that he could attract as many candidates as possible. This morning, he received a text from Adam, the assistant restaurant manager (and a Millennial) that said, "How about that R. S. manager! Anyone special in mind????" The text included a "thumbs-up" and a winking emoji.

Matthew's response was short and to the point: "This is not a conversation for text. We can talk on Tuesday."

Adam was upset. He was trying to lighten the mood. Why was Matthew always so grumpy?

1   What are some of the common work-related stereotypes for Millennials and Baby Boomers?

2   Why is it important to be aware of the generalizations that come with each generation?

3   Was Adam wrong in his approach? Would he have gotten a different response if Matthew were a Millennial? Was Matthew wrong in his response?

4   What are some ideas for bridging the generation gap?

The left-handed server

Case type: head case

Main subjects
Discrimination, diversity, recruiting / selection

Who's Who
• Thomas Waxer, Banquet Manager

Think point

Pre-employment tests can be a method to confirm or eliminate a candidate from the selection process. However, it is important to note that tests must be considered both reliable and valid.

14

The Royal Hotel offers its banquet guests a very formal type of service called "Silver" or "Russian" service. Thomas believes in consistency and elegance. He often admires servers as they line up in the ballroom of the Royal, all carrying serving platters in the same manner. He is convinced that guests value this consistency and grace.

When Thomas has doubts that potential candidates have gained enough experience in banquet service, he puts them through what he calls a "work sampling" test. This consists of carrying plates and portioning and serving fake food directly onto ten plates arranged on a round banquet table. He scores the candidate's performance on a scale of "A" to "F." Those with a score of "C" or less are eliminated.

This morning, while testing a candidate, Thomas noticed that he was carrying the platter with his right hand. "This is not correct," Thomas told him. "Did you read the job description?" Thomas pointed to the printed information material on the position (see Exhibit 5.1).

The server replied, "I'm truly sorry, sir. I can't transfer the food with my right hand. I was allowed to serve like this back in my country."

1   What are the advantages and disadvantages of work sampling tests?

2   What are some of the pitfalls of Thomas's pre-employment test?

3   Should Thomas force left-handed servers to carry platters with their left hand and portion the food with their right hand?

The case is based on the principles and situations described in the following:

The Culinary Institute of America. (2001). *Remarkable service* (pp. 185–192). New York, NY: Wiley.

Exhibit 5.1 Information material

Job description – banquet server

Key responsibilities

- Serve food and beverages in a friendly, courteous, and professional manner according to Royal's high standards of quality.
- Clear tables after service. Perform other duties as assigned, which may include assisting with setup and break down of function space and plating of meals.

Qualifications

- Ability to lift 40 pounds or more.
- Strong knowledge of Russian (Silver) food service style.

Royal Hotel – banquets training manual (excerpt)

The main goal of Silver or Russian service is to service fully cooked food while it is still hot and to serve it in an elegant manner. The server stands with feet together, to the left of the guest. Food is plated with the aid of a serving spoon and fork with the server's right hand. Servers move counterclockwise around the table.

Considerable skill, strength, and dexterity are required to perform proper platter service. Trays can be heavy and hot and must be held firmly in the left hand while the food is being served with the right hand from the guest's left. Practice is required to prevent dropping or breaking the food or spilling the sauce.

The online dirt

Main subjects
Discrimination, recruiting/selection

Who's who
• Betty Chu, Human Resources Manager
• Katherine Norton, Director of Human Resources

Think point

The reference verification process of a candidate is more prevalent with the use of social media and other online resources in present times than in the past. Think about the policy of the organization – how will such verifications be conducted?

"Betty, let's conduct our usual social media background check on this promising candidate," Katherine said and smiled. "Make a decision this afternoon; give him a call, and set up his interview for Monday. By the way, I am going to take off now; I need to do some shopping for the holiday party," she added as she left the HR office.

Once Katherine had left, Betty went online to check on the candidate for an open management position. At one of the popular social networking sites, she found the candidate's personal web page with the description of his main interests: "Sand, sun, and sex." In addition, Betty found a few mildly provocative pictures recently taken in a college party. One of them was portraying the candidate in underwear drinking from a half-pint beer mug.

1   Many companies are using search engines to conduct virtual background checks on candidates. What are the pros of this practice?

2   What are the risks involved in going online to research job candidates?

3   If you were Betty, what would you do now?

The case is based on the principles and situations described in the following:

Finder, A. (2006, June 11). *For some, online persona undermines a resume.* Retrieved December 7, 2007, from www.nytimes.com

Sundberg, J. (n.d.). How to stop employers digging your digital dirt. *The Undercover Recruiter.* Retrieved September 19, 2017, from http://theundercoverrecruiter.com/stop-employers-digging-your-digital-dirt-10-ways-clean-your-act-now/

Friendships at work

Main Subjects
Authority, credibility, feedback

Who's who
• Charlie Jones, Director of Engineering
• Brian White, Assistant Director of Engineering

Think point

It is understandable to make friends in one's place of work. Employees do spend a significant amount of time at their place of employment. There does remain an outstanding concern about those friendships when it comes to the role of authority in the workplace. While there might not be an official policy on time spent out of work with subordinates, it is important for associates with levels of authority to consider the impact that such connections could have on the workplace environment.

Meeting human resources requirements

Charlie sat down with Brian for their weekly one-on-one rap, and this week, he had a sensitive topic to discuss. "Brian," he started, "it's come to my attention that you've been hanging out a lot with a couple of the engineers outside of work."

"That's true," Brian responded, "but I didn't think that there was anything in the policy that said that I couldn't."

"No, there isn't . . ." Charlie agreed. "But I just don't think it's a good idea. How will they respect you if you're friends with them? You might have to write one of them up, you know."

1   What are the dangers of having friendships in the workplace?

2   What are the benefits of friendships in the workplace?

3   What does Brian need to be careful of?

4   Should Charlie pursue this further?

The incomplete schedule

Main subjects
Controlling costs, productivity

Who's who
• Judith Grace, Front Office Manager
• Dan Mazur, Director of Rooms
• Jane Peterson, Hotel Manager
• Marina Wright, Revenue Manager

Think point

Understanding all of the various standards that go into making a schedule can be overwhelming. While there is no set industry standard to productivity, each operation typically has its own guidelines to follow, which work in line with how the annual budget is created. Errors in making the schedule not only can impact the individual employees, but they can cause financial implications.

Judith had a crazy day. The Royal was fully booked, and she had only five minutes to look at the forecast and put together the schedule for the first week of December. Before leaving the hotel, she slid the schedule document under the door of the director of rooms. Judith was already making her tea at home when she received a voice mail from Dan.

> ## Voice mail
>
> "Hi, Judith, this is Dan speaking. Thanks for submitting your schedule for next week. Unfortunately, you missed Tuesday. To help you, I called Marina, who gave me some information. All right! Monday's occupancy will be 200 rooms; some of them – I guess 135 – will check out on Tuesday. According to Marina, Tuesday night, the hotel occupancy will be 240 rooms.
>
> "Would you mind leaving me a quick message with the missing information? Please keep in mind that Jane would like to review all schedules today.
>
> "Thanks, bye."

The Royal Hotel developed labor productivity standards[1] for each department. Judith knew that the front desk could use eight hours per shift (AM, PM, overnight), regardless of the occupancy. She also remembered that their labor productivity standards were based on the number of arrivals and departures. More than 100 arrivals and departures meant she was entitled to include another eight hours. When arrivals and departures exceeded 150, she could add another shift. Finally, for more than 300 arrivals and departures, she could schedule one additional agent shift.

> 1 What are some of the challenges a hospitality organization may face when creating productivity standards?
>
> 2 What are the implications if too many employees are scheduled?
>
> 3 Help Judith out by determining how many front desk agent hours she can schedule for Tuesday, December 2?

The case is based on the principles and situations described in the following:

Szende, P. (2013). Establishing labor standards and scheduling basics. In P. Szende (Ed.), *Hospitality management learning modules*. Boston, MA: Pearson Education, Inc.

Thompson, G. M. (1998). Labor scheduling, part 2. *Cornell Hotel and Restaurant Administration Quarterly*, 39(6), 26–37.

Note

1 Labor productivity standards.

- Productivity is the number of hours needed to service a hospitality unit.
- Labor standards utilize productivity ratios to identify the ideal amount of labor (including fixed and variable labor hours) to service incremental volumes of hospitality business.
- Labor standards serve as day-to-day operational guidelines, helping managers stay within budgetary guidelines.

The bartender's break

Main subjects
ADA, flexibility, job design/job description, productivity

Who's who
• Matthew Knorr, Director of Food and Beverage
• Emily Perkins, Lounge and Bar Manager
• Kalman Rosen, Barback

Think point

An employee working an eight-hour shift is entitled to one 30-minute meal break and two 15-minute breaks during the shift. In the operations of hospitality, this often means that someone has to cover that person's shift, as guests might be needing service. Each organization will need to determine who will assist in the coverage. It is important to review and update job descriptions on a regular basis to be inclusive of the flexibility that the industry requires.

"I need a little bit of assistance," Emily said when she called the F&B office.

Matthew ran down to the lounge.

"We have to send the bartender on break; could you watch the door for me?" Emily asked him.

As a "hands-on" manager, Matthew was happy to help out on the floor. He was, however, surprised that while Emily was making drinks behind the bar, the barback, Kalman, was chatting with a customer, and they were watching the ball game together on the flat screen TV placed behind the bar.

PM bartenders had a first dinner break covered by the AM bartenders, and they were also entitled to a shorter 15-minute break in the evening. Traditionally, managers were replacing the bartenders during the second break. Matthew believed that managers should be on the floor at all times to ensure that service is flawless; he could not understand why Kalman was not able to cover for the bartender.

The next day, Emily and Matthew met Kalman to discuss the issue. After praising the barback's overall performance, Matthew asked him to cover the bartender's second break starting next week. "You have been with the Royal Hotel for five years; I am sure you want to learn new skills and take on more challenging assignments," Matthew added.

"Sorry, Matthew, I am just not interested in covering the bartender's break. I am happy with what I am doing right now. By the way," Kalman added politely, "that's not even in my job description."

Matthew reminded the barback that job descriptions are not meant to be all-inclusive and jobs are subject to change and pointed to the disclaimer on the barback's job description:

"Other duties and responsibilities may be assigned."

"You know, Kalman, that nothing in this job description restricts my right to reassign duties and responsibilities to you. Let's meet again tomorrow to finalize this." Matthew ended the discussion.

1   List some of the positive and negative impacts of using job descriptions.

2   Evaluate Matthew's actions in dealing with the situation. What factors should he consider in his decision?

Exhibit 9.1 Job description – Bartender

TITLE: BARTENDER
DEPARTMENT: THE RIVERSIDE LOUNGE AND BAR
REPORT TO: LOUNGE AND BAR MANAGER
POSITION SUMMARY: Mixes and serves alcoholic and nonalcoholic drinks and food items to patrons of bar in a prompt and courteous manner.

ESSENTIAL JOB FUNCTIONS:

*   Knows all food and beverage items and daily specials and communicates them to the guest.

- Takes orders from customers, using upselling techniques.
- Mixes ingredients to prepare cocktails and other drinks.
- Rings guest checks, collects money for food and drinks served.
- Closes guest checks by credit cards, cash, or room charges, according to Royal operating procedures.
- Orders or requisitions liquors and supplies.
- Maintains a clean and efficient bar, both in and out of customer view.
- Monitors guest behavior and guest alcohol consumption to determine when alcohol service to the guest should cease.

ADDITIONAL RESPONSIBILITIES:

- Other duties and responsibilities may be assigned.

MINIMUM QUALIFICATIONS:

- High school diploma preferred.

This job requires the ability to perform the following:

- Handling, carrying, or pushing items weighing up to 50 pounds.
- Extensive periods of standing.
- Bending, stooping, kneeling, and lifting.

Licenses or certificates required

- Health/food handler cards as required by state government agency.
- Alcohol awareness certification.
- Must meet state legal age requirements.

Exhibit 9.2 Job description – barback

TITLE: BARBACK
DEPARTMENT: THE RIVERSIDE LOUNGE AND BAR
REPORT TO: LOUNGE AND BAR MANAGER
POSITION SUMMARY: Responsible for ensuring the quick and efficient servicing of the bar and lounge while providing excellent service.

ESSENTIAL JOB FUNCTIONS:

- Assists bartenders as directed; prepares garnishes and mixes.
- Replenishes supplies throughout shift.
- Familiar with all food and beverage items, as well daily specials, to respond accurately to any guest inquiry.
- Retrieves food orders from kitchen and delivers them to the bar.
- Maintains a clean and efficient bar, both in and out of customer view.

ADDITIONAL RESPONSIBILITIES:

- Other duties and responsibilities may be assigned.

MINIMUM QUALIFICATIONS:

- No formal education required.

This job requires the ability to perform the following:

- Handling, carrying, or pushing items weighing up to 50 pounds.
- Extensive periods of standing.
- Bending, stooping, kneeling, and lifting.

Licenses or certificates required

- Health / food handler cards as required by state government agency.
- Must meet state legal age requirements.

> ### Part summary
>
> This section covered the aspects of human resource management that precede the employee commencing their employment in an organization. Yet these decisions impact the employee experience once on site and working. Start with a clear organizational chart showing how associates will report to each other. Specifically define the responsibilities of each position in a detailed job description. Use this information to ensure that the candidates who are identified during the recruitment process and make the cut to selection will be the right fit for the organization.

Additional reading

Book

ADA

A source to understand the law from the American Bar Association in order to properly implement the policy so it will both benefit and enhance the workforce (Gorren, 2013).

Gorren, W. (2013). *Understanding the Americans with Disabilities Act* (Fourth Edition). Retrieved from www.americanbar.org/products/inv/book/214495/

Authority

Jonathan Raymond shares what he has learned over his 20 years of experience as an executive, entrepreneur, team leader, and leadership trainer. Through real-life examples, Jonathan brings his audience through a step-by-step approach in how to transform company culture through great leadership and management of people (Raymond, 2016).

Raymond, J. (2016). *Good authority. How to become the leader your team is waiting for*. Retrieved from http://catalog.2seasagency.com/book/good-authority/

Controlling costs

Understanding the importance of preparation and interpretation of financial information is key to operating a business (Oliver, 2006).

Oliver, L. (2006). The cost management toolbox: A manager's guide to controlling costs and boosting profits (First). New York: AMACOM.

Discrimination

This guidebook provides insight to protecting against and understanding how to prevent workplace discrimination (England, 2018).

England, D. C. (2018). The essential guide to handling workplace harassment and discrimination (4th ed.). Berkeley, CA: NOLA.

Challenges in the workplace can be identified when hiring only one classification of employee, in this case, only white workers (Roediger, 2007).

Roediger, D. R. (2007). The wages of whiteness: Race and the making of the American working class (Revised). Verso Books.

Job description

The following is a handbook that is designed to help HR mangers create a good job description, hire qualified employees, evaluate job performance, plan for the company's future needs, avoid legal traps, and troubleshoot a description (Mader-Clark, 2013).

Mader-Clark, M. (2013). *The job description handbook* (3rd ed.). Retrieved from https://store.shrm.org/The-Job-Description-Handbook

Organizational culture

In delivering happiness, Zappos CEO, Tony Hsieh, shares the different lessons he has learned in business and life, from starting a worm farm to running a pizza business, through LinkExchange, Zappos, and more (2013).

Hsieh, T. (2013). *Delivering happiness: A path to profits, passion, and purpose* (Reprint). New York, NY: Grand Central Publishing.

What leaders need to know to change organizations for the better is addressed when understanding culture and why it is important (Watkins, 2013).

Watkins, M. D. (2013, May 15). What is organizational culture? And why should we care? *Harvard Business Review*. Retrieved from https://hbr.org/2013/05/what-is-organizational-culture

The following article discusses key concepts pertaining to organizational culture and describes general strategies and HR practices that employers can use to create and sustain a strong business (Society for Human Resource Management, 2018).

Society for Human Resource Management. (2018, August 13). Understanding and developing organizational culture. Retrieved November 27, 2019, from the SHRM website: www.shrm.org/resourcesandtools/tools-and-samples/toolkits/pages/understandinganddevelopingorganizationalculture.aspx

Organizational structure

A well-designed structure induces specialization and competence, teamwork, accountability for results, innovation, and performance in every function within the organization (Meyer, 2017).

Meyer, N. D. (2017). Principle-based organizational structure: A handbook to help you engineer entrepreneurial thinking and teamwork into organizations of any size (1st ed.). NDMA Publishing.

Recruiting

The following is a must-read for attracting hourly employees. This book offers a proven step-by-step approach to recruiting top talent (Kleiman & Kleiman, 2002).

Kleiman, M., & Kleiman, B. (2002). *Recruit smarter, not harder*. Houston, TX: HTG Press.

Selection

This engaging work presents the latest research, court findings, and practices in human resources to equip organizations' selective programs (Gatewood, Feild, & Barrick, 2015).

Gatewood, R., Feild, H. S., & Barrick, M. (2015). *Human resource selection* (8th ed.). Boston: Cengage Learning.

The following is a solution-oriented guide to recruiting and cultivating the best workforce and how to keep it that way (Harvard Business Review, 2003).

Harvard Business Review. (2003). *Hiring and keeping the best people*. Boston: Harvard Business Review Press.

Journal

ADA

Despite the ADA being in place for nearly 30 years, there are still challenges; consider ways to improve a workplace's low employment by examining opportunities for persons with disabilities in the workplace (Ramsey, 2015).

Ramsey, M. (2015, October 1). The ADA at 25: The remaining challenges. Retrieved November 22, 2019, from SHRM website: www.shrm.org/hr-today/news/hr-magazine/pages/the-ada-at-25-the-remaining-challenges.aspx

Authority

Compliance with authority is necessary for the success of any organization's operation (Karakostas & Zizzo, 2016).

Karakostas, A., & Zizzo, D. J. (2016). Compliance and the power of authority. *Journal of Economic Behavior & Organization*, 124, 67–80. https://doi.org/10.1016/j.jebo.2015.09.016

Chain of command

There are ramifications for when the chain of command is not followed; consider this article for advice (Ayers, 2017).

Ayers, A. A. (2017). Who's the boss? The organizational impact of bypassing the chain of command. *Journal of Urgent Care Medicine*. Retrieved from www.jucm.com/whos-boss-organizational-impact-bypassing-chain-command/

Controlling costs

Effective management includes strategies to control costs (Buss, 2011).

Buss, H. (2011). Controlling conflict costs: The business case of conflict management. *Journal of the International Ombudsman Association*, 4(1), 54–62.

Discrimination

Various forms of discrimination in the workplace can contribute to occupational health issues (Okechukwu, Souza, Davis, & de Castro, 2014).

Okechukwu, C. A., Souza, K., Davis, K. D., & de Castro, A. B. (2014). Discrimination, harassment, abuse, and bullying in the workplace: Contribution of workplace injustice to occupational health disparities. *American Journal of Industrial Medicine*, *57*(5), 573–586. https://doi.org/10.1002/ajim.22221

Diversity

Analyzing workforce diversity and its impact on organizational productivity, researchers in this paper conclude that although "no two humans are alike," proper management of diversity can strengthen and increase productivity (Saxena, 2014).

Saxena, A. (2014). Workforce diversity: A key to improve productivity. *Procedia Economics and Finance*, *11*, 76–85. https://doi.org/10.1016/S2212-5671(14)00178-6

Recruiting

The Society for Human Resource Management's guide to understanding the process of recruiting and attracting talent (Breaugh, n.d.).

Breaugh, J. A. (n.d.). Recruiting and attracting talent. *SHRM Foundation*, 43.

This article provides an analysis of current recruitment methods and recommendations based on four identified major needs (Bergwerk, 1988).

Bergwerk, J. (1988). Recruitment and selection for company culture. *Journal of Managerial Psychology*, *3*(1), 9–15. https://doi.org/10.1108/eb004424

Selection

This paper explores the often-conflicting rights of all members involved in the hiring process and discusses whose are more important using real scenarios (Connerley et al., 2001).

Connerley, M. L., Arvey, R. D., Gilliland, S. W., Mael, F. A., Paetzold, R. L., & Sackett, P. R. (2001). Selection in the workplace: Whose rights prevail? *Employee Responsibilities and Rights Journal*, *13*(1), 1–13. https://doi.org/10.1023/A:1014466023589

The Society for Human Resource Management provides a guide to implementing formal selection assessments (Pulakos, 2005).

Pulakos, E. D. (2005). Selection assessment methods: A guide to implementing formal assessments to build a high-quality workforce. *SHRM Foundation*, 60.

Web links

ADA

www.ada.gov provides information and technical assistance on the provisions stated under the Americans with Disabilities Act ("ADA.gov homepage," n.d.).

ADA.gov homepage. (n.d.). Retrieved November 22, 2019, from www.ada.gov/

Authority

This article defines workplace authority and discusses topics such as maintaining workplace authority as management, earning it as an employee, the effects of positive workplace authority on profitability, and the negative economic consequences of power abuse (Mueller, 2017).

Mueller, D. (2017, September 26). What is workplace authority? Retrieved November 22, 2019, from Biz Fluent website: https://bizfluent.com/info-7758942-workplace-authority.html

This article provides five ways a manager can show authority, without yelling. These five tips include making it impersonal, changing your tone, getting to know your colleagues, knowing when and how to de-escalate things, and clarifying facts. Additionally, the author suggests actions such as conducting research before speaking, demonstrating seriousness through non-verbal communication, and choosing the right location for discussion (Quast, 2013).

Quast, L. (2013, August 12). How to exert authority at work without yelling or screaming. Retrieved November 22, 2019, from Forbes website: www.forbes.com/sites/lisaquast/2012/08/13/how-to-exert-authority-at-work-without-yelling-or-screaming/#3f82497a4852

Chain of command

The chain of command is one of the most difficult leadership concepts for small business owners or executives to implement (Grev, 2014).

Grev, I. (2014). How leaders should manage their chain of command. *The Business Journals*. Retrieved from www.bizjournals.com/bizjournals/how-to/growth-strategies/2014/06/how-leaders-should-manage-their-chain-of-command.html

Controlling costs

This article looks at ways to manage labor as a cost reduction strategy (Inc, 2015).

Inc, H. (2015, July 23). Managing labor costs: 5 ways you can improve your skills. Retrieved November 22, 2019, from Humanity website: www.humanity.com/blog/5-ways-to-better-manage-your-labor-costs.html

Discrimination

Learn about various types of employment discrimination, laws, legal protections, and how to handle discrimination issues (Doyle, 2019b).

Doyle, A. (2019b, November 18). Types of employment discrimination. Retrieved November 23, 2019, from The Balance Careers website: www.thebalancecareers.com/types-of-employment-discrimination-with-examples-2060914

Tips to help identify discrimination in the workplace are identified by this blogger (Alnaji, 2019).

Alnaji, C. (2019). Discrimination in the workplace happens: Here's how to spot it. Retrieved November 23, 2019, from Fairy God Boss website: https://fairygodboss.com/articles/discrimination-in-the-workplace-happens

Diversity

This article provides two examples of the challenges that come with managing a diverse workforce and guidelines to follow for an effective diversity program (C., 2017).

Victoria, C. (2017, June 29). Diversity and the workplace. Retrieved November 27, 2019, from Experience website: www.experience.com/advice/professional-development/diversity-and-the-workplace/

It goes in depth with eight benefits of workplace diversity. These eight include increased productivity, creativity, and profits; improved employee engagement; reduced turnover; better company reputation; wider range of skills; and cultural insight (Clarke, 2015).

Clarke, L. (2015, November 24). 8 amazing benefits of cultural diversity in the workplace. Retrieved November 27, 2019, from The 6Q Blog website: https://inside.6q.io/benefits-of-cultural-diversity-in-the-workplace/

Flexibility

Emphasizing the importance of flexibility, this article discusses why employers value flexible employees, why employees value flexible managers, and examples of the skill in action (Doyle, 2019a).

Doyle, A. (2019a, October 21). Why employers value flexible employees. Retrieved November 27, 2019, from The Balance Careers website: www.thebalancecareers.com/workplace-flexibility-definition-with-examples-2059699

Selection

This interesting take proposes including current employees in the selection process (Heathfield, 2019).

Heathfield, S. M. (2019, June 25). Employee involvement is key in a successful employee selection process. Retrieved November 29, 2019, from The Balance Careers website: www.thebalancecareers.com/employee-involvement-in-the-employee-selection-process-1919152

This article provides seven tips to help better your organization's selection process and chances of success (Hayton, 2018).

Hayton, E. (2018, June 27). 7 tips for a successful employee selection process. Retrieved November 29, 2019, from the Harver website: https://harver.com/blog/successful-employee-selection-process/

Part 2

Building your leadership credibility

How to use this part

This part examines the development of a leader in the hospitality industry. Being a leader can be challenging and, on many occasions, not viewed with a sense of credibility or respect by other managers or subordinates.

Key terms

The key terms found in the cases in this section are listed in the following, their definitions can be found on page xiv-xviii.

Anger	Harassment
Assertiveness	Humor/sarcasm
Authority	Incivility
Big picture	Influence
Buy-in	Leadership styles
Change	Meetings
Coaching	Open-door policy
Credibility	Organizational structure
Decision-making	Rapport
Defensiveness	Self-confidence
Delegation	Team building
Feedback	Training
Flexibility	Trust
Hands-on	Unpopular decisions

Kitchen camaraderie

Case type: head case

Main subjects
Recruiting/Selection, Self-Confidence

Who's who
• Pascal Gateau, Executive Chef
• Lori Grafton, Food and Beverage Assistant
• Matthew Knorr, Director of Food and Beverage

Think point

Building a team takes significant time and energy. While there is typically one person as the manager who serves as the leader of a department, it is the collective efforts of all the individuals in the department that create a culture of camaraderie and respect. The role of an executive chef is sometimes seen as demonstrating strong management skills whereby the line-level employees are less of a team and more individuals to the final product.

The topic of the food and beverage (F&B) meeting today was the importance of camaraderie.

Chef Gateau was enthusiastic about the subject and shared his view with the other managers.

Lori, the F&B assistant, kindly took notes and placed the draft meeting minutes on Matthew's desk. Here are some of the comments the chef made:

Food quality

I have total control over how I run my kitchen.
The ingredients are the star of my dishes.
I get great compliments for my dishes.
I feel like my cooking is instinctive cooking.
My plates are so hot that when you touch them, you are going to need a napkin.

Creating a team

I hire and promote people who complement me and have strengths where I need them.
I spend much time and energy building my team.
My team sees me as a strong member of the team.
I run my kitchen as a group effort and push my vision of perfection.
My team is dedicated and focused.
If I want my cooks to do their best work, I must supply them with the best ingredients.
I encourage my team to develop a habit of increasing guest interaction.

Closing comment

My advice for new employees is, don't let your ego get in the way.

The chef's performance appraisal was coming up, and Matthew definitely wanted to highlight areas of improvement.

1   What advice would you give Matthew?
2   Imagine that you are interviewing potential candidates who are systematically avoiding the word "I" when you ask them to speak about their past achievements. How would these applicants sound to you?

The case is based on the principles and situations described in the following:

Wilder, J. (2005, August). Kitchen camaraderie. *Santé*, *9*(5), 32.

Off-the-record

Case type: head case

Main subjects
Harassment, Open-Door Policy, Trust

Who's who
- Paul Bello, Purchasing Manager
- Anisa Schumacher, Purchasing Agent
- Corey Widman, Bellman

Think point

Serving in the role as a manager provides a potential opportunity where line-level employees may come to you to address areas of concern. Sometimes, these matters of concern might test your comfort level with their topic of trust as it relates to confidentiality.

"May I have a confidential meeting with you?" asked Anisa, one of the purchasing agents.

"Sure," answered Paul Bello, as he invited Anisa into his small office next to the loading dock.

"Please don't say anything to anyone," Anisa said.

"No worries." Paul smiled. "This will be between you and me; you have my word on this."

"This is about Corey, the bellman," continued Anisa. "He is harassing me, but I don't want anyone to know about the situation. . . . I'm in a family crisis situation," Anisa added and started to cry hysterically.

Paul's hands got sweaty, and he really did not know what to say now that Anisa had confided in him.

1   Is Paul obligated to honor this kind of employee request? Explain.

2   What should Paul have done differently?

3   Assume that you are Paul, and an employee from the F&B division is requesting a confidential meeting with you. What would be your response in that case?

Don't shoot the messenger

Main subjects
Buy-In, Change, Credibility, Influence, Unpopular Decisions

Who's who
• Shakia Andrews, Executive Housekeeper
• Angelica Hoang, Housekeeper
• Dan Mazur, Director of Rooms

Think point

The hospitality industry is well known for being a place of employment where turnover is high. In this case, when a new manager comes into the workplace, it's a matter of taking the time to understand the employees on the team and how best to communicate with them about new policies and procedures. In the event that the policies are not delivered in a credible fashion, it can be challenging to obtain buy-in from the line-level employees. Consider how the manager's credibility comes into play when trying to influence the acceptance of new changes.

Building your leadership credibility

The housekeeping department held an unusually well-attended meeting. Most of the time was dedicated to the new policy recently introduced by management. According to the new procedure, housekeepers are required to ensure that dirty room service carts do not remain in the hotel corridors. From now on, they will be asked to push the carts down to the back landings, located on each guest floor.

Heated words were exchanged as many housekeepers expressed anger and concern about the additional workload.

"I hear you guys. I am on your side. But you know how it is; she didn't allow me to do what I wanted. . . . Welcome to the Royal Hotel!" Shakia smiled, while gesturing toward the second floor where Dan's office is.

Angelica, one of the longstanding housekeepers, tried to calm the others down in a surprisingly compassionate tone of voice. "Ladies, please don't shoot the messenger; Shakia is not responsible for this new procedure."

1   Evaluate Shakia's actions in dealing with the situation. How do you explain her behavior?

2   How do you think employees perceive Shakia as a manager?

3   If you were in charge, how would you have handled the implementation of this new procedure?

The flashbacks

Main subjects
Assertiveness, authority, coaching, feedback, incivility, influence, meetings, organizational structure, rapport

Who's who
- Shakia Andrews, Executive Housekeeper
- Lori Canelle, Spa Manager
- Carlos Diaz, Guest Services Manager
- Judith Grace, Front Office Manager
- Robert Kunz, General Manager
- Dan Mazur, Director of Rooms
- Kalinda Stenton, PBX Manager
- Marina Wright, Revenue Manager

Think point

Facilitating a meeting takes practice, especially when you have employees or colleagues who have a more difficult time being corralled. Think about how you can address the time allocated to remain time-on-task. Managers should consider clearly setting the expectations prior to any meeting.

Dan couldn't fall asleep. Just a bad day! First of all, the Rooms Division meeting, with a full agenda, started 20 minutes late this afternoon, as Mr. Kunz stopped by and was causally speaking about various topics. "And that joke!" Dan remembered.

"Stop me if you've heard the latest joke," said Kunz, turning to the group. "The trouble with being a leader—" he started.

"I know," Marina interrupted. "Is that you can't be sure whether people are following you or chasing you," she finished with a chuckle.

No one else was laughing, and at once, everybody in the room became silent. Kunz was finally paged by the front desk and left the meeting.

That was just the start! Overall, Dan did not feel that the meeting had gone well, and he kept having flashbacks about various parts of it. He was constantly pondering what the best way to deal with similar occurrences in the future would be.

Flashback 1

At a previous Rooms Division meeting, Dan assigned a short, five-minute report on a specific topic to each department head. At today's meeting, Kalinda was scheduled to present her findings. However, Kalinda prepared not only the report but a longer PowerPoint presentation and had demanded from Dan, during the meeting, more time to present the slides to the managers. Dan was caught completely off guard.

Flashback 2

Shakia gave a brief overview on cleaning supplies that included a slide about how well housekeeping managed this expense line. Dan noticed a calculation error that entirely changed the accuracy of Shakia's data. The department actually spent more money than was budgeted. Dan politely mentioned the mistake. Marina also pointed out a small spelling error on the slide. Shakia was visibly outraged.

Flashback 3

After Shakia finished her overview, Lori asked her numerous questions about what cleaning supply she should use to disinfect the sauna.

Flashback 4

Judith spoke rarely and avoided eye contact; she was clearly not used to participating in discussions.

"Let's hear now from Judith," Dan prompted her in the middle of the meeting.

She blushed, feeling she was being put on the spot, and was unable to contribute.

Flashback 5

Everybody knew that Carlos and Lori disliked each other. In the past, Carlos often tried to make Lori look like a fool. While addressing the issue of setting up a crunch team, Lori suggested that Carlos should cross-train all employees on how to park a car. He answered Lori that her idea was really brainless, and he did not have the extra money to pay for the training hours. Lori got defensive and commented in detail on Carlos's questionable organizational skills during peak hours.

Flashback 6

The team was obviously struggling with the mystery shopper report follow-up.

Dan was seeking some consensus on whether the Rooms Division should involve other managers as well to perform regular room spot checks. However, the department heads were unable to reach a decision, and the group was unclear as to what steps to take next. Dan was desperately looking for the right way to refocus the group's energy and attention.

Flashback 7

Kalinda suggested that to improve the level of service, guests should be asked if they wished to be woken up in English, Spanish, or possibly in other languages.

"Kalinda, this is not a very useful idea," Dan told her.

At this point, the banquet houseman came in and asked if he could start setting up the room for dinner.

1   Do you agree with the following statement? "Incivility in meetings is affected by status. Those with greater power have more ways to be uncivil and get away with it." Please explain.

2   A variety of situations can arise when you chair a meeting.

   a   Identify the issues that are present in this case.
   b   What recommendations would you give to Dan in terms of addressing each issue effectively in the future?

3   Assume that Marina is too talkative in the meeting. How would you cut her off?

4   What general observations can be made to prevent such situations from reoccurring?

Exhibit 13.1 Meeting agenda

Royal Hotel
Rooms Division Meeting – Agenda
Bedford Meeting Room
Wednesday, January 10, 2018
2:00 PM

1   Overview of year 2017 – Dan
2   The floor is yours – Kalinda
3   Cleaning supplies – Shakia
4   Developing a crunch plan for guest services – brainstorming
5   Mystery shopper report follow-up
6   New business

The case is based on the principles and situations described in the following:

Bielous, G. (1996, June). Five ways to cope with difficult people. *SuperVision, 57*(6), 14–16.

Butler, A. S. (2013, December 19). *20 Techniques to improve meeting productivity: #5 Parking Lot*. Retrieved September 23, 2017, from www.avasbutler.com/20-techniques-to- improve-meeting-productivity-5-of-20-parking-lot/#.WcbLh7KGOUk

Cava, R. (2004). *Dealing with difficult people* (pp. 176–180). Buffalo, NY: Firefly Books.

Hamlin, S. (2005). *How to talk so people listen* (pp. 263–295). New York, NY: HarperCollins Publishers.

Lilley, R. (2002). *Dealing with difficult people* (pp. 125–137). London: Kogan Page.

Ramsey, R. D. (2000, October). Watch how you talk about your job. *SuperVision, 63*(10), 17–19.

Stone, F. (2003). *The manager's question and answer book* (pp. 76–95). New York, NY: Amacom.

The morning fun

Case type: incident case

Main subjects
Harassment, humor/sarcasm

Who's who
• Jane Peterson, Hotel Manager
• Brian White, Assistant Director of Engineering

Think point

You may have heard the phrase "Laughter is the best medicine." However, if humor is engaged as a practice, are there limits implemented as to avoid creating a hostile work environment? Humor and sarcasm can potentially lead to the creation of harassment in the workplace.

Jane often started her meetings with a quick "life lesson."

"I believe that laughter can make a difference. Humor lowers stress and promotes teamwork. When it comes to hiring employees, the Royal Hotel is always looking for people with a good sense of humor." This is how Jane started the safety meeting today.

"I have a joke," said Brian from engineering. At this point, he started to explain to the audience, "The top 10 reasons why a handgun is better than a woman."

Everyone was laughing in the room, including Jane. She looked around and said, "That's what I said! Fun boosts performance. No other female is in the room, and I'm not offended at all. Let's review the monthly accidents."

1   Evaluate the situation. What might be some of the issues in this case?

2   List those topics that you can joke about in the workplace. What are the subjects and situations that should be avoided?

3   Should the Royal management take any action?

The juice squeezer

Main subjects
Assertiveness, big picture, buy-in, change, controlling costs, decision-making, respect, unpopular decisions, trust

Who's who
• Wesley Edwards, Room Service Manager
• Matthew Knorr, Director of Food and Beverage
• Nick Willems, Room Service Server

Think point

When making decisions to control costs and to enhance the guest service experience, it is common to enlist the ideas and support of the front-line employees. This tactic will lead to a greater level of open communication and respect.

Wesley's last performance appraisal indicated that he needs to work on his people skills. He knows that trust and respect must be earned over time, with repeated experience. Therefore, he was happy when room service servers recently approached him with their idea of making fresh orange juice in the guest rooms. The employees' spokesperson, Nick, even showed Wesley a manual juice squeezer in a catalog and explained, "This will enhance the customers' value perception, and we can make more tips."

Unbeknownst to the servers, the Royal Hotel recently decided to purchase freshly squeezed orange juice from a local company, which was delivered every morning, to save money. Wesley was therefore hesitant with his answer.

Seeing this, Nick said with disappointment in his voice, "You guys just don't respect us and our ideas."

Deep inside, Wesley disliked Nick and didn't believe that he should be part of the Royal team.

Earlier that morning, Wesley had already made an appointment with Matthew to discuss the growing number of timing-related guest complaints and ways of keeping food and beverage (F&B) costs within budgetary guidelines.

Even though he had doubts about the viability of the employees' suggestion, he decided to further discuss the juice squeezer with Matthew. The F&B director carefully listened while Wesley explained the idea to him. At the end, the F&B director looked at Wesley somewhat annoyed and said, "As much as I appreciate that you shared this with me, I am more interested to hear what you told your team about their suggestion." When Wesley remained silent, Matthew suggested that he would get back to the employees.

1 Can managers respect those employees they mistrust or dislike?

2 Identify behaviors promoting and undermining trust in the following areas:

- Interpersonal skills.
- Fairness / consistency.
- Decision-making process.
- Information flow.
- Achievements / mistakes.
- Feedback / criticism.
- Problem and conflict resolution.

3 How do you think Wesley's willingness to address his team's idea with Matthew will further earn the employees' respect?

4 What problems might Matthew see concerning Wesley's effectiveness as a manager?

The service elevator

Main subjects
Anger, assertiveness, buy-in, change, rapport, unpopular decisions, team building,

Who's who
• Carlos Diaz, Guest Services Manager
• Matthew Knorr, Director of Food and Beverage
• Dan Mazur, Director of Rooms

Think point

When making decisions that will impact the service experience encountered by guests, it would be wise to include all of the parties involved in the process. Open lines of communication will assist in the support of an idea or rationalizing why an idea may not be suitable.

Carlos was furious at Dan. He swore at him and yelled, "That's the stupidest thing I've ever seen! How could you do something like that?" He slammed his fist against his desk, the vein in his temple pulsating. "Answer me! How could you do something so stupid?"

Every morning at the Royal Hotel, during heavy check-out periods, one of the service elevators is reserved for bell attendants so that they can efficiently transport luggage from guest rooms to the front door area. Yesterday, after lengthy discussion, Dan and Matthew agreed that room service would be using this elevator, as the hotel had been receiving a large number of complaints because of breakfast delivery delays.

Dan turned to Carlos and said to him, "Your behavior is not appropriate here at work," but the guest service manager was so angry that he couldn't even hear him.

> a   How do you think Dan should deal with Carlos?
>
> b   Use the seven steps outlined here to identify some options and strategies for Dan.
>
> c   Be creative. Where appropriate, identify statements and questions Dan could use.

Exhibit 16.1 Royal Hotel – management handbook (excerpts)

Dealing with anger

You goal is not to get rid of anger – it's to help the other person express his or her anger more calmly, so the two of you can solve the problem. When someone is angry at you, these skills can help you lower the intensity of his or her anger.

1) Deciding whether the other person really wants to work things out with you

Although we like to assume that the person does, it's possible that he or she is too emotional at the moment to want to work on it. To gain the other person's cooperation and willingness to do his or her part of the work, occasionally you may have to get upper management's help.

2) Being direct

Being direct means the following:

* Talking to the right person.
* Being specific and making clear what your goals or purposes are.

3) Acknowledging feelings

Acknowledge the anger, talk about it, listen to the person experiencing it, and validate it – before you try to talk about the facts or other issues. The angry person will be calmer and more reasonable if he or she first has a chance to be heard.

4) Finding something in common

When someone is angry at you, thinking about what you have in common can help prepare you to talk to him or her about the issue.

5) Depersonalizing

A major source of anger and conflict is taking things too personally. To depersonalize, you must ask yourself whether what you heard (or think you heard) is related to work, or whether it is a personal attack. If it is related to work, focus on the work issue involved and disregard the personal references.

6) Identifying the real issues

The key – once feelings are acknowledged and common ground is established – is getting to the real issues.

Getting to the real issues helps you move past misinterpretations, vague impressions, and assumptions and enables you to deal with the facts.

7) Letting go

In anger and conflict, the need to let go means that even though you've taken all the preceding steps, you still can't make the other person do what you want and you can't make things turn out the way you want. What you've done is allow for what you want to happen – and the response is in the other person's hands.

The case is based on the principles and situations described in the following:

McClure, L. (2000). *Anger and conflict in the workplace*. Manassas Park, VI: Impact Publications.

Claudia's training assignment

Main subjects
Assertiveness, defensiveness, feedback, rapport

Who's who
- Shakia Andrews, Executive Housekeeper
- Claudia Kawata, Management Trainee
- Manuel Mercadante, Houseman
- Mary Sims, Catering Coordinator
- Kelly Woodstock, Catering Manager

Think point

Management training programs are an excellent way for new entrants into the industry to quickly learn and develop the necessary skills to become an entry-level manager. Regardless of the position, feedback can be something hard both to deliver and to receive. Learning how to respond to feedback in a positive manner is a practiced approach.

Six months ago, Claudia was hired to be part of the Royal Management Training Program. This is a self-paced, individual program designed to provide candidates with the leadership skills necessary to become entry-level managers. The key component of this program is rotating through just about every department at the Royal Hotel. As part of the schedule, Claudia had to perform a variety of learning activities. According to the training guideline, this month, she had to focus on developing coaching abilities. Today, she had to complete some assignments on "Delivering Constructive Feedback."

Starting next week, Claudia will attend a one-week classroom session to recap the material she has covered over the first six months. Let's assist her.

1   Claudia, these are the discussion questions for your classroom training session next week:

a   Many people resist critical feedback; receivers are likely to disagree with critiques. Please explain.

b   Employees need to receive feedback regarding their performance. At the same time, feedback often results in performance declines. Why? To explain, please consider the following areas:

- Feedback's focus and purpose.
- Number of sources.
- Individual factors – employee.
- Individual factors – supervisor.
- Organizational factors.

2   Written assignment A – communication patterns

- Please review the following managerial statements. Identify mistakes and if necessary suggest an alternative approach for the managers that build rapport.
- Recommend alternative employee answers as well for the mini-scenario only. Be creative.
- Please read Exhibit 17.1 before starting this exercise.

Statement M: Manager E: Employee	Your comments	Alternative managerial approach
M: You are doing an amazing job here at the Royal, but I am concerned about your work on this project.		
M: (handing a folder to the employee) This doesn't work. The memorandum needs fixing.		
Mini-scenario		
M: I can't believe you haven't done the schedule.		
E: I am in the middle of doing some other stuff.		
M: Great! This is what we call the Royal attitude.		
E: Sorry, I'm busy; this is my eighth consecutive shift.		
F: Well, welcome to the hotel industry.		
E: I do my best.		
M: I warn you, your annual appraisal is coming up.		

Statement M: Manager E: Employee	Your comments	Alternative managerial approach
M: Look at this table setup. Only a very sloppy person would accept it. I'm being very reasonable about this.		
M: You must remember that . . .		
M: (watching how the employee talks to a guest on the phone) You really have an attitude problem.		
M: (glancing at the employee's desk) You're really disorganized.		
M: You're well organized.		
M: You're aggressive.		
M: You're confident.		
M: It's not professional to show up late.		
M: I'm happy to see that your work is getting better.		
M: Your presentation was well received.		
M: You have been showing disrespect for Mike again.		
E: (sharing his medical condition)		
M: Well, over 50, this can happen. I'm sorry!		
M: You never complete work by the deadline.		

3   Written assignment B – communication patterns

You witnessed that the following statement was made by Shakia, a Royal manager:

"Manuel is not a team player. I need to sit down with him." Assume that you serve as Shakia's coach. Identify and ask her a few questions in order to make her feedback session with Manuel a successful one. (Please review the concepts in Exhibit 17.1 again.)

4   Written assignment C – interpersonal styles

You are Kelly, the catering manager. You have drafted a long and rather complicated wedding proposal for an important client. You have agreed with Mary, the catering coordinator that it will be ready at four o'clock to allow time for last-minute changes. It is now half past four, and there is still no sign of the proposal. Identify a passive, an aggressive, and an assertive way of approaching the coordinator.

Please review Exhibit 17.2 before starting this exercise.

5   Written assignment D – assisting techniques

- Please review the following managerial statements. Suggest solutions that build rapport.
- Please read Exhibit 17.3 before starting this exercise.

M: Manager E: Employee

Statement	Suggested solution
"You" and "I" statements	
M: When you interrupt me, you are being rude.	
M: You let me down.	
Closed and open questions	
M: Why did you do that?	
M: Surely you can recognize the error, can't you?	
Paraphrasing	
E: I am overloaded. I have too many assignments.	
Mirroring	
E: Honestly, I've had it! The hotel is bombarding me with new assignments to the point where there's no way I can finish the shift report.	
E: I'm doing twice as much work as Mary is, and it's unfair.	
Reframing	
E: You're sneaky! I can't believe that you brought this up to Dan behind my back.	
Higher-up M: You're a slacker, and you're not pulling your weight here at the Royal.	

Exhibits

Royal Hotel – Management Training Manual (excerpts)
 Delivering constructive feedback
 The way managers deliver feedback strongly influences its effectiveness.
 Presented in the following (Exhibit 17.1) are guidelines intended for effective feedback.

Exhibit 17.1 communication patterns

- Conflict often arises out of our patterns of communication. Many responses that we give and receive from others fall somewhere on these nine communication continua. Our ability to comprehend patterns of communication will enhance relationships with those with whom we communicate.

- Each continuum represents a type or category of response that we may either give to others or receive from others. The line also represents a range of responses with each of the categories. The extreme ends of the continua are examples of opposite comments or responses. Any particular response may fall at an extreme end or somewhere along a continuum.
- The pattern of responses we give and receive defines the quality of our interpersonal relationships. It is important to study our communication patterns to make necessary adjustments that may improve our relationships with others.

Note: The usage of the following nine communication continua is often simultaneous. These overlapping patterns complement as well as weaken or strengthen each other.

Corrective ◄──────────────────────────► **Reassuring**

Corrective feedback is used to alter a behavior that is ineffective or inappropriate. Under the best of circumstances, the subordinate will probably feel a little defensive or embarrassed.

(Focus on errors)

Reassuring feedback is used to reinforce behavior that is effective and desirable.
  If a supervisor concentrated on what employees were doing well, then superior work is what those employees would become aware of.

(Focus on excellence)

Defensive ◄──────────────────────────► **Supportive**

Defensive behaviors

- Messages carry judgments and evaluation of others or their ideas.
- One attempts to control the conversation or situation.
- Messages suggest the speaker is trying to direct others.
- Messages demonstrate lack of interest or indifference.
- There is no room for differing ideas or viewpoints.

  When a defensive communication style is utilized, the receiver most often responds defensively.

Supportive behaviors

- Messages are clear, specific statements without loaded words or judgmental cues.
- A problem orientation is not imposing.
- Speaker's talk is unplanned and free of hidden motives.
- Messages convey interest and understanding and are responsive to the other's feelings and thoughts.
- Equality is based on mutual trust and respect.

A supportive climate is built on understanding. When using this style of communication, a manager is concerned and willing to listen to the explanation offered by the subordinate.

Superiority ← → **Equality**

Superiority

People generally respond negatively to superior messages. They produce defensiveness and hard feelings.

Equality

These messages have the opposite effect. Those who receive them often regard them as being supportive.

Solution giving ← → **Problem inquiry**

Solution giving

At this end, we give solutions without exploration or inquiry about what the problem might be. A supervisor who gives solutions may negatively affect the decision-making ability of his or her employees.

Problem inquiry

Engaging in problem inquiry often helps others to discover their own solution to their problem or conflicts. Problem inquiry uses questions to expand the conversation, open up our thoughts, and enrich our exploration of the problems; it helps us gain insight into our problems.

Evaluative / Judgmental ← → **Descriptive**

Evaluative/Judgmental

Evaluative responses only communicate one's interpretation of events or data. Evaluative words, especially negative ones, are likely to cause a defensive reaction.

Descriptive

Illustrations or examples are enabling the recipients to make a concrete connection with what the feedback giver is talking about. Feedback givers should be able to give multiple illustrations of the behavior that was of concern and that led to their conclusion.

General ◄───► Specific

General / Global

The vagueness makes the feedback difficult to interpret correctly. Global or blanket statements often produce defensiveness.

Specific

Unless the feedback is specific, very little learning or reinforcement is possible.

Focus on attitude ◄───► Focus on behavior or actions

Attitude

The more that feedback is molded in terms of attitude, the more it will be perceived as a personal attack and the more difficult it will be to deal with.

Behavior/Actions

Separate the people from the problem. People have total control over their own behavior. Employees may be held accountable for their actions.

Ignore feelings ◄───► Empathy

Ignore Feelings

Ignoring feelings can cause conflict and damage relationships.

Empathy

Empathetic responses provide senders an opportunity to discuss their feelings if they choose. These responses usually expand the conversation as people open up and discuss their inner feelings. They send the unspoken message that you care about others.

Absolute ◄───► Conditional

Absolute

Absolute language oversimplifies the truth and limits understanding to simplistic, black-and-white concepts. Absolute responses are seldom accurate. They leave no room for variability, flexibility, or uncertainty and could undermine employees' self-esteem.

Conditional

On the conditional end of the continuum are responses that fairly address the situation. The manager is taking into consideration a variety of possible solutions or approaches from which to choose.

Exhibit 17.1 is in part based on the information from Goodwin, C. and Griffith, D.B. (2007). *The Conflict Survival Kit: Tools for Resolving Conflict at Work* (pp. 99–111). Upper Saddle River: NJ: Pearson.

Exhibit 17.2 Interpersonal styles

Every time we speak, we choose and use one of three basic communication styles: passive, assertive, and aggressive.

Passive	Assertive	Aggressive
* Passivity is not speaking up for your own rights and interests. * Submissive people give in, even at their own expense, to avoid the discomfort of potential confrontation.	* Assertiveness is speaking up for your own rights and interests without violating the rights and interests of others. * Assertive people stand their ground; they are factual and straightforward.	* Aggressiveness is acting for your own rights and interests in a way that violates the rights and interests of others. * Aggressive people quickly escalate a conversation into adversarial.

Exhibit 17.3 Assisting techniques

"You" and "I" statements

- Beginning with "You" is more likely to convey the impression that you blame the other person and that you are certain only your perceptions are correct. If the other person then responds with a "You" statement, assigning responsibility back to you, negative feelings may escalate, and it may become harder to reach an understanding. In most cases, "You" messages provoke a defensive response and an argument.
- By beginning the message with "I" rather than "You," the focus is less on blaming and more on helping the receiver understand the perceptions of the feedback giver. An "I" message is an honest statement in that it discloses to the other person how you genuinely feel.

Closed and open questions

Questioning has a special place in coaching. Asking good questions enables us to understand people on their own terms.

- Closed-ended questions prompt a very short, predictable answer. Closed questions tend to be straightforward, and we can use them when we want specific information. These questions generally do not lend themselves to continued conversation and may be perceived by the person being questioned as hostile or provoking.

- We can encourage the flow of information by asking more open-ended questions. An open-ended question invites a person to explain his or her point of view. They are more likely to de-escalate emotion and encourage others to "open up" and share thoughts, feelings, and opinions.

Paraphrasing

- A paraphrase is a restatement in your own words of what you think the sender is saying in his or her message. A paraphrase will demonstrate to the sender how accurately you understand the contents of a message.
- Paraphrasing helps clarify meaning in two ways. First, by offering the speaker your version of what you've heard, you test your understanding. Second, a paraphrase demonstrates your attention and interest, thus "rewarding" the speaker and encouraging further sharing and at a deeper level.

Mirroring

- When we mirror, we hold a mirror up to the other person – describing how they look or act. We respectfully acknowledge the speaker's feelings or emotions.
- The purpose of reflecting is to let the speaker know that you understand how he or she feels about a particular topic or issue. Reflective statements are short declarative statements without indicating agreement or disagreement.
- Mirroring bad feelings helps to lower the emotional temperature.

Reframing

- It is difficult to maintain an attitude of curiosity and control over our emotions while we are being accused and blamed. One tool we can use as listeners is reframing. Reframing is a way of responding to a comment that changes its "frame," or subjective aspects, while maintaining its essential content.
- Statements can be reframed in ways that make them more positive, more future-oriented, and much more constructive.
- Through the reframing process, we can turn negative or hostile statements into problems to be solved collaboratively.

The case is based on the principles and situations described in the following:

Cannon, M. D., & Witherspoon, R. (2005). Actionable feedback: Unlocking the power of learning and performance improvement. *Academy of Management Executive*, 19(2), 120–134.

Collins, S. D. (2005). *Managing conflict and workplace relationships* (pp. 54–55, 72–73). Mason, OH: Thomson South-Western.

Gillen, T. (1992). *Assertiveness for managers* (p. 315). Brookfield, VT: Gower.

Goodwin, C., & Griffith, D. B. (2007). *The conflict survival kit: Tools for resolving conflict at work*. Upper Saddle River: NJ: Pearson.

Guilar, J. D. (2001). *The interpersonal communication skills workshop* (pp. 52, 69–70). New York, NY: Amacom.

Karp, H. (2005). The lost art of feedback. In J. Gordon (Ed.), *Pfeiffer's classic activities: For developing new managers* (pp. 251–262). Indianapolis, IN: Wiley and Pfeiffer.

Newman, D. R., & Hodgetts, R. M. (1998). *Human resource management: A customer-oriented approach* (67–77). Upper Saddle River, NJ: Prentice Hall.

Silberman, M., & Hansburg, F. (2000). *PeopleSmart: Developing interpersonal intelligence* (pp. 95–117). San Francisco, CA: Berrett-Koehler Publishers, Inc.

Silverman, S. B., Pogson, C. E., & Cober, A. B. (2005). When employees at work don't get it: A model for enhancing individual employee change in response to performance feedback. *Academy of Management Executive*, *18*(2), 135–147.

Sonnenschein, W. (1997). *The diversity toolkit* (pp. 126–128). Lincolnwood, IL: Contemporary Books.

Case 18

The six leadership styles

Case type: application case

Main subjects
Authority, buy-in, change, coaching, credibility, decision-making, influence, leadership styles, trust

Who's who
• Shakia Andrews, Executive Housekeeper

Think point

There is a variety of known leadership management styles. Understanding these styles and how best to communicate can assist in having a positive influence among subordinates.

Shakia recently completed a Royal leadership seminar to learn how different leadership styles affect performance and results. She called a housekeeping management meeting for this afternoon to explain to assistant managers the importance of being flexible and not relying on only one leadership style. To illustrate the difference between styles, she came up with the following scenario:

"We are considering a new system of rotating rooms for housekeepers so that everyone gets a turn at the most expensive guest rooms and the best tips."

62

She closed her eyes and imagined using each of the six major leadership styles. (See Exhibit 18.1.)

1   How would you approach the housekeeping employees? For each leadership style, write a one-paragraph script for Shakia. Be creative.

2   Discuss the impact that each style can have on the housekeeping work climate.

3   How do you think housekeeping employees will perceive Shakia as a manager in each of these situations?

Exhibit 18.1 Royal Hotel – management handbook (excerpts)

The six leadership styles

The best, most effective leaders act according to one or more of six distinct approaches to leadership and skillfully switch between the various styles depending on the situation.

	Coercive	Authoritative	Affiliative	Democratic	Pacesetting	Coaching
The leader's modus operandi	Demands immediate compliance	Mobilizes people toward a vision	Creates harmony and builds emotional bonds	Forges consensus through participation	Sets high standards for performance	Develops people for the future
The style in a phrase	"Do what I tell you."	"Come with me."	"People come first."	"What do you think?"	"Do as I do, now."	"Try this."
When the style works best	In a crisis, to kick-start a turnaround, or with problem employees	When changes require a new vision, or when a clear direction is needed	To heal rifts in a team or to motivate people during stressful circumstances	To build buy-in or consensus or to get input from valuable	To get quick results from a highly motivated and competent team	To help an employee improve performance or develop long-term strengths

Adapted excerpt by permission of *Harvard Business Review*.

From "Leadership that gets results" by Goleman, D., *78*(2), 78–90.

Copyright © 2000 by the Harvard Business School Publishing Corporation; all rights reserved.

> ## Part summary
>
> This section covered the aspects of developing a manger into a leader, an individual who is well respected by subordinates and who has the credibility to make positive operating decisions. Consider methods of communication as the first line of defense to operating successfully. Various leadership styles were also examined.

Additional reading

Books

Authority

Through his decades of experience in consulting with corporations and teaching MBA students the nuances of organizational power, Pfeffer, in his book, helps readers understand organizational dynamics but, more specifically, how and why people succeed (Pfeffer, 2010).

Pfeffer, J. (2010). *Power: Why some people have it – and others don't*. Retrieved from www. gsb.stanford.edu/faculty-research/books/power-why-some-people-have-it-others-dont

Big picture

This book provides ideas, insight, tips, and tools for HR professionals looking to further develop their career and success (Ulrich, Younger, Brockbank, & Ulrich, 2012).

Ulrich, D., Younger, J., Brockbank, W., & Ulrich, M. (2012). *HR from the outside in: Six competencies for the future of human resources* (1st edition). New York: McGraw-Hill Education.

A company's success lies upon five drivers: cash, profit, assets, growth, and people. Readers are provided with practical knowledge and advice to help individuals see and contribute to the bigger picture of an organization (Cope, 2012).

Cope, K. (2012). *Seeing the big picture: Business acumen to build your credibility, career, and company* (1st edition). Austin, TX: Acumen Learning.

Change

This international bestseller serves as a practical toolkit and guide on how to manage change with positive results (Kotter, 2012).

Kotter, J. P. (2012). *Leading change* (1R edition). Boston, Mass: Harvard Business Review Press.

Coaching

Respected Dr. Angus McLeod gathered the best fundamental practices in coaching in this comprehensive handbook that is designed to help HR managers and coaches who evaluate performance (McLeod, 2003).

McLeod, A. (2003). *Performance coaching: The handbook for managers, H.R. professionals and coaches* (1st ed.). United Kingdom: Crown House Publishing.

Feedback

The following is book of gathered insights from neuroscience and psychology that provides practical advice on how to turn feedback into something productive (D. Stone & Heen, 2014).

Stone, D., & Heen, S. (2014). *Thanks for the Feedback: The science and art of receiving feedback well (even when it is off base, unfair, poorly delivered, and, frankly, you're not in the mood)* (1st ed.). New York, NY: Penguin Group USA.

Flexibility

Author Peter Reilly discusses flexibility in its five different types to emphasize its management benefits of reducing costs, improving quality and service, increasing productivity, hedging against change, and meeting supply needs (Reilly, 2001).

Reilly, P. A. (2001). *Flexibility at work: Balancing the interests of employer and employee* (1st ed.). United Kingdom: Gower Publishing, Ltd.

Hands-on

The following is a book that challenges readers to rethink their attitude toward work and realize that not every person is suited for an office life (Crawford, 2011).

Crawford, M. B. (2011). *The case for working with your hands, or, why office work is bad for us and fixing things feels good* (1st ed.). London: Penguin Viking.

Harassment

The following is a tutorial book that provides steps for investigation regarding workplace harassment, a sample of a harassment policy, and a memo initiating investigation (Oppenheimer & Pratt, 2002).

Oppenheimer, A., & Pratt, C. (2002). *Investigating workplace harassment: How to be fair, thorough, and legal*. Retrieved from https://store.shrm.org/Investigating-Workplace-Harassment-How-to-Be-Fair-Thorough-and-Legal-Practical-HR-Series

Incivility

This book looks at how managers and employees can improve their workplace with civility (Porath & Pearson, 2016).

Porath, C., & Pearson, C. (2016). *Mastering civility: A manifesto for the workplace*. New York: Grand Central Publishing.

Influence

The following is a book that introduces tools to help leaders build influence, promote their interests, and get buy-in (Oade, 2010).

Oade, A. (2010). *Building influence in the workplace: How to gain and retain influence at work* (2010 edition). Basingstoke, New York: Palgrave Macmillan.

Leadership styles

This book provides a comprehensive overview of the most commonly used leadership styles in business (Sandling, 2014).

Sandling, J. (2014). *Leading with style: The comprehensive guide to leadership styles.* Retrieved from www.goodreads.com/work/best_book/42943225-leading-with-style-the-comprehensive-guide-to-leadership-styles

Meetings

A book for project managers and team leaders to learn meeting tools to maximize engagement from participates and get great input (Turmel, 2014).

Turmel, W. (2014). *Meet like you mean it: A leader's guide to painless and productive virtual meetings.* Illinois: Achis Marketing Services.

Organizational structure

Business firms around the world are experimenting with new organizational designs, changing their formal architectures, their routines and processes, and their corporate cultures as they seek to improve their current performance and their growth prospects (Roberts, 2004).

Roberts, J. (2004). *The modern firm: Organizational design for performance and growth* (1st ed.). New York: Oxford University Press.

Rapport

Through a close look at scholarly research and science, this book goes in depth about rapport and how to create it and provides practical applications to maintain it (Angelo, 2015).

Angelo, G. (2015). *Rapport: The art of connecting with people and building relationships* (*Rapport, how to build rapport, how to connect with people, rapport building, connecting people, building relationships*) (1st ed.). Scotts Valley, CA: CreateSpace Independent Publishing Platform.

Self-confidence

Written by the leading authority on self-esteem science, this book provides a rigorous yet approachable look into what constitutes self-esteem (Branden, 1995).

Brandon, J. (2014, October 6). 10 ways to build your confidence at work. Retrieved from Inc.com website: www.inc.com/john-brandon/10-ways-to-build-your-confidence-at-work.html

Negative peer relationships, especially with a boss, can greatly undermine employee confidence, but there are ways to improve management techniques to avoid this (Smith, 2012).

Smith, J. (2012, March 6). How to be more confident at work. Retrieved November 29, 2019, from *Forbes* website: www.forbes.com/sites/jacquelynsmith/2012/03/06/how-to-be-more-confident-at-work/#47de6f05d9b2

Team building

This book outlines the five common dysfunctions that teams face and suggests a powerful model and steps to overcome them in the context of a fable (Lencioni, 2002).

Lencioni, P. (2002). *The five dysfunctions of a team: A leadership fable* (1st ed.). San Francisco, CA: Jossey-Bass.

This collection of *Harvard Business Review* articles compiles ten inspiring and useful perspectives on superior team building (Harvard Business Review, 2011).

Harvard Business Review. (2011). *Harvard business review on building better teams* (1st ed.). Boston: Harvard Business Review Press.

Training

With a research-based approach presented in a lively, engaging tone, this book takes training professionals through exercises and tools that set new standards for the training industry (Stolovitch, & Keeps, 2011).

Stolovitch, H. D., & Keeps, E. J. (2011). *Telling ain't training: Updated, expanded, enhanced* (2nd ed.). Alexandria, VA: Association for Talent Development.

Ray Noe, a seasoned training and human resources professor and manager, combines experience, new technology and research, and an evolving sense of how to effectively train into a book filled with development practices that add value to both the employee and the employer (2016).

Noe, R. A. (2016). *Employee training & development* (7th ed.). Hoboken, New Jersey: McGraw-Hill Professional Publishing.

Trust

This best-selling book breaks down the concept of trust in a comprehensive way and offers sample scripts and skills to help readers build trusting relationships (Feltman, 2011).

Feltman, C. (2011). *The thin book of trust: An essential primer for building trust at work.* Bend, OR: Thin Book Publishing.

Journals

Big picture

This article identifies big strategic questions that every leader should spend time evaluating and wrestling with how to answer. Tips include making choices in the negative, pretending you have no money, talking to the unusual suspects, and existing at the macro and micro levels simultaneously (Johnson, 2016).

Johnson, E. (2016). How leaders can focus on the big picture. *Harvard Business Review.* Retrieved from https://hbr.org/2016/11/how-leaders-can-focus-on-the-big-picture

Change

The interconnected functions of training, development, and innovation are components of organizational change (Sartori, Costantini, Ceschi, & Tommasi, 2018).

Sartori, R., Costantini, A., Ceschi, A., & Tommasi, F. (2018). How do you manage change in organizations? Training, development, innovation, and their relationships. *Frontiers in Psychology*, *9*, 313. https://doi.org/10.3389/fpsyg.2018.00313

Decision-making

This study identifies the factors influencing success in decision-making among organizational leaders and managers in organizations' practices (Obioma Ejimabo, 2015).

Obioma Ejimabo, N. (2015). The influence of decision making in organizational leadership and management activities. *Journal of Entrepreneurship & Organization Management*, *04*(02). https://doi.org/10.4172/2169-026X.1000138

Delegation

Designed for busy managers, this book serves as a guide with included tips, exercises, self-assessments, and worksheets to understand the "easy-to-master five-step process for effective delegation" that teaches how to determine which tasks to delegate, identifying the right person for the job, assigning the task, monitoring progress while providing feedback, and evaluating performance (McIntosh & Luecke, 2009).

McIntosh, P., & Luecke, R. A. (2009). *The busy manager's guide to delegation*. Retrieved from www.oreilly.com/library/view/the-busy-managers/9780814414743/

Consisting of advice, this book will teach readers how to establish a productive environment, assigning the right work to the right people, conducting an effective hand-off meeting, and monitoring without micromanaging (Harvard Business Review, 2014).

Harvard Business Review. (2014). *Delegating work (HBR 20-minute manager series)*. Retrieved from https://store.hbr.org/product/delegating-work-hbr-20-minute-manager-series/16999

Harassment

Sarcasm, despite its role, can instigate conflict and be a catalyst for creativity (Huang, Gino, & Galinsky, 2015).

Huang, L., Gino, F., & Galinsky, A. D. (2015). The highest form of intelligence: Sarcasm increases creativity for both expressers and recipients. *Organizational Behavior and Human Decision Processes*, *131*, 162–177. https://doi.org/10.1016/j.obhdp.2015.07.001

Influence

Employees at all organizational levels have influence over their subordinates, their colleagues, and even their bosses. This article offers some practical solutions to help employees more fully recognize their influence over other members of the organization (Bohns & Flynn, 2013).

Bohns, V. K., & Flynn, F. J. (2013). Underestimating our influence over others at work. *Research in Organizational Behavior*, *33*, 97–112. https://doi.org/10.1016/j.riob.2013.10.002

Leadership styles

The following is a review paper that summarizes literature on leadership styles and their effect on the quality of work life (Nanjundeswaraswamy & Swamy, 2014).

Nanjundeswaraswamy, T. S., & Swamy, D. R. (2014). Leadership styles. *Advances in Management*, 7(2). Retrieved from www.mnsu.edu/activities/leadership/leadership_styles.pdf

The following essay addresses topics such as, to name a few, HRM, HR's importance as a source of competitive advantage, leadership, its different styles, employee job satisfaction, and cultural influences ("Human resource management," 2018).

Human resource management: Leadership styles. (2018, July 25). *UKEssays.Com*. Retrieved from www.ukessays.com/essays/management/human-resource-management-and-leadership-style-management-essay.php

Meetings

This study provides illustrative comments on the effectiveness / ineffectiveness of and forms of improvement for workplace meetings (Geimer, Leach, DeSimone, Rogelberg, & Warr, 2015).

Geimer, J. L., Leach, D. J., DeSimone, J. A., Rogelberg, S. G., & Warr, P. B. (2015). Meetings at work: Perceived effectiveness and recommended improvements. *Journal of Business Research*, 68(9), 2015–2026. https://doi.org/10.1016/j.jbusres.2015.02.015

Open-door policy

This journal article suggests the open-door policy improves trust, communication, and motivation with employees and also provides an outline of characteristics of effective policies (Shenhar, 1993).

Shenhar, A. (1993). Keeping management's door open: How to establish an open door policy that works. *Leadership & Organization Development Journal*, 14(2), 8–12. https://doi.org/10.1108/01437739310032665

Self-confidence

This review of literature shows the significance of self-esteem in relation to an employee's identity, responsiveness, and professional presence (Jan, Khan, Khan, Khan, & Saif, 2015).

Jan, F., Khan, M. R., Khan, I., Khan, S., & Saif, N. (2015). The employees' self-esteem: A comprehensive review. *Public Policy and Administration Research*, 5(5), 52–56.

Team building

This article will make you view team building as an investment and implement it as such (Scudamore, 2016).

Scudamore, B. (2016, March 9). Why team building is the most important investment you'll make. *Forbes*. Retrieved from www.forbes.com/sites/brianscudamore/2016/03/09/why-team-building-is-the-most-important-investment-youll-make/#31a9d6fc617f

Empirical research shows that teams can be improved through a variety of teamwork training techniques (McEwan, Ruissen, Eys, Zumbo, & Beauchamp, 2017).

McEwan, D., Ruissen, G. R., Eys, M. A., Zumbo, B. D., & Beauchamp, M. R. (2017). The effectiveness of teamwork training on teamwork behaviors and team performance: A systematic review and meta-analysis of controlled interventions. *PLOS ONE*, 12(1), e0169604. https://doi.org/10.1371/journal.pone.0169604

Training

This article breaks down the shortcomings and negative connotation that training carries in most workplaces and proposes a time-tested learning model that any organization can benefit from using (Meyer, 2014).

Meyer, S. J. (2014, July 1). Why workplace learning fails, and why it's time to ban the fire hose. *Forbes*. Retrieved from www.forbes.com/sites/stevemeyer/2014/07/01/why-work place-learning-fails-and-why-its-time-to-ban-the-fire-hose/#7e56d3e96365

The following qualitative research analyses the existing literature and case studies on training in relation to employee performance in order to develop a checklist for management to evaluate employees that is adaptable to all businesses (Elnaga & Imran, 2013).

Elnaga, A. A., & Imran, A. (2013). The effect of training on employee performance. *European Journal of Business and Management, 5*(4), 137–147.

Unpopular decisions

Here, *Fortune* offers steps and real-world examples regarding how to announce unpopular decisions in the best way to alleviate tensions between management and employees (Covin, 2016).

Covin, G. (2016, June 8). Here's the right way to make unpopular decisions. *Fortune*. Retrieved from https://fortune.com/2016/06/08/leadership-unpopular-decisions/

A best-selling author breaks down the different excuses executives offer to avoid making tough decisions and empowers readers to adjust their mind-set when it comes to decision-making (Carucci, 2018).

Carucci, R. (2018, April 13). Leaders, stop avoiding hard decisions. *Harvard Business Review*. Retrieved from https://hbr.org/2018/04/leaders-stop-avoiding-hard-decisions

Web links

Authority

Authority is a quality by which your employees recognize and respect you as a managerial person of prestige. This article discusses how an individual may establish an attitude of authority in the workplace by displaying his or her leadership qualities, providing employees with what they need to perform their tasks, keeping customers in front of your employees' minds, acting with consistency, and striving for balance between an overly directive and an overly collaborative environment (Paige, n.d.).

Paige, A. (n.d.). How to establish attitude of authority in the workplace. Retrieved November 22, 2019, from Chron.com website: https://smallbusiness.chron.com/establish-attitude-authority-workplace-10114.html

Big picture

The author discusses innovative solutions for strategic thinkers, how to develop a strategic mind-set, and examples of provocative questions to ask (Bing, 2013).

Bing, L. A. (2013, July 26). Big-Picture mentality: How to develop strategic leadership skills. Retrieved November 23, 2019, from www.blackenterprise.com/big-picture-mentality-how-to-develop-strategic-leadership-skills/

This lesson reviews the concept of understanding the big picture in a workplace in addition to identifying the advantages of having this knowledge (Haire, n.d.).

Haire, L. (n.d.). The benefits of understanding the big picture at work. Retrieved November 23, 2019, from https://study.com/academy/lesson/the-benefits-of-understanding-the-big-picture-at-work.html

This blog post puts into perspective what it would be like to have employees fully engaged in the big picture of the organization. Specifically, the article discusses how to get employees engaged and how understanding the big picture leads to successful strategy execution (Haudan, 2017).

Haudan, J. (2017, June 28). Engaging your employees in the big picture. Retrieved November 23, 2019, from Root Inc. website: www.rootinc.com/blog/engaging-employees-big-picture/

Buy-in

This video lesson discusses how employee buy-in promotes engagement and willingness to work hard. It is, therefore, a very significant component to understand and develop in the workplace (Davis, 2018).

Davis, O. (2018). *Employee buy-in: Definition and explanation – video & lesson transcript.* Retrieved from https://study.com/academy/lesson/employee-buy-in-definition-lesson-quiz.html

This article discusses the value of teamwork, incentives to employee buy-in, and barriers to team buy-in (Half, 2017).

Half, R. (2017, April 25). How (and why) to get employee buy-in on projects. Retrieved November 24, 2019, from Robert Half website: www.roberthalf.com/blog/management-tips/how-and-why-to-get-employee-buy-in-on-projects

According to this article, establishing employee buy-in begins with "knowing your why" to find purpose and build an exceptional work culture (Renjen, 2012).

Renjen, P. (2012, September 26). How to get employee buy-in to build exceptional culture. *Fast Company.* Retrieved from www.fastcompany.com/3001573/how-get-employee-buy-build-exceptional-culture

This article takes the approach of "selling in" to an idea by "describing and defending." The idea behind this approach is to develop an idea, sell it to ourselves first, and then go about selling it to others (Hedges, 2015).

Hedges, K. (2015, March 16). How to get real buy-in for your idea. *Forbes.* Retrieved from www.forbes.com/sites/work-in-progress/2015/03/16/how-to-get-real-buy-in-for-your-idea/#19bb68a44044

Change

As the next organizational shift approaches, this article discusses the psychological rationale behind employee backlash while providing tips on how to get employees excited about significant changes (Hao & Yazdanifard, 2015).

Hao, M. J., & Yazdanifard, R. (2015). How effective leadership can facilitate change in organizations through improvement and innovation. *Global Journal of Management and Business Research: Administration and Management*, 15.

The following article puts into perspective the need for mutual understanding between an employer and employee amid the process of change (Reh, 2019).

Reh, F. J. (2019, February 4). The gentle way to implement change in the workplace. Retrieved November 24, 2019, from The Balance Careers website: www.thebalancecareers.com/managing-change-managing-people-s-fear-2275302

Coaching

Now moving away from the past performance-related focus in coaching, this article addresses the shift that has been taking place toward a more future-focused coaching style in recent years (Skidmore, 2018).

Skidmore, K. (2018, May 29). The purpose of coaching in the workplace has changed. Retrieved November 24, 2019, from Flash Point Leadership website: www.flashpointleadership.com/blog/the-purpose-of-coaching-in-the-workplace-has-changed

Decision-making

The following *Forbes* article discusses methods to encourage employees to practice decision-making and why employees should be involved in it (Kappel, 2018).

Kappel, M. (2018, April 4). How to encourage employee involvement in decision making. *Forbes*. Retrieved from www.forbes.com/sites/mikekappel/2018/04/04/how-to-encourage-employee-involvement-in-decision-making/#3fb71b716561

The following article identifies matters to consider when in need to make the best possible decision for the company. This includes gathering information, evaluating if the decision would be good for the company, considering the long term, understanding that there are no perfect solutions, and avoiding being stubborn (Issid, 2016).

Issid, J. (2016, January 7). Making difficult decisions at work. Retrieved November 24, 2019, from Monster website: https://hiring.monster.ca/employer-resources/workforce-management/hr-management-skills/making-decisions-at-work/

Defensiveness

Identifying the negative impacts of defensive behavior, this article provides a list of five steps for individuals to manage their defensiveness (Cramm, 2015).

Cramm, S. (2015, January 12). Defensive behavior and the bosses that provoke it. Retrieved November 27, 2019, from Strategy+business website: www.strategy-business.com/blog/Defensive-Behavior-and-the-Bosses-That-Provoke-it?gko=84169

This article identifies four ways to communicate with defensive people by refraining from reacting defensively, shifting the focus to the other person, asking questions to understand them, and moving toward a resolution (Roselle, 2018).

Roselle, B. (2018, November 2). 4 ways to communicate better with defensive people. *The Business Journals*. Retrieved from www.bizjournals.com/bizjournals/how-to/human-resources/2018/11/4-ways-to-communicate-betterwith-defensive-people.html

The *Harvard Business Review* identifies a procedure called "three strikes and you're in" to think through before becoming defensive in a situation (Goulston, 2013).

Goulston, M. (2013, November 15). Don't get defensive: Communication tips for the vigilant. *Harvard Business Review*. Retrieved from https://hbr.org/2013/11/dont-get-defensive-communication-tips-for-the-vigilant

Delegation

In addition to identifying reasons why managers may not delegate work, a preparation checklist called the "Delegator's Dozen" is provided in this article to help managers delegate effectively (Lloyd, 2012).

Lloyd, S. (2012). Managers must delegate effectively to develop employees. Retrieved November 27, 2019, from SHRM website: www.shrm.org/resourcesandtools/hr-topics/organizational-and-employee-development/pages/delegateeffectively.aspx

Hands-on

The following article suggests five reasons why employers should take the hands-on approach for employee training on soft skills (Wigston, 2019).

Wigston, S. (2019, May 9). 5 reasons to take a hands-on approach to soft skills training. Retrieved November 27, 2019, from Training Industry website: https://trainingindustry.com/blog/leadership/5-reasons-to-take-a-hands-on-approach-to-soft-skills-training/

This *New York Times* article discusses the need for hands-on learning experience, as the world will remain abstract and distant and the passions for learning will not be engaged without it (Crawford, 2009).

Crawford, M. B. (2009, May 21). The case for working with your hands. *New York Times*. Retrieved from www.nytimes.com/2009/05/24/magazine/24labor-t.html

Harassment

The U.S. government website for the Equal Employment Opportunity Commission informs about the laws surrounding harassment and the liability that an employer is automatically responsible for (EEOC, n.d.).

EEOC. (n.d.). Harassment. Retrieved November 27, 2019, from US Equal Employment Opportunity Commission website: www.eeoc.gov/laws/types/harassment.cfm

The following article discusses when workplace harassment becomes unlawful, states and companies that may have broader definitions of workplace harassment, types of harassment, topics that should not be asked at job interviews to avoid harassment, the boundary for acceptable behavior, and laws surrounding the topic (Doyle, 2019).

Doyle, A. (2019, November 18). Types of employment discrimination. Retrieved November 23, 2019, from The Balance Careers website: www.thebalancecareers.com/types-of-employment-discrimination-with-examples-2060914

Incivility

The following article discusses incivility at the workplace, the problems that it can create, what managers can do about it, and how to reduce rudeness in the workplace (Mankodi, 2018).

Mankodi, T. (2018, December 24). Workplace incivility and rudeness needs to stop. Here's why. Retrieved November 27, 2019, from Ascend: Harvard Business Review website: https://hbrascend.org/topics/workplace-incivility-and-rudeness-needs-to-stop-heres-why/

This *Forbes* article addresses the negative effects of incivility, especially when it is ignored, and how leadership can establish a zero tolerance for incivility (Murrell, 2018).

Murrell, A. (2018, July 16). Stopping the downward spiral of workplace incivility. Retrieved November 27, 2019, from Forbes website: www.forbes.com/sites/audreymurrell/2018/07/16/stopping-the-downward-spiral-of-workplace-incivility/#5a2ec7ef54ef

Influence

This article leads to five leadership books that provide influence (Kinni, 2008).

Kinni, T. (2008, February 29). Five books that will amplify your ability to lead through influence. *Harvard Business Review*. Retrieved from https://hbr.org/2008/02/five-books-that-will-amplify-y

This paper gives evidence that suggests employees are constrained by cognitive biases that lead them to underestimate their influence over others in the workplace (DeMers, 2015).

DeMers, J. (2015, January 15). 7 ways to build influence in the workplace. Retrieved November 27, 2019, from Inc. website: www.inc.com/jayson-demers/7-ways-to-build-influence-in-the-workplace.html

This *Forbes* article introduces techniques on how to influence others in the workplace through speaking organically, catering to the audience, and visualizing the end goal (Gibbs, 2018).

Gibbs, R. (2018, April 25). How to influence others in the workplace, regardless of your position. Retrieved November 27, 2019, from the Forbes website: www.forbes.com/sites/forbescoachescouncil/2018/04/25/how-to-influence-others-in-the-workplace-regardless-of-your-position/#77ee8a5b74cd

Leadership styles

The following article discusses the different leadership styles of autocratic, bureaucratic, laissez faire, and democratic (Foote, 2013).

Foote, T. (2013, January 27). Different leadership styles: What suits your workplace? Retrieved November 27, 2019, from Fun Team Building Company – The Leader's Institute website: www.leadersinstitute.com/different-leadership-styles-what-suits-your-workplace/

Meetings

This article identifies six different types of meetings (Linton, 2019).

Linton, I. (2019, February 5). Types of meetings in the workplace. Retrieved November 27, 2019, from Chron.com website: https://smallbusiness.chron.com/types-meetings-workplace-36827.html

Open-door policy

This author addresses ideas on how to make an open-door policy work (Waagen, 2017).

Waagen, A. (2017, March 22). How to make an open-door policy work. Retrieved November 27, 2019, from the Business Journals website: www.bizjournals.com/bizjournals/how-to/human-resources/2017/03/how-to-make-an-open-door-policy-work.html

This is the first in a series of posts examining myths about why employees don't speak up (Detert, Burris, & Harrison, 2010).

Detert, J. R., Burris, E. R., & Harrison, D. A. (2010, May 24). Good communication goes beyond open door policies. *Harvard Business Review*. Retrieved from https://hbr.org/2010/05/good-communication-goes-beyond

This author provides a few ways you can maintain a productive workday with an open-door policy (Boitnott, 2016).

Boitnott, J. (2016, August 2). 7 ways workers can have an open-door policy without going crazy. Retrieved November 27, 2019, from the Entrepreneur website: www.entrepreneur.com/article/280015

Rapport

This article discusses the importance of building rapport with team members and provides 82 ways on how to accomplish that ("82 ways how to build rapport with anyone you work with," 2019).

82 ways how to build rapport with anyone you work with. (2019, July 4). Retrieved November 29, 2019, from Lighthouse: A blog about leadership & management advice website: https://getlighthouse.com/blog/how-to-build-rapport/

Self-confidence

Here are some strategies and exercises to implement or encourage employees to take action on to boost self-confidence (2015).

The article provides ten tips for boosting workplace confidence and taking ownership (Brandon, 2014).

Branden, N. (1995). *The six pillars of self-esteem*. New York: Bantam.

Team building

This work provides a how-to guide for turning everyday moments into opportunities to build a "we" not "me" workplace culture (Goyette, 2016).

Goyette, P. (2016, February 16). 5 ways team building activities improve workplace performance. Retrieved November 29, 2019, from the Eagle's Flight website: www.eaglesflight.com/blog/5-ways-team-building-activities-improve-workplace-performance

The basis of team unity is an understanding of the organization's mission and objectives. Here are 12 tips for workplace team building (Heathfield, 2019).

Heathfield, S. M. (2019, July 30). If you want to build successful teams, use these 12 tips. Retrieved November 29, 2019, from The Balance Careers website: www.thebalancecareers.com/tips-for-team-building-1918512

Training

A brief overview of the benefits of well-structured training in the workplace (Frost, 2019).

Frost, S. (2019, February 5). The importance of training & development in the workplace. Retrieved November 29, 2019, from Chron.com: https://smallbusiness.chron.com/importance-training-development-workplace-10321.html

The following is a simple guide to aid in finding the best training method for desired outcomes and five popular methods (Andriotis, 2018).

Andriotis, N. (2018, December 27). 5 popular employee training methods for workplace training. Retrieved November 29, 2019, from the ELearning Industry website: https://elearningindustry.com/how-choose-training-methods-for-employees

Trust

The Kellogg School of Management at Northwestern University has compiled a list of insights as to what companies and individuals can do to establish trust (E. Stone, 2019).

Stone, E. (2019, February 12). Take 5: How to build trust in the workplace. Retrieved November 30, 2019, from Kellogg Insight website: https://insight.kellogg.northwestern.edu/article/take-5-how-to-build-trust-in-the-workplace

By encouraging self-reflection and providing ten ways that effective leaders build trust, *Psychology Today* gives a look into trust building and condenses the knowledge of the author's book into a short read (Russell, 2012).

Russell, N. S. (2012, August 20). 10 ways effective leaders build trust. Retrieved November 30, 2019, from Psychology Today website: www.psychologytoday.com/blog/trust-the-new-workplace-currency/201208/10-ways-effective-leaders-build-trust-0

Unpopular decisions

This article focuses on communication of unpopular decisions and provides a model and emphasis on values to help you implement the best approach (Kay, 2017).

Kay, M. (2017, February 16). Communicating unpopular decisions to team members. Retrieved November 30, 2019, from the AboutLeaders website: https://aboutleaders.com/communicating-unpopular-decisions-to-team-members/

This six-step guide will leave you feeling confident in your tough decision and help you understand the reactions you may expect to get (Xu, 2016).

Xu, K. (2016, March 3). 6 ways to execute unpopular (but wise) decisions. Retrieved November 30, 2019, from the Corp! website: www.corpmagazine.com/uncategorized/6-ways-to-execute-unpopular-but-wise-decisions/

In an age of kinder, less dominant leaders, the prospect of upsetting employees is fear-inducing and challenging. This article pushes the importance of trust and transparency to retain good rapport with staff in the face of unpopular decisions (Scharfenberg, 2018).

Scharfenberg, D. (2018, November 14). As leadership styles lean kinder, how do bosses make unpopular decisions? *Boston Globe*. Retrieved from www.bostonglobe.com/magazine/2018/11/14/leadership-styles-lean-kinder-how-bosses-make-unpopular-decisions/gASpsRDfOkAvwxaUO4iVMM/story.html

Part 3

Building and managing performance

How to use this part

It is a manager's responsibility to build upon the performance of an employee to further develop his or her skills. The methods and ways that a manager communicates with subordinates can be important to continuing to develop open communication and trust. Coach-and-counsel sessions and annual performance appraisals are two of the ways that managers can develop the employee's performance to meet or exceed standard operating procedures.

Key terms

The key terms found in the cases in this section are listed here. Their definitions can be found on page xiv–xviii.

ADA
Authority
Chain of command
Coaching
Discrimination
Diversity
Feedback
Job design
Job description
Performance appraisal
Productivity
Religion
Self-confidence
Work systems

Sorry, I don't drink!

Case type: incident case

Main subjects
Discrimination, diversity, performance appraisal, religion

Who's who
- Jennifer Ortiz, Restaurant Manager
- Masoud Mustafa, Server Assistant

Think point

The hospitality industry employs a diverse spectrum of associates. One measure of the diversity can be religious affiliation and observation. Religious preference should not be deemed as a form of discrimination.

Jennifer was about to finish Masoud's performance evaluation. He was one of the most efficient server assistants; he was ready to be promoted to a server.

As they discussed career plans, Jennifer told Masoud, "The only area you should really focus on now is wine knowledge. I would like to sign you up for an upcoming wine appreciation course.

"I'm sorry, Jennifer. I don't drink!" Masoud told her.

"But we are in the restaurant industry. You need to know about wines," Jennifer insisted.

"I'm an observant Muslim, and I would like to be a server in this five-star hotel," answered Masoud quietly.

1   Do you agree with Jennifer that Masoud should have some wine knowledge?

2   Please advise Jennifer to establish career goals for Masoud.

Oops

Main subjects
Authority, credibility, gossip

Who's who
• Alison Finley, Credit Manager
• Carlos Diaz, Guest Services Manager
• Yuan Yao, Assistant Director of Finance

Think point

Socializing outside of the workplace is a common occurrence for associates. However, there can be times in which the behaviors carried out during those experiences can be grounds for gossip to travel through the rumor mill or grapevine. Some companies may address this directly in their employee handbook, and others may not. One of the factors an associate should consider before engaging in outside of work encounters or in the consumption of alcohol is what impact such actions could have on his or her credibility as an employee or a manager.

Building and managing performance

Last week was the Royal Hotel holiday party for the managers. Alison was well behaved at the official event, but when she went out with a bunch of the managers afterward, she had a bit too much to drink at the after party, and Carlos gave her a ride home. The rumor mill is now swirling with talk about what happened between her and Carlos. This afternoon, she has a meeting with Yuan, and she's nervous that he will bring it up.

1   Should Alison be nervous about her meeting with Yuan?

2   What mistakes did Alison make?

3   How should Alison handle this situation?

4   Should Yuan bring the incident up with Alison at all?

Tyler the overnight houseman

Main subjects
Coaching, productivity

Who's who
• Shakia Andrews, Executive Housekeeper
• Tyler O'Grady, Overnight Houseman

Think point

Observation is one approach to monitoring the performance of employees in the workplace. In an attempt to continuously improve the performance and productivity of employees, observation and coach-and-counseling sessions are approaches to utilize.

This evening, Shakia had to stay late to help with the turndown service, and so she decided to wait until the overnight housemen arrived. Depending on the hotel occupancy, two or three employees were scheduled. Overnight housemen were in charge of the Royal Hotel's complimentary shoeshine service. Shakia was chatting a little bit with the employees and opted to observe them while they were polishing shoes.

Tonight, one of the housemen was Tyler. He had been at the Royal Hotel for over a year, and no complaint had ever been received about his performance. Tyler was dependable and meticulous but very, very slow.

Shakia watched as Tyler unhurriedly removed the laces to get access to the tongue of the shoe to prevent staining the laces. He then applied the polish to the shoe in slow, circular movements to ensure that the polish reached the inside of the creases. At the end, he meticulously, at a snail's pace, buffed the shoe until all traces of dullness had disappeared and the shoe shined to perfection.

Shakia admired his thoroughness, but Tyler took twice as long as the other housemen. Shakia was wondering how she could quicken his pace.

> The overnight houseman's job description included the following job requirements:
>
> Perform routine work or the same task over and over again.
> This person must have the ability to lift, pull, and push a moderate amount of weight.
> This is a fast-paced position that will involve occasional customer interaction.

> 1 Describe the problem behavior.
>
> 2 What could be causing this behavior?
>
> 3 Highlight some of the consequences that the problem behavior has on others.
>
> 4 Outline some techniques supervisors could use to deal with the issue.

The case is based on the principles and situations described in the following:

Albright, M., & Carr, C. (2002). *Solving on-the job people problems* (pp. 151–154). Paramus, NJ: Prentice Hall.

Gentle hints

Main subjects
ADA, coaching

Who's who
• Jean Andres, Front Desk Agent
• Dan Mazur, Director of Rooms
• Allen Winston, Regular Hotel Guest

Think point

The hospitality industry employees a diverse set of employees from various cultures. On occasion, the hygiene practices of individuals might not be the same as what we come to expect in the United States. While these are extremely difficult and awkward conversations to have, it is a matter of professionalism to coach an employee.

Upon check-out, Mr. Winston, one of the regular guests, approached Dan in the lobby. "Listen, Dan, I had a great stay, but I need to share something with you. Jean, your front desk agent, is an excellent employee, and I appreciate all that he does, but unfortunately, he has a slight hygiene problem. Hmm, I wanted to tell you last month; it's his body odor and bad breath, I guess," said Mr. Winston slightly embarrassed. "You may want to give him some gentle hints," continued the guest. "Otherwise, I will say, 'Hi, Jean,' instead of 'Hello' next time I'm back." Mr. Winston smiled and walked to his car.

Dan returned to his office and was wondering how he should deal tactfully with this sensitive issue.

1   Identify potential reasons for the situation.

2   Highlight and evaluate possible actions Dan could take.

3   Who should deal with hygiene problems when they arise?

The slacker

Main subjects
Job design/job description, productivity, work systems

Who's who
• Jennifer Ortiz, Restaurant Manager
• Tim Campbell, Server Assistant

Think point

Standard operating procedures (SOP) are designed to make an organization have an outline or breakdown to how service should be delivered in a timely fashion to improve the guest experience. With the advances of technology, the SOP should be re-examined on a frequent basis to ensure they are still relevant. When training occurs, the use of the SOP serves as the guideline to ensuring employees are properly trained to perform within the time frame outlined.

Building and managing performance

Every time Jennifer came to the restaurant, she had the impression that Tim, one of the server assistants, was "goofing off." Even when the restaurant was packed, he was typically standing in a corner, waiting to complete the next service step.

Server assistants were assigned to work with a certain number of servers. They were rarely helping each other. Server assistants received a portion of the tip from their respective servers.

For managers, it was most frustrating to see his slow motion while host persons and managers had to reset tables all the time. Jennifer barely had time to interact with guests and deal with other issues. Every time Tim was asked to help clear or reset tables in others sections, he claimed that he was busy with his own tables.

According to the notes of assistant managers, Tim was already advised to pull his own weight. Tim believed that he was doing his job as outlined in his job breakdown.

Jennifer knew that Tim and other server assistants should be more productive. She was rather desperate as she was reviewing the task breakdown. Some of the people around her did what they had to do but nothing more.

Selected service steps as outlined in the Royal Standard Operation Procedures:

Task Breakdown	Steps	Responsibility	Timing Standard
1.	Greet guest at the door	Host/hostess	
2.	Escort and seat guest	Host/hostess	Within 2 minutes of arrival
3.	Explain the menu, take beverage order	Server	
4.	Serve bread and butter	Server assistant	Within 2 minutes of being seated
5.	Serve beverages	Server	Within 6 minutes of order taken
6.	Take food order	Server	
7.	Serve food items	Server	Within 15 minutes of order taken
8.	Clear table	Server assistant	Within 3 minutes of all guest's finishing.
9.	Serve dessert	Server	
10.	Serve coffee	Server	
11.	Place check	Server	
12.	Reset table	Server assistant	Within 4 minutes of guests' departure

1 What seems to be happening in the restaurant? Describe the problem behavior.

2 What could be causing this behavior?

3 What recommendation might you have to improve the system? What further actions could Jennifer take in this situation?

Yasmine's appraisal

Case type: application case

Main subjects
Coaching, feedback, performance appraisal

Who's who
- Matthew Knorr, Director of Food and Beverage
- Yasmine Lewis, Hostess
- Jennifer Ortiz, Restaurant Manager

Think point

The annual performance appraisal is an opportunity to examine the performance of an employee over a one-year time period. They are intended to be a positive experience, whereby the employee can receive both positive and constructive feedback to review the last year and seek ways to continuously improve. It is up to the manager to ensure the feedback session occurs with the employee in a timely fashion tied to his or her anniversary date or the time period designated for conducting reviews. Preparation for reviews is another important aspect on the behalf of the manager.

Jennifer glanced at her wall calendar. "It's already September. I should really sit down with Yasmine and do her yearly appraisal." She sighed.

The breakfast rush was over, and in addition, the weekly food and beverage meeting was cancelled because Matthew, the F&B director, was still on vacation. So, Jennifer called the assistant manager on duty to cover the door for Yasmine while she was being reviewed for her annual appraisal. Jennifer printed the document and decided to quickly read it while waiting for Yasmine.

> 1   Let's help Jennifer. Read through the performance documentation (Exhibits 24.1 and 24.2). What mistakes did she make? Use your imagination, and revise the statements where appropriate.
>
> 2   How should managers keep track of employees' performance?
>
> 3   Should Jennifer go over the employee's appraisal with her manager before she reviews it with Yasmine?

The case is based on the principles and situations described in the following:

Chan, J. F., & Lutovich, D. (1994). *Writing performance documentation: A self-paced training program*. San Anselmo, CA: Advanced Communication Designs, Inc.

Falcone, P. (1999). Rejuvenate your performance evaluation writing skills. *HR Magazine*, 44(10), 126–136.

Society of Human Resource Management. (1996, March). *Performance appraisals: A collection of samples* (2nd ed.). Alexandria, VA: SHRM.

Exhibits

Exhibit 24.1: Royal Hotel – Manager's handbook (excerpts)
Exhibit 24.2: Yasmine's performance appraisal

Exhibit 24.1 Royal Hotel – Manager's handbook (excerpts)

Writing employee performance appraisals – guidelines

- When you evaluate an employee's performance, you need to consider behavior and results that you have observed or measured. You then need to decide whether the person's performance met, failed to meet, or exceeded expectations.
- It is the conclusions you draw from the facts that should lead to specific decisions and actions. The documents you write must not only communicate your conclusions; they must include the details that clearly support those conclusions.
- A description is only useful if the details it includes are specific and complete. Instead of relying on subjective terms and vague statements that can be misunderstood, use objective language that describes observations.
- Acceptable performance documentations tell employees clearly what they are doing well and what they need to improve.
- Performance appraisals are to be completed in a timely manner.

Exhibit 24.2

THE ROYAL HOTEL

Employee performance appraisal

NAME: Yasmine Lewis

JOB TITLE: Hostess

APPRAISAL PERIOD:

APPRAISAL PREPARED BY:
Jennifer Ortiz, Restaurant Manager

NEXT LEVEL APPROVAL:

EVALUATOR SIGNATURE:

EMPLOYEE SIGNATURE:

DEPARTMENT: Harvest Room Restaurant

DATE IN POSITION: 7/1/2017

From 7/1/2017 To 6/30/2018

DATE APPRAISAL GIVEN: 9/2/18

DATE: ____/____/____

DATE: ____/____/____

DATE: ____/____/____

My signature acknowledges that this performance summary has been discussed with me.

1. Levels of performance

Exceeds standards — Performance and results achieved consistently exceed the standards and expectations for the position requirements.

Meets standards — Performance and results achieved generally meet the standards and expectations for the position requirements.

Below standards — Performance and results achieved consistently do not meet the standards and expectations for the position requirements.

2. Situation overview

- The Harvest Room is one of the Royal Hotel's highest revenue-generating outlets and is considered one of the top restaurants in the city.
- Yasmine transferred from the Stewarding Department to the Harvest Room in July 2017.
- She has come a long way from where she started. Yasmine was "thrown in" right in the thick of the busy season as the opening hostess.

3. Performance factors

ES = Exceeds standards   MS = Meets standards   BS=Below standards

ES	MS	BS

Job knowledge & comprehension

ES		

- She is very professional.
- Yasmine is a quick learner. She has been a guiding light when it comes to the training of other hosts/hostesses.

Work quality

		BS

- Yasmine does not complete the reservation book adequately.
- In addition, she is often forgetful.
- Yasmine does not like answering the reservation hotline.
- More passion for perfection is needed.

Productivity / work habits

ES		

- She is very organized in regards to the upkeep of the host stand.
- Yasmine is a team player.
- Yasmine knows her limitations; she is very vocal when it comes time for management assistance.

Grooming

ES		

- Yasmine exhibits appropriate grooming; she is better dressed than the other AM hostess.

Initiative / problem solving

	MS	

- Although this area has yet to truly be tested, Yasmine should focus on quickly resolving issues that may arise and learn to properly use her resources to multi-task.

Interpersonal skills

	MS	

- Unfortunately, she received numerous complaints regarding her attitude.
- Although she is a nice person, she doesn't take criticism well. She has a tendency to be condescending when interacting with management.
- This is something we would like Yasmine to take note of and improve on.

Customer relations

ES		

- Yasmine is good with Royal customers.

Attendance and punctuality

		BS

- Yasmine incurred a high number of incidents of tardiness over the last 12 months.
- We expect better attendance.
- She did not show up for work on Sunday, 6/29/2018.

Total

4. Overall rating

	MS	

To conclude, Yasmine is one of the key players of the Harvest Room and a valuable part of the Royal Hotel. She has been climbing uphill since she started, and she will continue to learn as time goes by. Yasmine has become settled in her position.

5. Recommendations for future development

- Fine-tuning the service quality and becoming more knowledgeable will broaden her radar and eye for detail.
- She needs to be "warm and fuzzy" with others.

Yasmine, you recently expressed interest in becoming a supervisor. You are on the right track! Keep it up, and you may get a promotion sooner than you think.

6. Employee comments

The case is based on the principles and situations described in the following:

Chan, J. F., & Lutovich, D. (1994). *Writing performance documentation: A self-paced training program*. San Anselmo, CA: Advanced Communication Designs, Inc.

Falcone, P. (1999). Rejuvenate your performance evaluation writing skills. *HR Magazine*, 44(10), 126–136.

Society of Human Resource Management. (1996, March). *Performance appraisals: A collection of samples* (2nd ed.). Alexandria, VA: SHRM.

> ## Part summary
>
> This section covered the aspects to employee development through the use of coach-and-counseling sessions. Constructive feedback is important for the manager to deliver but can be hard for the employee to receive. Managers should consider their words and actions carefully in the preparation for any meeting with an employee, whether it be for disciplinary reasons, coaching, or to deliver an annual performance appraisal. The way that a manager communicates with subordinates can lead to being a trusted individual who has the confidence of the staff; done incorrectly, that trust can be extinguished.

Additional reading

Books

Coaching

This *Wall Street Journal* bestseller by Michael Bungay Stanier unpacks the necessary questions that need to be asked in order to develop an effective coaching method that leads to great results (2016).

Stanier, M. B. (2016). *The coaching habit: Say less, ask more and change the way you lead forever* (1st ed.). Vancouver, B.C.: Page Two: Box of Crayons.

Discrimination

Utilizing statistics, this book introduces readers to race and gender barriers in the workplace (Cohn, 2000).

Cohn, S. (2000). *Race, gender, and discrimination at work* (1st ed.). London: Routledge Westview Press.

The following is the story of one of the first women hired at Goodyear and her fight for equal pay and fairness, including the historic discrimination case and how her determination became a victory for the nation (Ledbetter & Isom, 2013).

Ledbetter, L., & Isom, L. S. (2013). *Grace and grit: My fight for equal pay and fairness at Goodyear and beyond* (1st ed.). Penguin Random House.

Diversity

The majority-culture workplace has evolved; this book discusses why it's imperative for businesses to have a diverse workforce and identifies ways that it can be accomplished (Braswell, 2019).

Braswell, P. (2019). *Let them see you*. London: Penguin Random House.

Feedback

Packed with extensive research, this book provides 16 tools for self-assessment and planning and guidelines to give helpful feedback to employees (Carroll, 2014).

Carroll, A. (2014). *The feedback imperative: How to give every day feedback to speed up your team's success* (1st ed.). Austin, TX: River Grove Books.

Job design

This book is designed to help readers understand research, theory, and the practical aspects of job design by examining innovations in manufacturing technologies, techniques, and philosophies and how these affect work design, research, and practice (Parker, Parker, & Wall, 1998).

Parker, S. K., Parker, S., & Wall, T. D. (1998). *Job and work design: Organizing work to promote well-being and effectiveness*. Thousand Oaks, CA: SAGE.

Performance appraisal

A thoroughly tested, distinctive alternative to the appraisal process that draws on well-established principles of organizational behavior, this book is practical and easy to use – featuring case studies, interviews, and useful templates (Baker, 2013).

Baker, T. (2013). *The end of the performance review: A new approach to appraising employee performance* (1st ed.). Hampshire, United Kingdom: Palgrave Macmillan.

Productivity

This influential business book guides readers on how to approach professional and personal tasks for stress-free productivity (Allen & Fallows, 2015).

Allen, D., & Fallows, J. (2015). *Getting things done: The art of stress-free productivity* (Revised). London: Penguin Books.

Religion

This book analyzes the current dynamic of religion in U.S. companies and proposes a model of respectful pluralism to create an accepting workspace (Hicks, 2003).

Hicks, D. A. (2003). *Religion and the workplace: Pluralism, spirituality, leadership*. https://doi.org/10.1017/CBO9780511615474

Journals

ADA

The purpose of the Americans with Disabilities Act (ADA) is to put into perspective how a candidate with a disability may be viewed and treated under the law during the selection and hiring process for employment of a customer service position at a large financial services corporation (Klimoski & Palmer, 1993).

Klimoski, R., & Palmer, S. (1993). The ADA and the hiring process in organizations. *Consulting Psychology Journal: Practice and Research*, 45(2), 10–36. https://doi.org/10.1037/1061-4087.45.2.10

Chain of command

It is important to understand the importance of the chain of command (Kelchner, 2019).

Kelchner, L. (2019, February 4). The importance of following the chain of command in business. Retrieved November 22, 2019, from Chron.com website: https://smallbusiness.chron.com/importance-following-chain-command-business-23560.html

Discrimination

Subtle discrimination in the workplace undermines employee and organizational functioning (Jones, Arena, Nittrouer, Alonso, & Lindsey, 2017).

Jones, K. P., Arena, D. F., Nittrouer, C. L., Alonso, N. M., & Lindsey, A. P. (2017). Subtle discrimination in the workplace: A vicious cycle. *Industrial and Organizational Psychology*, *10*(1), 51–76. https://doi.org/10.1017/iop.2016.91

Diversity

Successfully managing workplace diversity could lead a company to better financial gain due to a result in more satisfied, committed, and better-performing employees (Patrick & Kumar, 2012).

Patrick, H. A., & Kumar, V. R. (2012). Managing workplace diversity: Issues and challenges. *SAGE Open*, *2*(2), 1–15. https://doi.org/10.1177/2158244012444615

Performance appraisal

This article addresses the current dissatisfactions with appraisal systems, which will continue until they are revised to accommodate the "how" as well as the "what" in performance (Levinson, 1976).

Levinson, H. (1976, July 1). Appraisal of what performance? *Harvard Business Review* (July 1976). Retrieved from https://hbr.org/1976/07/appraisal-of-what-performance

Productivity

This article looks at productivity as the amount of value produced divided by the amount of cost (or time) required to do so (Fuller, 2016).

Fuller, R. (2016, April 19). The paradox of workplace productivity. *Harvard Business Review*. Retrieved from https://hbr.org/2016/04/the-paradox-of-workplace-productivity

The following research displays the benefits and penalties to workplace productivity (Haynes, Suckley, & Nunnington, 2017).

Haynes, B., Suckley, L., & Nunnington, N. (2017). Workplace productivity and office type: An evaluation of office occupier differences based on age and gender. *Journal of Corporate Real Estate*, *19*(2), 111–138. https://doi.org/10.1108/JCRE-11-2016-0037

Religion

A senior lecturer at Harvard Business School attributes managing religion at work to having the right attitude (Gerdeman, 2018).

Gerdeman, D. (2018, September 27). Religion in the workplace: What managers need to know. *HBS Working Knowledge*. Retrieved from http://hbswk.hbs.edu/item/religion-in-the-workplace-what-managers-need-to-know

This thorough read from the Society of Human Resource Management discusses faith-focused and faith-friendly businesses as well as many other factors to consider when managing varying religious beliefs (Grossman, n.d.).

Grossman, R. J. (n.d.). Religion at work. *SHRM*. Retrieved from www.shrm.org/hr-today/news/hr-magazine/pages/religion-at-work.aspx

Work systems

A new generation of research suggests that HR flexibility plays a key role in allowing high-performance work systems to materialize into improved organizational performance (Beltrán-Martín, Roca-Puig, Escrig-Tena, & Bou-Llusar, 2008).

Beltrán-Martín, I., Roca-Puig, V., Escrig-Tena, A., & Bou-Llusar, J. C. (2008). Human resource flexibility as a mediating variable between high performance work systems and performance. *Journal of Management*, 34(5), 1009–1044. https://doi.org/10.1177/01492 06308318616

Web links

ADA

Adata.org provides information, guidance, and training on the Americans with Disabilities act (ADA National Network, n.d.).

ADA National Network. (n.d.). What is the Americans with disabilities act (ADA)? Retrieved November 22, 2019, from https://adata.org/learn-about-ada

This official government site of the U.S. Department of Labor published the provisions under ADA (U.S. Department of Labor, n.d.).

U.S. Department of Labor. (n.d.). Americans with Disabilities Act. Retrieved November 22, 2019, from www.dol.gov/general/topic/disability/ada

Authority

In the role of management, there will more than likely be a time where an employee will challenge your authority. This video provides tips and ways on how to handle these employees and situations (Management Is a Journey, 2019).

Management Is a Journey. (2019). *How to handle employees who challenge your authority.* Retrieved from www.youtube.com/watch?v=8SirouS8ueo&feature=youtu.be

Chain of command

Understand the various chains of command structures (Heathfield, 2018).

Heathfield, S. M. (2018, September 16). Understanding the chain of command in your workplace. Retrieved November 22, 2019, from The Balance Careers website: www.thebalancecareers.com/chain-of-command-1918082

Coaching

This article addresses six steps to follow in order to be an effective and supportive coach (Heathfield, 2019).

Heathfield, S. M. (2019, August 2). 6 steps help you coach employees effectively. Retrieved November 24, 2019, from The Balance Careers website: www.thebalancecareers.com/use-coaching-to-improve-employee-performance-1918083

Discrimination

The U.S. government and the Equal Employment Opportunity Commission (EEOC) provides details to each protected class and discrimination type (U.S. Equal Employment Opportunity Commission, n.d.).

U.S. Equal Employment Opportunity Commission. (n.d.). Types of discrimination. Retrieved November 23, 2019, from EEOC website: www.eeoc.gov/laws/types/

Diversity

Identified benefits of workplace diversity include diverse backgrounds of talent, skills, and experiences; inspiration of innovation; open doors for a business through language skills; a growth in the talent pool; and improved employee performance in an inclusive environment (Deering, 2015).

Deering, S. (2015, October 12). What are the benefits of diversity in the workplace? Retrieved November 27, 2019, from the Undercover Recruiter website: https://theundercoverrecruiter.com/benefits-diversity-workplace/

The six addressed benefits of a diverse workforce include a variety of perspectives, increased creativity, increased productivity, reduced fear with improved performance, boost of brand reputation, and global impact (Stringfellow, 2019).

Stringfellow, A. (2019, July 17). 6 benefits of cultural diversity in the workplace. Retrieved November 27, 2019, from Wonolo website: www.wonolo.com/blog/6-benefits-of-having-a-diverse-workforce/

Performance appraisal

This article examines what happens when our performance is compared with those of colleagues, with implications for how performance reviews should be conducted (Gaskell, 2018).

Gaskell, A. (2018, June 21). The right and wrong way to conduct performance appraisals. Retrieved November 29, 2019, from the Forbes website: www.forbes.com/sites/adigaskell/2018/06/21/the-right-and-wrong-way-to-conduct-performance-appraisals/

Productivity

This article discusses the meaning of workplace productivity, benefits of a productive workplace, effects of low productivity, causes of low workplace efficiency, and ways to improve workplace productivity (Donohoe, 2018).

Donohoe, A. (2018, October 25). What is workplace productivity? Retrieved November 29, 2019, from the Biz Fluent website: https://bizfluent.com/info-7972229-workplace-productivity.html

Religion

The U.S. Equal Employment Opportunity Commission's official definition and laws regarding religious discrimination (U.S. Equal Employment Opportunity Commission, n.d.).

U.S. Equal Employment Opportunity Commission. (n.d.). Religious discrimination. Retrieved November 29, 2019, from U.S. Equal Employment Opportunity Commission website: www.eeoc.gov/laws/types/religion.cfm

Self-confidence

An additional 15 ways to increase self-confidence at work and view it as one of your most significant assets (Wheatman, n.d.).

Wheatman, D. (n.d.). Increasing self-confidence in the workplace. Retrieved November 29, 2019, from LiveCareer website: www.livecareer.com/resources/jobs/networking/increasing-self-confidence-in-the-workplace

Work systems

The chief excellence officer at Great Systems explains the factors that impact work systems, how to evaluate your current one, and steps to improve it in order to maximize outcomes (McManus, 2018).

McManus, K. (2018). Do you have great work systems? Retrieved November 30, 2019, from https://greatsystems.com/great-work-systems/

Part 4

Encouraging others

How to use this part

Consider how the manager can encourage the associates in the workplace by offering rewards to enhance the motivation of the individual. Organizations seek to tie work performance in a motivating way to rewards. Identify ways to provide feedback in a respectful way during coach-and-counsel sessions to improve employees' engagement with the organization.

Key terms

The key terms found in the cases in this section are listed here. Their definition can be found on page xiv–xviii.

Coaching
Feedback
Job design
Job description
Motivation
Organizational politics
Organizational structure
Promotion
Respect
Rewards
Work systems

I am just a part-timer

Main subjects
Coaching, motivation, rewards, work systems

Who's who
• Betty Chu, Human Resources Manager
• Leslie Rudick, Candidate

Think point

Business levels in a hospitality organization demand a variety of staffing options. In addition to full-time employees, many organizations will hire part-time employees. These employees may be individuals who presently work another full-time job, may be a parent looking for "mothers' hours" or students looking for limited hours. Creativity in hiring, training, and retaining the part-time employees is critical for success.

Encouraging others

Betty, from HR, called Leslie this morning. "I am delighted to inform you that we can offer you now a part-time position at the front desk."

"Great," answered Leslie. "I've finished my midterms. I can't wait to start this weekend job."

"All right, the next step for you is to attend our two-day orientation on Monday and Tuesday next week," explained Betty.

"Oops," answered Leslie, "I have classes on both these days, and I cannot miss more classes."

"You know, Leslie, without completing the orientation, you may not be employed in this hotel. Would you like to call me back?" Betty said.

For Leslie, this front-desk position was only a stopover in her pursuit of a career elsewhere. But she considered herself a hardworking and productive individual. Leslie had had various short-term positions in the past, and Betty's call provoked the usual feeling of being a temporary worker who is easily replaceable.

1   What are the advantages of using part-time employees?

2   Consider ways of hiring that can help the Royal Hotel lengthen the part-time relationship.

3   What recommendations would you give to Royal management in terms of offering training for part-timers in more creative ways?

4   Most part-timers don't intend to stay with one employer for years. How can management maximize the value of the time part-timers spend with Royal Hotel?

Housekeeping guest satisfaction scores

Case type: head case

Main subjects
Motivation, rewards

Who's who
• Shakia Andrews, Executive Housekeeper

Think point

Despite the development of standardized operating procedures for operating efficiency, employees typically will produce better results when an opportunity for rewards exists. Despite offering rewards, it is important to understand your employees and what types of rewards will motivate them to deliver better results. The two types of rewards include intrinsic and extrinsic. Intrinsic rewards are received by the individual directly through task performance. Satisfaction is derived from the job itself, such as pride in one's work, a feeling of accomplishment, or being part of a team. Extrinsic rewards are external to the job and provided by the employer. Benefits provided by the employer are usually money, promotion, or other such incentives.

Encouraging others

Shakia was desperate. The guest satisfaction scores for the Housekeeping Department had been extremely low for the past year. Though the housekeeping management procedures had been in place for several years, nearly all of the guestroom attendants had been employed by the Royal Hotel for less than two years. Shakia was not sure what had caused the perceived level of service and cleanliness to suffer.

1   Why are the guest service scores for the Housekeeping Department usually low?

2   Housekeeping managers often realize that probably the hardest part of their job is to motivate their staff. Explain.

3   Where should Shakia begin to raise the guest satisfactions scores?

4   To maintain the commitment of housekeepers, identify creative intrinsic[1] and extrinsic[2] rewards.

The case is based on the principles and situations described in the following:

Frye, W. D. (2007, July/August). Determining why housekeeping guest service scores are low. *The Rooms Chronicle, 5.*

Notes

1   Intrinsic rewards are received by the individual directly through task performance. (Satisfactions derived from the job itself, i.e. such as pride in one's work, a feeling of accomplishment, or being part of a team.)

2   Extrinsic rewards are external to the job and provided by the employer. (Benefits provided by the employer, usually money, promotion, or other benefits.)

The dead-ender

Main subjects
Motivation, organizational structure, promotion, rewards

Who's who
• Carlos Diaz, Guest Services Manager
• Amy Polak, Assistant Front Office Manager
• Marina Wright, Revenue Manager

Think point

Promotion from within can serve as a positive motivational tool for employees as well as managers to move up the career ladder. Depending on the size of the organization and the length of service of other current employees / managers, there can be a plateau for opportunities. A good business practice to retain the managers waiting for the next opportunity is to look at how the additional skills needed can be developed, as well as identifying other ways to retain associates.

Encouraging others

Amy felt that she had stayed in the same job for too long, far longer than originally promised.

She joined the Royal Hotel as an assistant front office manager four years ago.

She enjoyed her job. Many of the front-desk agents who worked under her wings had become "Employee of the Month." Lately, she was wondering why she was never considered for the "Manager of the Quarter" award.

Her problem was that while she was always busy, she wasn't learning anything new. She'd seen all the issues before. Besides boredom or the sense that everything was too repetitive, she felt that she had been taken for granted.

What had driven Amy was her desire to become a hotel manager. Both of the past two directors of rooms said they were satisfied with her performance but explained to her that the Rooms Division had no prospects for promotion in the near future. She remembered that Marina and Carlos had started their careers also at the front desk, and now they were both department heads.

Amy felt that career opportunities had become limited for her. The career ladder was blocked.

She loved the Royal Hotel, but in the last one or two years, she'd found herself thinking about leaving.

1   What are some of the reasons for employees reaching a stage where growth or movement has stopped?

2   What are some of the benefits of being temporarily plateaued?

3   What may be some of the negative effects of plateauing on the person and organization?

4   Individuals often become "indispensable" and are prevented from promotions. What are the consequences of this practice?

5   What are some the techniques to motivate employees in the absence of promotion opportunities?

The case is based on the principles and situations described in the following:

Bardwick, J. M. (1986). *The plateauing trap: How to avoid it in your career . . . your life*. New York: Amacom.

Tainted occupations

Main subjects
Job design/job description, motivation

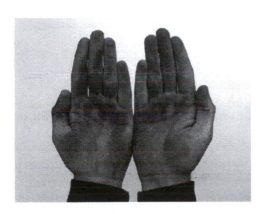

Who's who
• Matthew Knorr, Director of Food and Beverage
• Merrick Lew, Assistant Chief Steward

Think point

One of the typical ways that individuals advance in the hospitality industry is through experience. Another perspective is that a college degree should advance you faster into the industry. For those who have spent time and money to earn a college degree, the expectations for faster acceleration are a component of concern. Family and friends, outside of the hospitality industry, might find it harder to understand the positions / work entailed and determine there are stigmas to being employed in the field. For the individual working in the field, it is important to have a goal and understand the organizational structure to develop oneself to get to the intended position.

Encouraging others

Merrick recently graduated from a prestigious hospitality program. His dream has always been to become a food and beverage director. The Royal Hotel offered him the assistant chief steward position. Originally, Merrick was hoping to start in a customer contact position, but Matthew convinced him that this job would help him to achieve his career goals.

When he accepted the position, he immediately called his parents to share the news. His dad was impressed by the title. He asked Merrick what the position exactly consisted of.

"Actually, I will be in charge of the hotel's china / glass / silver budget," answered Merrick. He felt slightly embarrassed and did not say that actually he would be the boss of the dishwashers.

1   Dirty work refers to occupations that are viewed by society as physically, socially, or morally tainted. Most dirty work occupations appear to have relatively low prestige (i.e., function of status, power, education, income). Please provide a few examples of dirty occupations in the hotel industry.

2   What challenges do managers in dirty work occupations face?

3   What tactics can a manager use to neutralize the attributes of the work that render it seemingly dirty?

4   How can management enhance occupational dignity and esteem in dirty work positions?

The GM's morning round

Main subjects
Feedback, motivation, organizational politics, respect

Who's who
- Shakia Andrews, Executive Housekeeper
- Lori Canelle, Spa Manager
- Evelyn Collins, Room Service Assistant Manager
- Carlos Diaz, Guest Services Manager
- Brooke Garofalo, Front Desk Agent
- Jarrett Geller, Hotel Guest, Conference Organizer
- Evan Grafton, Valet Parker
- Amber Kerkorian, Spa Supervisor
- Robert Kunz, General Manager
- Jason Lim, Front Desk Agent
- Debbie Murphy, Sales Manager
- Fiona O'Brien, Public Relations Manager
- Kristen Palmer, Regular Restaurant Guest
- Jane Peterson, Hotel Manager
- Zachary Savin, Restaurant Server
- Sabrina Schmidt, Bartender
- Dylan Shaw, Bartender
- David Steele, Security Manager
- Hailey Valletta, Assistant Revenue Manager

An effective strategy that management can utilize is management by walking around (MBWA). When a general manager walks around the property and engages with the employees, it can increase the level of respect for that manager. Consider what is the best way to interact with employees in the most effective manner.

The Royal's executive committee invited a famous motivational speaker to the last management retreat. Robert Kunz spent the entire weekend reviewing the handout they were given.

He learned a lot about positive reinforcement and other morale-boosting strategies that could work at the Royal Hotel. Monday morning, he decided to get out of the executive office suite to engage hotel employees at all levels.

Stop 1 – Sales

He decided to begin his round at the Sales Department. "Good morning, Mr. Kunz," Debbie, the sales manager, greeted him.

"Hello, Debbie, I am so happy that I bumped into you," Mr. Kunz told her. "I need to tell you that you do an amazing job with our clients; keep up the good work." The GM smiled and proceeded to the restaurant to have a coffee.

Stop 2 – Restaurant

"I'm sure this is the day Mr. Kunz will say something!" Zachary, one of the servers, murmured to himself. The other day, Ms. Palmer, one the regular guests, mentioned to Zachary that she had sent a letter to Mr. Kunz a month ago. Ms. Palmer mentioned that she had specifically asked Mr. Kunz to praise his outstanding performance. Zachary was at first uncomfortable with what Ms. Palmer had done, but at the same time, he was excited about the possibility of being personally recognized by Mr. Kunz.

As usual, Mr. Kunz was happy with Zachary's service. He finished his cappuccino, signed the check, and left the restaurant.

"See you, Mr. Kunz. . . maybe tomorrow," Zachary told him and started to clean the table.

Stop 3 – Reservation

After his coffee, he briefly visited the reservation office. Hailey, the assistant manager, was about to finalize the ten-day forecast. "I've come to personally congratulate you, Hailey, for your accurate forecasts. What would I do without you?" Mr. Kunz told her, while studying the printout and slowly walking down the corridor between the cubicles.

Stop 4 – Front desk

"Good morning, Brooke! I heard so much about you! Mr. Geller, who organized the two-day pharmaceutical conference this week couldn't stop mentioning your name." Mr. Kunz greeted one of the front desk agents.

Brooke felt very good about Mr. Kunz's kind approach. She already knew that using names could personalize interactions. It was a little thing, but it worked. At the same time, she felt somewhat confused about the situation. She had been off the last two days, and she'd never met Mr. Geller. As soon as Jason, the other front desk agent finished a guest check-out, she walked over to him and proudly said, "You know, Mr. Kunz knows my name."

"Yes, he asked me two minutes ago what the name of the other front desk agent was," Jason said. "By the way, I authorized a late check-out to Mr. Geller in room #325. He is the nicest guest I've ever had," he added and acknowledged the next guest in line.

Stop 5 – Guest services

Evan, a long-time employee, was the valet parker this morning. Mr. Kunz approached him with uncontrollable enthusiasm. "Absolutely super! That was really great how you pulled this expensive car. We are all very impressed. Well done."

Carlos overheard the conversation and looked puzzled. He wanted to sit down this morning with Evan and have a serious heart-to-heart with him. Evan was a pleasant person but did only the minimum, the kind of person who never deviates from the book.

Stop 6 – Housekeeping

Mr. Kunz liked to stop by housekeeping, as he believed that those employees deserved daily stimulation.

Shakia had just started the pre-shift briefing when he arrived. Housekeepers were informed on what was going on at the Royal, including who was checking in so that everyone was on the same page. To lift employee spirits, Kunz provided kudos to all the employees by saying that he'd always dreamed of managing an "all-star team" and gave everyone a pin for uniforms that said, "Bravo." At the end of the meeting, he took a photo of the entire staff wearing the new pin. It would be great for the bulletin board. For his next housekeeping visit, Mr. Kunz had just signed a rush order this morning for T-shirts that said, "Pat on the back."

Stop 7 – Room service

Evelyn, one of the AM assistant managers in room service, was inspecting an order when Mr. Kunz arrived. The hotel was fully booked the night before, and Kunz had heard from Jane earlier that Evelyn had asked for help. "Well done! You handled the crunch situation this morning very effectively," the general manager told her. "It's too bad, that even with extra assistance, hotel corridors are full of dirty room service carts," added Mr. Kunz.

Stop 8 – Spa

He continued his tour at the spa. At 9:30 AM, Jane paged Kunz and informed him that Lori had called out sick and said she thought that Amber, the morning supervisor, should stay longer, as many VIP guests had made massage appointments.

The general manager approached Amber, who was serving fresh lemonade to guests.

"I can't tell you, Amber, how much we appreciate how you help us maintain our high service standards." He started the conversation with her.

"It's my job," she answered pleasantly. Amber was astonished, as she had never received any kind of compliment regarding her performance here at the Royal.

"By the way," Mr. Kunz said and smiled, "would you be available to pick up an extra shift this afternoon?"

Stop 9 – Lounge

Sabrina and Dylan, the two bartenders, were polishing martini glasses when Mr. Kunz showed up. "Here is our 'top mixologist'! How proud we are of you," shouted Kunz and pointed toward Sabrina.

One of the local magazines published a "Beloved Bartender" section every three years. They named the top bartenders in the city, did a little profile on them, and listed their favorite cocktail recipes. A journalist had contacted Fiona a few months ago, and they decided together that Sabrina should be featured in the magazine.

"You see, Dylan, you should be more like Sabrina," Kunz said and turned to the other bartender.

Stop 10 – Security

The GM concluded his morning round in the small security office.

He came to praise David for his professionalism during the power outage the day before.

Mr. Kunz had a firm handshake. David noticed that when Mr. Kunz shook his hand, he used his other hand, covering the shake, and held his hand for longer than normal. Mr. Kunz asked David to remain seated. He was standing with hands on hips, elbows out to the sides. David felt slightly uncomfortable, as the general manager took up lots up of space. Also, Mr. Kunz placed his hand twice on his arm during the conversation and interrupted him a few times.

1 Evaluate the manager's effectiveness in motivating his employees in each situation as follows.

   a   What key mistakes is Mr. Kunz making?
   b   Describe the effect of his approach on employees.
   c   What suggestions would you make to Mr. Kunz?

2 Do we need to praise every time employees do a good job?

3 Employees don't always react to praise in a gracious way. Why?

4 Telling employees, "You're doing a great job," isn't specific enough. Develop a list of "openers" that you can use to keep praise specific.

The chef's incentive program

Main subjects
Controlling costs, motivation, rewards

Who's who
- Pascal Gateau, Executive Chef
- Matthew Knorr, Director of Food and Beverage
- Robert Kunz, General Manager
- Jane Peterson, Hotel Manager

Think point

Controlling expenses is a critical piece of the business operation. In the food and beverage department, those expenses are controlled by maintaining a food cost percentage that is at or below budget on a monthly basis. Typically, the responsibility falls to both the executive chef and the food and beverage director to maintain accuracy in costs. One motivational strategy is to implement a financial reward for meeting certain goals. Consider whether it is better to go with an individual or team approach to the goal.

The executive committee meeting was short today. Mr. Kunz asked everyone to further cut costs and then abruptly left the meeting room. Jane looked at Matthew and asked him while smiling, "So, how could F&B contribute to the welfare of the Royal Hotel?"

Encouraging others

Matthew looked at the next year's F&B budget and sighed.

"You'll need to institute an aggressive incentive program based on food cost saving for the chef," continued Jane.

"Should I give him a substantial bonus if he reaches our goal?" asked Matthew.

"My suggestion is that instead of a single goal level with the bonus being 'all or nothing,' you should create multiple goal levels with a different bonus level attached to each; basically, the higher the goal level attained, the higher the reward," Jane concluded.

1 Describe the disadvantages of individual monetary incentives.

2 What are the advantages of creating multiple goal levels with a different bonus level attached to each?

3 In order to achieve a food cost percentage below budget, develop an individual incentive program for the chef. Assuming that the food revenue budget is maintained, determine the award values based on improvement. (Ten percent of the saving is typically a good benchmark.)

4 Write a brief memorandum to the chef outlining the program. Make sure that the chef sees a clear link between his efforts and the incentive payout.

5 What are the pitfalls associated with incentives based solely on cost control? How could Matthew improve the chef's incentive program?

Additional information

Budgeted yearly food revenue: $2,000,000
Budgeted food cost: 25.5%

The case is based on the principles and situations described in the following:

Locke, E. A. (2004). Linking goals to monetary incentives. *Academy of Management Executive*, 18(4), 130–133.

> ## Part summary
>
> This part examines the opportunity to use reward as a tool for motivation of employees to meet or exceed the expectations of budgetary performance. There are two different types of motivations, intrinsic and extrinsic, which will drive the intent of employees. As a manager, identify ways to create performance goals tied to rewards as a retention tactic. Identify ways to be present and engage with staff in a positive, professional manner for operational effectiveness.

Additional reading

Books

Feedback

In her *New York Times* and *Wall Street Journal* bestseller, a former executive at Google and Apple Kim Scott shares her unique approach to effective management known as radical candor, or the idea that a good boss needs to care personally and challenge directly employees on their team (K. Scott, 2017).

Scott, K. (2017). *Radical candor: Be a kick-ass boss without losing your humanity* (1st ed.). Retrieved from www.amazon.com/Radical-Candor-Kim-Scott/dp/B01KTIEFEE

Job description

This article provides a four-step guidance on constructing a job description (Schambers, 2015).

Schambers, A. (2015, August 14). Job descriptions: The foundation of human resources. *Grand Rapids Business Journal*. Retrieved from www.grbj.com/articles/83063-job-descriptions-the-foundation-of-human-resources

Job design

An employees' excellent performance and well-being are core aspects that many organizations aim to achieve. Job design theory provided strong implications and guidelines to help practitioners to achieve such goals (Al-Zoubi, 2008).

Al-Zoubi, M. (2008). *Job design and employees well-being and performance: A future perspective*. Saarbrucken, Germany: VDM Verlag.

Motivation

In this *New York Times* bestseller, Daniel H. Pink draws on four decades of scientific research on human motivation and examines three elements of true motivation – autonomy, mastery, and purpose (2009).

Pink, D. H. (2009). *Drive: The surprising truth about what motivates us* (1st ed.). New York, NY: Riverhead Books.

Encouraging others

This book discusses the nature of motivation, what it results in, and how to keep it going (Banks, 1997).

Banks, L. (1997). *Motivation in the workplace: Inspiring your employees* (illustrated edition). West Des Moines, Iowa: Amer Media Inc.

Organizational politics

Get ahead, gain influence, and get what you want; office politics are an unavoidable fact of life in every workplace (McIntyre, 2005).

McIntyre, M. G. (2005). *Secrets to winning at office politics*. Retrieved from https://us.macmillan.com/secretstowinningatofficepolitics/mariegmcintyre/9780312332181

Organizational structure

Here's a guide that shows managers how to choose the best organizational design for their business from five basic structures identified by the author. Readers will discover how to avoid typical mistakes, especially those pertaining to conflict among different divisions (Mintzberg, 1992).

Mintzberg, H. (1992). *Structure in fives: Designing effective organizations* (1 edition). Upper Saddle River, NJ: Pearson.

Promotion

This book talks about why timing is more important than talent, how corporations make promotion decisions, career mistakes to avoid, what women in the workforce need to know, and 12 proven strategies for promotion (Asher, 2014).

Asher, D. (2014). *Who gets promoted, who doesn't, and why: 12 things you'd better do if you want to get ahead* (2nd ed.). Plano, TX: Potter/Ten Speed/Harmony/Rodale.

Rewards

A how-to book on compensation and reward systems from expert Thomas Wilson (1994).

Wilson, T. B. (1994). *Innovative reward systems for the changing workplace* (4th printing). New York: McGraw-Hill.

This book provides managers with essential rewards, tips, and strategies to ensure recognition is shown (Bowen, 2000).

Bowen, R. B. (2000). *Recognizing and rewarding employees* (1st ed.). New York: McGraw-Hill Education.

Journals

Motivation

This study examines what kinds of factors drive motivation and to what extent these factors influence performance (Shahzadi, Javed, Pirzada, Nasreen, & Khanam, 2014).

Shahzadi, I., Javed, A., Pirzada, S. S., Nasreen, S., & Khanam, F. (2014). Impact of employee motivation on employee performance. *European Journal of Business and Management, 6*(23), 159–167.

Organizational politics

Both theoretical and empirical research on organizational politics are discussed in this article (Ferris & Kacmar, 1992).

Ferris, G. R., & Kacmar, K. M. (1992). Perceptions of organizational politics. *Journal of Management, 18*(1), 93–116. https://doi.org/10.1177/014920639201800107

Promotion

This article examines favoritism as a bias or undue influence for promotion (Tyler, 2012).

Tyler, K. (2012, June 1). Undeserved promotions. *SHRM.* Retrieved from www.shrm.org/hr-today/news/hr-magazine/pages/0612tyler.aspx

Respect

This study argues that there are two types of respect: "we" are valued in this organization, and the organization values "me." The work explores the important distinction and implications (Rogers & Ashforth, 2017).

Rogers, K. M., & Ashforth, B. E. (2017). Respect in organizations: Feeling valued as "we" and "me." *Journal of Management, 43*(5), 1578–1608. https://doi.org/10.1177/014920 6314557159

Rewards

The following is a handbook from the Society for Human Resource Management for planning and executing total rewards strategies (Heneman & Coyne, 2007).

Heneman, R. L., & Coyne, E. E. (2007). Implementing total rewards strategies: A guide to successfully planning and implementing a total rewards system. *SHRM Foundation, SHRM Foundation's Effective Practice Guidelines Series, 54.*

Research shows that various factors influence employee motivation and satisfaction and a manager must realize the effects that different reward strategies can have (Baskar & Rajkumar, 2013).

Baskar, P., & Rajkumar, P. (2013). A study on the impact of rewards and recognition on employee motivation. *International Journal of Science and Research (IJSR), 4,* 1644.

Using self-determination theory and an understanding of psychological mechanisms, the how and the whys of reward satisfaction were tested in this study (Thibault Landry & Whillans, 2018).

Thibault Landry, A., & Whillans, A. (2018). The power of workplace rewards: Using self-determination theory to understand why reward satisfaction matters for workers around the world. *Compensation & Benefits Review, 50*(3), 123–148. https://doi.org/10.1177/0886368719840515

Work systems

In finding that an effective human resources influence can intensify the results of high-performance work systems, this study concluded that the universalistic and contingency perspectives are complementary rather than incompatible (Jeong & Choi, 2016).

Jeong, D. Y., & Choi, M. (2016). The impact of high-performance work systems on firm performance: The moderating effects of the human resource function's influence. *Journal of Management & Organization*, 22(3), 328–348. https://doi.org/10.1017/jmo.2015.38

Web links

Coaching

Giving a personal look into his own experience and career at Facebook, Justin Rosenstein shares what he has learned to be the three most important and effective areas to address in regards to coaching (Rosenstein & Schwartz, 2018).

Rosenstein, J., & Schwartz, C. (2018, January 23). How to coach teammates: A key responsibility of effective leaders. *Wavelength by Asana*. Retrieved from https://wavelength. asana.com/coaching-workplace-why-examples/

This article provides an overview of the HR competency of coaching in a business environment (SHRM, 2019).

SHRM. (2019, August 16). Coaching in a business environment. Retrieved November 24, 2019, from SHRM website: www.shrm.org/resourcesandtools/tools-and-samples/toolkits/pages/coachinginabusinessenvironment.aspx

Motivation

This article presents eight ideas on how to inspire motivation in the workplace by learning what people want, setting realistic goals, providing employee recognition, utilizing training and development, providing autonomy to high-performing employees, celebrating holidays and creating traditions, tapping into employee discretionary energy, and promoting your personal growth and motivation (Heathfield, 2019b).

Heathfield, S. M. (2019b, November 20). 8 ideas on how to inspire motivation in the workplace. Retrieved November 27, 2019, from The Balance Careers website: www.thebalancecareers.com/does-your-workplace-inspire-motivation-1918742

This article addresses the importance and benefits of employee motivation and provides tips on how to increase it in the workplace (R., 2016).

R., H. (2016, January 27). Why employee motivation is important (& how to improve it). Retrieved November 27, 2019, from The 6Q Blog website: https://inside.6q.io/employee-motivation-important/

Organizational politics

This *HBR* article looks at the four different types of terrains for organizational politics: the woods, the weeds, the rocks, and the high ground (Jarrett, 2017).

Jarrett, M. (2017, April 24). The 4 types of organizational politics. *Harvard Business Review*. Retrieved from https://hbr.org/2017/04/the-4-types-of-organizational-politics

Organizational structure

This article address various types of organizational structures and connects via links to the other four parts in the series (Morgan, 2015).

Morgan, J. (2015, July 6). The 5 types of organizational structures: Part 1, the hierarchy. Retrieved November 29, 2019, from the Forbes website: www.forbes.com/sites/jacobmorgan/2015/07/06/the-5-types-of-organizational-structures-part-1-the-hierarchy/#642ed7e65252

Promotion

This is a quick read that discusses three steps to take before deciding to promote an employee, management methods to preserve the respect of the passed-over employee, and strategies to rebuild the team (Campbell & Friend, 2011).

Campbell, P., & Friend, J. (2011, August 20). Managing the employee promotions process. Retrieved November 29, 2019, from the Edward Lowe Foundation website: https://edwardlowe.org/managing-the-employee-promotions-process-2/

Respect

This article provides an overview of recognizing and building respect for a more positive workplace (Heathfield, 2019a).

Heathfield, S. M. (2019a, November 19). How you can best demonstrate respect in your workplace. Retrieved November 29, 2019, from The Balance Careers website: www.thebalancecareers.com/how-to-demonstrate-respect-in-the-workplace-1919376

Rewards

The following is an overview of monetary and non-monetary incentives and their effects on morale and workplace balance (S. Scott, 2019).

Scott, S. (2019, February 5). Rewards and incentives in the workplace. Retrieved November 29, 2019, from the Chron.com website: https://smallbusiness.chron.com/rewards-incentives-workplace-11236.html

This article provides a look at how the best rewards programs will help alleviate a lot of common HR issues (Entrepreneur Contributors, 2005).

Entrepreneur Contributors. (2005, January 10). The best ways to reward employees. Retrieved November 29, 2019, from the Entrepreneur website: www.entrepreneur.com/article/75340

Work systems

For a basic overview of work systems, this is a great resource to start with (Burke, 2017).

Burke, A. (2017, September 26). What is a work system in an organization? Retrieved November 30, 2019, from the Biz Fluent website: https://bizfluent.com/info-10007600-work-system-organization.html

Part 5

Dealing with problem behaviors

How to use this part

Consider the various ways that employees from different backgrounds and generations can bring variety to the set of behaviors they have in the workplace. Management is considered to be the governing authority in an organization to mediate and bring the team together and not let individuals create a negative environment. Consider how you might remedy these various behaviors in the workplace.

Key terms

The key terms found in the cases in this section are listed here. Their definitions can be found on pages xiv–xviii.

Analytical	Incivility
Authority	Meetings
Big picture	Organizational politics
Bullying	Organizational structure
Chain of command	Perfectionism
Change	Performance appraisal
Coaching	Rapport
Decision-making	Recruiting
Feedback	Respect
Flexibility	Selection
Gossip	Trust
Harassment	Workaholism
Humor / sarcasm	Work systems

INTRODUCTION

Culture promotes behavioral norms

Company culture describes the company, how it is managed, how it reacts to external challenges, and how workers respond to their work environment. Company culture can be divided into three general categories: constructive, passive/defensive, and aggressive / defensive (Cooke & Szumal, 2000; Human Synergistics Internatonal, n.d.).

The constructive culture is the most desirable and the least often found. It is typified by the following norms:

- Achievement
- Self-actualizing
- Humanistic, encouraging
- Affiliative

Passive / defensive cultures are characterized by the following norms:

- Approval
- Conventional
- Dependent
- Avoidance oriented

Aggressive / defensive cultures encompass the following norms:

- Oppositional
- Power oriented
- Competitive
- Perfectionistic

References

Cooke, R. A., & Szumal, J. L. (2000). Using the organizational culture inventory to understand the operating cultures of organizations. In N. M. Ashkanasy, C. P. M. Wilderom, & M. F. Peterson (Eds.), *Handbook of organizational culture and climate* (pp. 147–162). Thousand Oaks, CA: Sage Publications, Inc.

Human Synergistics International. (n.d.). *The human synergistics circumplex*. Retrieved August 17, 2017, from www.humansynergistics.com/about-us/the-circumplex

Note: Circumplex style names, descriptions, and items are copyrighted and used by permission. From Organizational Culture Inventory by Robert A. Cooke and J. Clayton Lafferty, 1987, Plymouth, MI: Human Synergistics International. Copyright © 1987, 2017 by Human Synergistics, Inc. Used by permission.

Inappropriate behaviors in the workplace

Human behavior is shaped by various factors, and organizational members may not always behave in ways consistent with their company's prevailing culture.

However, it is obvious that defensive cultural norms (both passive and aggressive) will negatively impact employees' behavior.

In this chapter, we will present all sorts of difficult employees – more often to be encountered in organizations with nonconstructive cultures. Each difficult person with his or her particular form of difficult behavior presents a unique challenge for the management. Unfortunately, no one has the perfect solution for handling such people; at the same time, if we look for patterns of behavior, we can prepare ourselves for dealing with them.

Section A

Behaviors promoted by passive/defensive cultures

Peter is the nicest manager!

Main subjects
Coaching, feedback, self-confidence, trust

Who's who
• Judith Grace, Front Office Manager
• Peter Klema, Assistant Front Office Manager

Think point

Long-term employees can be individuals who either work to make the organization better or work against the success of change. Consider how you can work to earn the trust of a long-term employee and how you can get him or her on board with you to work collaboratively to make positive required changes.

Judith called Peter, one of the assistant front office managers, to her office.

"What can I do for you?" Peter asked with a big smile on his face.

Judith felt very comfortable with Peter. Peter was a long-term employee and always had a friendly word for everyone. He was one of those employees who never said, "No."

"This is regarding the new shift checklists." Judith started the conversation. "I emailed you the proposal a while ago," she continued. "Do you have any thoughts, anything that you didn't like about the change?"

"It's great!" said Peter.

"Hmmm, all right, in that case, could you make sure it is implemented as soon as possible?" Judith asked. "As you know, Peter, I will be on vacation for the next two weeks, and I count on you."

"No problem, Judith. It will be introduced next week," Peter said and as he was leaving the office jokingly added, "It's always a pleasure doing business with you, Judith."

When Judith got back from vacation, she noticed that the staff was still using the old shift checklists, which did not include important new procedures to be completed.

1   Describe the benefits of this type of behavior.

2   Identify potential reasons for the difficult behavior.

3   Highlight some of the consequences that the problem behavior has for others.

4   How would you handle the situation now?

5   Outline some techniques Judith should have used in the first place to handle the situation.

The "invisible" accounting clerk

Main subjects
Coaching, feedback, rapport, self-confidence

Who's who
• Mike Lee, Accounting Manager
• Jack Aggott, Accounts Receivable Clerk

Think point

Communication skills are a necessary component to all positions. However, some individuals are found to be more introverted than extroverted. In the hospitality industry, where most employees tend to demonstrate extroversion, it can be hard sometimes to identify how best to understand an individual who is shy or introverted.

Mike Lee, the accounting manager, sighed as Jack was leaving his office. He had a very hard time communicating with Jack. Jack was shy and kept a low profile, but what bothered Mike the most was that every time he asked him a question, all he was getting in response was a "yep" or a "nope." He did not sense any negativity or calculated aggression in this behavior. Jack joined the Royal Hotel nine months earlier as an accounts receivable clerk. He was responsible for processing billing for hotel guests and functions. Mike also noticed in the weekly accounting meetings that Jack never had anything to contribute. Jack was almost an "invisible" character of the hotel. Mike was wondering who signed off on Jack's probationary review three months earlier without making any comments on Jack's communication skills. Mike was wondering how to deal with Jack.

1   Describe the problem behavior.

2   Identify potential reasons for the difficult behavior. Why do so many people describe themselves as shy?

3   What are some of the negative consequences of shyness in the workplace?

4   How would you increase shy employees' comfort level?

The wishy-washy manager

Main subjects
Coaching, decision-making, feedback

Who's who
• Matthew Knorr, Director of Food and Beverage
• Emily Perkins, Lounge and Bar Manager

Think point

Decision-making skills are required for managers in the hospitality industry in order to demonstrate success. Indecisiveness can lead to loss of productivity, confusion, and the perception of lack of interest. One approach to supporting employees in expanding their ability to make timely decisions is to empower them; demonstrate and show the level of support you have for the employee to make his or her own decisions. Should the decision made not turn out with the best outcomes, having a positive feedback session to address the situation and decision-making process in a non-threatening manner is a coaching practice to continue to develop employees.

After the food and beverage meeting, Matthew asked Emily to stay back for a minute. "Emily, have you made up your mind? Do you think we should increase the bar par stock level? We discussed this last month."

"Do I have to decide now? What do you think I should do?" Emily replied.

"Well, you are the bar manager . . ." insisted Matthew.

"Why don't you decide on this, Matthew? I promise I'll go with the flow," answered Emily with a charming facial expression.

At this point, Matthew was paged and had to leave the meeting-room.

1   Describe the problem behavior.

2   Identify potential reasons for the difficult behavior.

3   Highlight some of consequences that the problem behavior has for the operation.

4   If you were Matthew, how would you handle the situation?

I was just kidding!

Main subjects
Feedback, humor/sarcasm, incivility, meetings, respect

Who's who
- Carlos Diaz, Guest Services Manager
- Dan Mazur, Director of Rooms
- Kalinda Stenton, PBX Manager

Think point

Humor can sometimes be a way to communicate or to ease fear or uncomfortable situations. On occasion, humor might turn to sarcasm or be shared at the expense of another individual. This inappropriate sharing can lead to incivility among team members.

Carlos Diaz raised his hand during the divisional meeting.

"Go ahead, Carlos," Dan said.

"Actually, I put together a citywide valet parking price comparison," Carlos told him.

"Wow, did you do this all by yourself?" said Kalinda and turned her thumb down laughingly.

Some started to laugh. Carlos laughed with the others, but he also felt bad about the situation. Kalinda was a good colleague and had finished her first year as PBX manager, but it was obvious that she would like to move to a position with increased responsibility soon. As he looked at Kalinda, she quickly mumbled to him, "I was just kidding." He didn't think that Dan could hear Kalinda's sarcastic comment as he was briefly answering a phone call. Carlos was wondering how he should follow up on this.

1   Describe the problem behavior.

2   Identify potential reasons for the difficult behavior.

3   Highlight some of the consequences that the problem behavior has for others.

4   Outline some techniques supervisors could use to deal with the issue.

5   How could Carlos address Kalinda's behavior?

Did you hear what Lori did last night?

Main subject
Feedback, gossip

Who's who
• Lori Canelle, Spa Manager
• Yvonne Clark, Director of Sales and Marketing
• Debbie Murphy, Sales Manager
• Brian White, Assistant Director of Engineering

Think point

Regardless of the size of the hospitality operation, the opportunity to connect with colleagues and discuss personal matters outside of work or speculate on the behaviors of others is a practice that happens. In most instances, this practice of spreading rumors, creating gossip, or adding to the grapevine is in poor taste and can impact the culture of others working in the same property. This behavior can be considered more detrimental for those who are managers over simple line-level employees.

It was a hot day in July. After the sales meeting, Yvonne and Debbie stayed back for small talk around the water cooler. Debbie smiled and asked Yvonne, "Did you hear what Lori did last night?"

"I am sure you will tell me. What would I do without you? How else would I know what is really happening in this hotel?" answered Yvonne.

"Well, I heard from a good source that Lori and Brian, you know the guy from engineering?" Debbie went on with her story, with some juicy details.

1   Describe the problem behavior.

2   Identify potential reasons for the difficult behavior.

3   Highlight some of the consequences that the problem behavior has for others.

4   Describe the communication failure that occurred in this case.

5   Outline some techniques Yvonne should have used to deal with this specific issue.

6   How can managers further combat this problem and minimize gossip's damaging effects?

Behaviors promoted by aggressive/defensive cultures

It won't work!

Main subjects
Change, coaching, feedback, meetings

Who's who
- Bruce Baber, Assistant Catering Manager
- Laura Coe, Assistant Catering Manager
- Petra Wolf, Assistant Catering Manager
- Kelly Woodstock, Catering Manager

Think point

Brainstorming can be a process used to identify a creative flow of ideas for new projects. One aspect that is critical when facilitating a session is to establish the ground rules for sharing. One of the most common is to allow everyone to share ideas without additional questions, being negative, or putting the idea down. Once all ideas are on the table—or in most instances, on a flip chart or dry-erase board—then the team can start to address each idea for its merit. The one thing that is constant is change. Change can be a hard aspect for some individuals, especially if they have been employed at the same location for a long length of time; their adverse reactions or poor negative past experiences can come across as being closed down and off-putting to others.

"I am sorry to tell you guys, but we are behind budget," Kelly said at the start of the catering meeting. "We all agree that the meetings market is lucrative. What techniques do you think we should use to reach those folks?" she asked and looked at the three catering assistant managers, Bruce, Laura, and Petra.

Both Petra and Laura came up with some ideas. Petra suggested that a carefully planned sales blitz[1] may be the right technique. She energetically stood up and started to put some buzzwords on a flip chart on how she would organize it. "Last month, we identified 500 prospects; to qualify new business, I suggest that we should do a three-day sales blitz and—" Petra explained.

Bruce interrupted her. "Yeah, and who would do it?"

Petra was ready with the answer. "Spring break is coming up in four weeks. Let's hire some sales-oriented college students from the local hospitality program to reinforce our team."

Bruce cut Petra off again. "We tried that a couple of years ago. It's intrusive and won't work. Let's move on."

Petra wanted to explain that it would not be an unannounced cold call. The prospective clients would be advised ahead of time, but she changed her mind and sat down.

Kelly looked puzzled and asked if anyone would like to continue the discussion with some other ideas. As no one responded, Kelly moved to the next point on the agenda.

Laura, the junior catering manager who originally wanted to present her plan, slowly put her paperwork away. It was not the first time that Bruce shot down ideas. Laura joined the Royal Hotel last year; during her interview, Kelly made her believe that creativity and innovation were important for the hotel. She now felt disappointed.

1 Describe the problem behavior.

2 Identify potential reasons for the difficult behavior.

3 Highlight some of the consequences that the problem behavior has for others.

4 Describe the communication failure that occurred in this case.

5 Outline some techniques managers could use to deal with negative people.

Note

1 Sales blitz

A sales blitz focuses on contacting potential clients in a concentrated area over a brief period of time.

That's just how the chef is!

Main subjects
Bullying, chain of command, coaching, feedback, harassment, incivility,
performance appraisal, self-confidence

Who's who
• Pascal Gateau, Executive Chef
• Matthew Knorr, Director of
Food and Beverage
• Katherine Norton, Director of
Human Resources

Think point

Even televised entertainment demonstrates that a chef in the kitchen can be
considered a tyrant or have a strong, demanding expectation in the way the
kitchen is operated. Despite what the media does to embellish such behavior,
it is not a positive HR practice to behave in such a way. The use of exit
interviews is a way to obtain information from employees, prior to their
departure, about their working experience. If you want to remain competitive,
then it's important to collect this data but most important to do something
with it.

Aggressive/defensive cultures

Matthew was troubled by the results of the quarterly turnover and exit interview summary. According to the document, five kitchen employees resigned. Four employees claimed that the chef was the cause of their departure. Here are some comments employees made:

"The chef regularly loses his temper and verbally abuses us."
"Gateau is well known as a tyrant; he yelled and screamed at us all the time."
"The chef took advantage of me and treated everyone like scum."
"He is always giving me dirty looks; he has unreasonable expectations."
"Why do you think so many people last only a few months?"

Surprisingly, one of the employees who left for family reasons spoke very highly about the executive chef: "I loved this place! I came to the Royal Hotel right after military school, and Chef Gateau helped me a lot to become a team player and a good chef de partie. Advancement is based on individual ability and achievement. I will be back one day."

Matthew remembered that the other day, he stepped into the chef's office to check something with him regarding the menu; he told him that he would rather meet with him elsewhere, as the kitchen was his territory.

Matthew knew that resigning employees exaggerate sometimes but decided to briefly discuss the results with Katherine after the executive committee meeting. She carefully listened to Matthew and replied quietly, "That just how the chef is."

1   Describe the problem behavior.

2   What is the difference between harassment and bullying?

3   Identify potential reasons for the difficult behavior. How does this behavior affect the work environment?

4   Highlight some of consequences that the problem behavior has for others.

5   It seems that the chef can get away with his inappropriate behavior. Highlight some potential reasons.

6   Outline some techniques management could use to deal with the chef.

7   Could you identify two specific HR techniques (a) one to avoid hiring potential bullies (b) and a performance appraisal technique in order to curtail workplace incivility?

The expert

Main subjects
Authority, coaching, self-confidence

Who's who
• Bob Biel, Assistant Housekeeping Manager
• Shakia Andrews, Executive Housekeeper
• Chloe Reilly, Housekeeper

Think point

Many hotels employee individuals who have worked countless hours and decades of their life in the same location. Many room attendants in the Housekeeping Department have dedicated their life's work to the job. On most occasions, line-level positions will be held by individuals who do not have a college education. Young managers who have recently earned a college degree can sometimes have an inflated sense of self-confidence. It requires a delicate balance to bring the college graduate to a level of reality without tarnishing his or her enthusiasm for the job while working together to improve the functions for productivity that might be lacking.

Aggressive/defensive cultures

Bob recently graduated from a prestigious hospitality program. He joined the Royal Hotel a year earlier as an assistant housekeeping manager with the hope that he could become a department head after completing his first year. Bob was very dynamic and productive; he distinguished himself as a knowledgeable employee. At the same time, Shakia, his supervisor, often felt that Bob's management style was overbearing. The other day, she overheard how Bob was giving feedback to a long-time housekeeper: "Chloe, that's not the right way to do that. I know better than you how to roll the pillows and the bedspread toward the headboard."

Bob constantly gave unwanted advice to everyone and knew everything. She also noticed that other assistant managers never socialized with Bob, and morale was down in the office.

The last incident occurred that morning when Shakia arrived. "How is everything, Bob?" she asked as she entered the office.

"Good, Shakia. I told the housekeepers this morning not to use sanitizer when cleaning the bathroom floor; the all-purpose cleaner is more than enough."

"Bob, it is our standard to mop the floor with a sanitizer," Shakia replied.

"I thought that we need to save money," Bob said.

"Let's sit down this afternoon before you leave," Shakia answered.

1 Describe Bob's behavior.

2 Identify potential reasons for Bob's difficult behavior.

3 Highlight some of the consequences that the problem behavior has for others.

4 Outline some techniques Shakia should use to deal with Bob.

Jeff, you test my patience!

Main subjects
Analytical, big picture, coaching, feedback

Who's who
- Jeff Gillespie, Assistant Banquet Manager
- Thomas Waxer, Banquet Manager

Think point

Consider if you are an individual who has the ability to see the big picture and lay out a plan to get there or if you are more of a person who finds that the devil is in the details. Our industry requires both types of individuals; however, they need to be aligned to the correct position or properly trained for the requirements of the job.

Aggressive/defensive cultures

Thomas was surprised when Jeff, the new assistant banquet manager, arrived with a stack of professional books and "how-to guides."

"Don't worry, Thomas. I'm not a perfectionist," Jeff told him.

Thomas smiled, as he could not remember the last time he had five minutes to read a book in the office.

In the weekly event meetings, Jeff was very attentive. At the same time, Thomas noticed that Jeff always recalculated forecasts and pricing estimates sent by catering. Jeff spent hours analyzing the banquet event orders and suggested the implementation of mathematical probability analysis to reduce the risk of underestimating the number of no-shows. This last idea tested Thomas's patience, and he stopped the project.

A few weeks earlier, when Jeff was in charge, a wedding guest was complaining that the buffet was not decorated well enough and the event overall was lacking creativity. Also, Jeff forgot to send up the leftover cake to the bridal suite. Aside from this incident, Thomas was happy with Jeff, but sometimes, he wondered if banquet management was the right job for Jeff.

1 Describe the problem behavior.

2 Identify potential reasons for the difficult behavior.

3 Highlight some of the consequences that the problem behavior has for others.

4 Outline some general techniques supervisors could use to deal with similar issues.

5 What should Thomas do?

The perfect change of light bulbs

Case type: issue case

Main subjects
Big picture, coaching, perfectionism

Who's who
• Charlie Jones, Director of Engineering
• Katherine Norton, Director of Human Resources
• Brian White, Assistant Director of Engineering

Think point

The concept of being a perfectionist can be overbearing to some individuals. When the demands of a perfectionist are holding people to a higher standard or one that is unrealistic, it can begin to erode the level of confidence the subordinates or peers have in that person.

Aggressive/defensive cultures

"Should we have lunch together?" Charlie suggested to his assistant, Brian.

"Sure, I will join you in a second," Brian answered and started to straighten every stack on his desk before leaving the office.

Charlie was patiently waiting while Brian made sure that all books, pens, and folders were perfectly aligned. "Did you have a chance to send out the memo regarding energy-saving techniques?" he asked Brian.

"I will do it first thing tomorrow morning; I just want to run a quick spell check," explained Brian.

"I thought we reviewed the memo last week?" Charlie interrupted.

Brian worked very hard and tried to go several steps beyond "going that extra mile." He recently launched a new engineering initiative. In this new program, Brain was offering new techniques to employees on how to replace light bulbs perfectly.

Katherine mentioned to Charlie the other day that one of the engineering employees was complaining in HR about Brian. According to the employee, Brian was intolerant of even the slightest mistakes. He could dwell on errors for days, and most of the engineers worked in constant fear of slipping up. As they were walking down to the cafeteria, Charlie was wondering what to tell his assistant.

> 1 Describe the problem behavior.
>
> 2 Identify potential reasons for the difficult behavior.
>
> 3 Highlight some of consequences that the problem behavior has for others.
>
> 4 Outline some techniques Charlie could use to deal with the issue.

The case is based on the principles and situations described in the following:

Raudsepp, E. (1990). Is perfectionism holding your career back? *Supervision, 51*(8), 3–5.

The "bleeding heart" of the hotel

Main subjects
Coaching, flexibility, workaholism

Who's who
• Jennifer Ortiz, Restaurant Manager
• Paul Yurkonis, Assistant Restaurant Manager

Think point

Working in the hospitality industry where a business is open extended hours or 24/7 can be a direct line of challenge for an individual who tends to be a workaholic. This can force an individual to constantly be working. While it is important to remain flexible so work can be accomplished according to the hours of operation and when extended occupancy or business levels demand it, it is also important to find a balance.

Aggressive/defensive cultures

The restaurant was rather slow that day, and Jennifer was ready to leave. "Are you heading home soon too?" Jennifer asked Paul, one of the assistant managers.

"I have some paperwork to finish," answered Paul.

Jennifer was hesitating a moment and asked him, "Would you like me to stay and help you?"

"No, I will just do it by myself. Thanks anyway." Paul smiled and turned the computer on.

Paul had been at the Royal much longer than Jennifer, and when she joined the hotel, she quickly realized that Paul was the "bleeding heart" of the hotel. He came in early and left late – every single day. Jennifer noticed that Paul was even around on his days off. Paul was very dependable and willing, and still, he somehow made Jennifer feel that his great attitude was not appreciated. Flexibility and hard work were expected throughout the hotel, as stated in the manager's handbook:

> "As a manager, you may be required to put in excess hours to complete assignments and projects related to your position."

Jennifer certainly valued Paul's efforts, but she was concerned as well. She was unsure if she should address the situation.

1   Describe the problem behavior.

2   Identify potential reasons for the difficult behavior.

3   Highlight some of consequences that the problem behavior has for the operation.

4   Outline some techniques managers could use to deal with similar issues.

Breaking down the barriers

Main subjects
Organizational structure, team building, work systems

Who's who
- Shakia Andrews, Executive Housekeeper
- Judith Grace, Front Office Manager
- Robert Kunz, General Manager
- Dan Mazur, Director of Rooms
- Jane Peterson, Hotel Manager

Think point

A successful approach that many companies utilize is that of an employee satisfaction survey. It is typically conducted on an annual basis to obtain information and feedback from employees in an anonymous fashion. While it is great to collect this information, it is critical that management actually do something with that information. Otherwise, employees will feel that their time is wasted and comments will not improve the working environment. There can also be conflict among various departments. As the general manager, you must work to build the team up together in a collective manner.

Dan was rather shocked as he was reviewing the results of the yearly employee survey.

Here are some of the issues highlighted by front office employees:

- "There are excessive delays in getting rooms clean for arriving guests."
- "Housekeepers are just too slow and lazy. They don't care about guests. All they want to do is get through the day and get home. They don't care about the pressure we're under down here."
- "Dear management! Do you know why customer satisfaction is falling? If we don't communicate among each other, don't you think that the guests are going to notice that?"
- "When someone is missing a pillow or a towel, it takes forever to get them to the room, which makes all of us look terrible. You can't hide this stuff from guests."
- "Dan is telling us to cut labor; Jane and Robert tell us to schedule as many front desk agents as needed to provide quality service."
- "Those maids make so much in tips and have no clue how difficult our job is; let's outsource housekeeping."

Here are some of the issues highlighted by housekeeping employees:

- "Bad information from the front desk about priorities for guest rooms."
- "Last-minute surprises about large groups checking into the hotel at the same time (they used to have all-staff meetings prior to the arrival of a big group)."
- "Unwillingness of front desk and concierge employees to pitch-in outside their specific job responsibilities during busy times."
- "Poor treatment of housekeeping staff by front desk crew. Where does the lack of respect issue come from? And how big of a problem is it? I think it's fairly typical for the guest services people downstairs to see us . . . as being less important than they are. It's not completely unique."
- "Yeah, but why should we work hard, anyway? We don't get many tips. And even if we bust our butts and turn our rooms around quickly, no one really appreciates us."
- "It's no wonder two of our best housekeepers left us last month. And no one ever helps us. You'd think one of the guys in the monkey suits standing downstairs might come upstairs every once in a while and vacuum or something."
- "Those front desk clerks, they don't talk to housekeepers upstairs until there's an emergency. And by then, it's too late. And when the emergency is over, they don't even think to go upstairs and say thank you. It's like they're too good or something. And when they call us, they act like we're second-class citizens. They look down at us. We're the ones who have to keep this beautiful hotel in good shape."
- "Rooms are not ready on time because no one downstairs tells anyone upstairs which rooms they need first."

Minutes after Dan received the results, he also got two voice mails, one from Judith and another one from Shakia.

Judith left the following message: "Dan, can you believe those maids? What do you want me to learn from them? I will stop by later. Bye."

Shakia said, "Hi, Dan, I guess you received it too. Don't you think Judith and her team have a silo mentality?[1] You know that my people work very hard, and they know what their priorities are; can I come to see you?"

1 Describe the situation in the Rooms Division.

2 Identify some underlying reasons for the situation.

3 Highlight some consequences that the situation causes.

4 What can be done to tear down silos, reduce conflicts, and increase collaboration?

Your action plan should be organized as follows:

a Strategic decisions (culture / "big picture")
b Organizational structure / work design
c Programs aimed at fostering co-operation / preventing workgroup arrogance
d Performance management
e Rooms Division policies and procedures

The case is based on the principles and situations described in the following:

Lencioni, P. (2006). *Silos, politics, and turf wars*. San Francisco: Jossey-Bass.

Note

1 Silo mentality

Team members perceive their role in the organization purely in terms of the activities within their own specific department (silo).

> ### Part summary
>
> This section covered the concept that the one thing that is constant is change. Individuals can sometimes be resistant to change. It is the responsibility of a good manager to try to bring together the team, develop individuals, and prevent negative or counterproductive behavior from infiltrating the workplace.

Additional reading

Books

Analytical

Learn how to sustain success through best-practice data management, technology usage, partnering, and skill building by establishing an analytical mind-set through two key skills: storytelling and visualization (Guenole, Ferrar, & Feinzig, 2017).

Guenole, N., Ferrar, J., & Feinzig, S. (2017). *The power of people: Learn how successful organizations use workforce analytics to improve business performance.* New York: Pearson FT Press.

The goal of the following book is to inform, transform, and empower your HR decisions by placing a heavy emphasis on the need for HR professionals to understand and apply data analytics (Waters, Streets, McFarlane, & Johnson-Murray, 2018).

Waters, S., Streets, V., McFarlane, L., & Johnson-Murray, R. (2018). *The practical guide to HR analytics: Using data to inform, transform, and empower HR decisions.* Retrieved from https://store.shrm.org/The-Practical-Guide-to-HR-Analytics-Using-Data-to-Inform-Transform-Empower-HR-Decisions

Predictive HR Analytics shows step-by-step how to carry out analysis and interpret the results of HR metrics to get the most out of the HR function (Edwards & Edwards, 2016).

Edwards, K., & Edwards, M. (2016). *Predictive HR analytics: Mastering the HR metric* (1st ed.). Kogan Page.

Bullying

This book talks about what bullies do and how to stop them at work (Daniel & Metcalf, 2016).

Daniel, T. A., & Metcalf, G. S. (2016). *Stop bullying at work: Strategies and tools for HR, legal, & risk management professionals* (2nd ed.). Alexandria, VA: Society For Human Resource Management.

Decision-making

A four-step process called WRAP (widen your options reality test) counteracts the biases in our lives to help us make the right decision at the right moment (Heath & Heath, 2013).

Heath, C., & Heath, D. (2013). *Decisive: How to make better choices in life and work* (1st ed.). Danvers, MA: Currency.

Flexibility

This handbook is designed to help you transform and break free from inflexible, 40-hour work weeks by providing ways to fit work requirements with life obligations (Blades & Fondas, 2010).

Blades, J., & Fondas, N. (2010). *The custom-fit workplace: Choose when, where, and how to work and boost your bottom line* (1st ed.). San Francisco, CA: Jossey-Bass.

Gossip

This book presents a sociological perspective on the functions of gossip and rumor in different types of social settings and advice on how to handle it in the workplace (Ballano, 2017).

Ballano, D. V. O. (2017). *Handling rumors and gossip in business, the workplace, and everyday life*. Retrieved from www.bookworks.com/book/handling-rumors-gossip-business-workplace-everyday-life/

Meetings

This book provides step-by-step systems to have focused and time-effective meetings (Herold, 2016).

Herold, C. (2016). *Meetings Suck: Turning one of the most loathed elements of business into one of the most valuable* (1st ed.). Austin, TX: Lioncrest Publishing.

Organizational politics

This handbook offers a broad perspective on the intriguing phenomena of power, influence, and politics in the modern workplace; their meaning for individuals, groups, and other organizational stakeholders; and their effect on organizational outcomes and performances (Vigoda-Gadot & Drory, 2006).

Vigoda-Gadot, E., & Drory, A. (Eds.). (2006). *Handbook of organizational politics*. Northampton, MA: Edward Elgar Pub.

Perfectionism

Readers discover the key characteristics of a healthy family system, along with the single most important lesson of all – perfection does not exist (Smith, 2013).

Smith, A. (2013). *Overcoming perfectionism: Finding the key to balance and self-acceptance* (Revised, Updated edition). Health Communications Inc. EB.

Performance appraisal

This book features concise sections on how to write the evaluation and handle tricky legal issues and verbally discusses the evaluation; also included is a directory of thousands of words and phrases appropriate for any type of written evaluation (Sandler & Keefe, 2003).

Sandler, C., & Keefe, J. (2003). *Performance appraisals phrase book: The best words, phrases, and techniques for performance reviews* (1st ed.). Avon, MA: Adams Media.

Rapport

This book discusses rapport, four tips in using body language to help build trust, and examples of its application (Evans, 2014).

Evans, B. (2014). *Building rapport: The best techniques for instant rapport building with anyone*. Success First Publishing.

Workaholism

This guidebook offers everything from identification of a workaholic and an understanding of the mental state that it entails to how family and children can help and are affected to solutions to curb the addictive patterns (Robinson, 2014).

Robinson, B. E. (2014). *Chained to the desk: A guidebook for workaholics, their partners and children, and the clinicians who treat them* (3rd ed.). New York: NYU Press. JSTOR.

Through a look into the emotional side of the makeup of a workaholic, this best-selling book suggests new strategies to achieve work-life balance (Killinger, 1997).

Killinger, B. (1997). Workaholics: The respectable addicts. Canada: Firefly Books.

Work systems

This book serves as a guidebook for managers by providing a non-hierarchical model rooted in theory on how to improve performance and strengthen dynamics. You will be challenged to use your own past experience to look past the surface chaos and focus on strategic implementation that will match your intentions (Hoebeke, 1994).

Hoebeke, L. (1994). *Making work systems better: A practitioner's reflections* (1st ed.). New York: Wiley.

Journals

Analytical

HR analytics will become an established discipline that has a proven impact on business outcomes and will have a strong influence in operational and strategic decision-making (van de Heuvel & Bondarouk, 2017).

van den Heuvel, S., & Bondarouk, T. (2017). The rise (and fall?) of HR analytics. *Journal of Organizational Effectiveness: People and Performance*, 4(2), 157–178. https://doi.org/10.1108/JOEPP-03-2017-0022

Authority

This article distinguishes four types of authority: capacity-based, ontological, moral, and charismatic (Alasuutari, 2018).

Alasuutari, P. (2018). Authority as epistemic capital. *Journal of Political Power*, 11(2), 165–190. https://doi.org/10.1080/2158379X.2018.1468151

Bullying

This article introduces a social exchange perspective to the study of workplace bullying (Parzefall & Salin, 2010).

Parzefall, M.-R., & Salin, D. M. (2010). Perceptions of and reactions to workplace bullying: A social exchange perspective. *Human Relations*, *63*(6), 761–780. https://doi.org/10.1177/0018726709345043

This journal reviews definitions and descriptions of workplace bullying and its consequences (Appelbaum, Semerjian, & Mohan, 2012).

Appelbaum, S. H., Semerjian, G., & Mohan, K. (2012). Workplace bullying: Consequences, causes and controls (part one). *Industrial and Commercial Training*, *44*(4), 203–210. https://doi.org/10.1108/00197851211231478

Coaching

This article describes some of the practical techniques and tools used in the practice of coaching and identifies different types of coaching, such as in diversity, cross-cultural interaction, health, transition, and so on (Jones, Woods, & Guillaume, 2016).

Jones, R. J., Woods, S. A., & Guillaume, Y. R. F. (2016). The effectiveness of workplace coaching: A meta-analysis of learning and performance outcomes from coaching. *Journal of Occupational and Organizational Psychology*, *89*(2), 249–277. https://doi.org/10.1111/joop.12119

Decision-making

Understanding that decision-making is a skill that employers' value, this article discusses what the skill is, the process of decision-making, the different types of decision-making skills, ways to problem solve and work collaboratively, utilizing emotional intelligence to control emotions to convey opinions, and using logical reasoning in addition to providing examples of this skill being used in action (Doyle, 2019).

Doyle, A. (2019, May 31). Find out the reasons why employers value decision-making skills. Retrieved November 24, 2019, from The Balance Careers website: www.thebalancecareers.com/decision-making-skills-with-examples-2063748

To strengthen one's own handling of difficult situations, this article provides seven ideas to support the development of a great decision maker (Petty, 2019).

Petty, A. (2019, June 25). 7 ideas to support your development as a great decision maker. Retrieved November 24, 2019, from The Balance Careers website: www.thebalancecareers.com/how-to-make-better-decisions-at-work-3961619

Both skills of decision-making and assertiveness serve as traits that are appealing to employers. This article reviews the importance of the two skills and what good decisions, bad decisions, positive assertiveness, and negative assertiveness may look like in the workplace (Kokemuller, n.d.).

Kokemuller, N. (n.d.). Importance of decision making & assertiveness in the workplace. Retrieved November 24, 2019, from the Chron.com website: https://work.chron.com/importance-decision-making-assertiveness-workplace-2651.html

Gossip

This article by the *Harvard Business Review* identifies strategies for open communication to minimize office gossip (Bassuk & Lew, 2016).

Bassuk, A., & Lew, C. (2016, November 11). The antidote to office gossip. *Harvard Business Review*. Retrieved from https://hbr.org/2016/11/the-antidote-to-office-gossip

Humor / sarcasm

There is a place for sarcasm between people who trust each other, but it can be toxic when overdone or used in the wrong context (Bernstein, 2015).

Bernstein, E. (2015, August 24). People love your sarcasm, really. *Wall Street Journal*. Retrieved from www.wsj.com/articles/people-love-your-sarcasm-really-1440451942

Meetings

This article argues that most business meetings are disruptive and unnecessary (Johansson, 2015).

Johansson, A. (2015, April 8). Why meetings are one of the worst business rituals. Ever. Retrieved November 27, 2019, from the Entrepreneur website: www.entrepreneur.com/article/244499

Organizational politics

This article examines the various relationships of organizational politics types (Maslyn, Farmer, & Bettenhausen, 2017).

Maslyn, J. M., Farmer, S. M., & Bettenhausen, K. L. (2017). When organizational politics matters: The effects of the perceived frequency and distance of experienced politics. *Human Relations*, 70(12), 1486–1513. https://doi.org/10.1177/0018726717704706

Organizational structure

The article examines how types of organizational structure provide the appropriate conditions for the development of organizational learning (Inocencia, 2011).

Inocencia, M. M. (2011). The influence of organizational structure on organizational learning. *International Journal of Manpower*, 32(5/6), 537–566. https://doi.org/10.1108/014377 21111158198

Perfectionism

This article examines the pros and cons to being a perfectionist (Swider, Harari, Breidenthal, & Steed, 2018).

Swider, B., Harari, D., Breidenthal, A. P., & Steed, L. B. (2018, December 27). The pros and cons of perfectionism, according to research. *Harvard Business Review*. Retrieved from https://hbr.org/2018/12/the-pros-and-cons-of-perfectionism-according-to-research

Performance appraisal

Employee performance has traditionally been accorded prime focus by human resource managers. As a result, a number of performance appraisal techniques have over time been devised to help establish employee's performance (Idowu, 2017).

Idowu, A. (2017). Effectiveness of performance appraisal system and its effect on employee motivation. *Nile Journal of Business and Economics*, 3. https://doi.org/10.20321/nilejbe.v3i5.88

Rapport

This research article discusses the necessity of rapport for good relationships between occupational therapists and patients (Furnham, King, & Pendleton, 1980).

Furnham, A., King, J., & Pendleton, D. (1980). Establishing rapport: Interactional skills and occupational therapy. *British Journal of Occupational Therapy*, 43(10), 322–325. https://doi.org/10.1177/030802268004301005

Recruiting

HR departments are beginning to implement artificial intelligence into their recruiting process (Castellanos, 2019).

Castellanos, S. (2019, March 14). HR departments turn to AI-enabled recruiting in race for talent. *Wall Street Journal*. Retrieved from www.wsj.com/articles/hr-departments-turn-to-ai-enabled-recruiting-in-race-for-talent-11552600459

Respect

This articles offers a look at how to evaluate the respect in your organization with an emphasis on the importance of respectful leadership in the eyes of employees (Rogers, 2018).

Rogers, K. (2018, July 1). Do your employees feel respected? *Harvard Business Review*, (July–August 2018). Retrieved from https://hbr.org/2018/07/do-your-employees-feel-respected

Trust

The Reina Trust Building Institute has implemented their research and two decades of assisting leaders in building and rebuilding trust into one book. This work focuses on rebuilding and recovering from workplace betrayals and takes readers through a proven seven-step process to help everyone involved (Reina & Reina, 2010).

Reina, D., & Reina, M. (2010). *Rebuilding trust in the workplace: Seven steps to renew confidence, commitment, and energy* (1st ed.). San Francisco, CA: Berrett-Koehler Publisher.

Workaholism

University of Pennsylvania's Wharton School professor of management makes an important distinction between work addiction and working long hours and gives insight into consequences and practical advice (Rothbard, 2018).

Rothbard, N. (2018, April 11). You may be a workaholic if. *Harvard Business Review*. Retrieved from https://hbr.org/ideacast/2018/04/you-may-be-a-workaholic-if

This article discusses the antecedents and consequences of workaholism from a scientific perspective (M. A. Clark, 2016).

Clark, M. A. (2016, April). Workaholism: It's not just long hours on the job. *American Psychological Association*. Retrieved from www.apa.org/science/about/psa/2016/04/workaholism

This study delves into the health and circumstantial causes of workaholism, the machines and methods, and the lack thereof with which we measure the condition (Andreassen, 2014).

Andreassen, C. S. (2014). Workaholism: An overview and current status of the research. *Journal of Behavioral Addictions*, 3(1), 1–11. https://doi.org/10.1556/JBA.2.2013.017

Aggressive/defensive cultures

Work systems

This study emphasizes the importance of relational coordination among employees as a bridge between high-performance work systems and improved performance outcomes (Gittell, Seidner, & Wimbush, 2009).

Gittell, J. H., Seidner, R., & Wimbush, J. (2009). A relational model of how high-performance work systems work. *Organization Science*, *21*(2), 490–506. https://doi.org/10.1287/orsc.1090.0446

Web links

Analytical

The following is a factsheet on HR analytics by the numbers (van Vulpen, 2015).

van Vulpen, E. (2015). What is HR analytics (people analytics)? Human resources analytics. Retrieved November 23, 2019, from AIHR website: www.analyticsinhr.com/blog/what-is-hr-analytics/#seventh

Being able to work with data and having firm analytical skills and soft people skills are essential to work in HR nowadays. The source suggests five specific skills that are believed to be important for an HR manager to have (Terrill & Martin, 2014).

Terrill, J., & Martin, J. (2014, July 8). Analytical skills importance in HR today. Retrieved November 23, 2019, from TerrillConnect–Compliance, Regulatory & Company News website: www.jwterrill.com/wp/2014/07/08/analytical-skills-importance-in-hr-today/

This website provides applications, tools, and FAQ ("HR analytics," n.d.).

HR analytics: Everything you need to know. (n.d.). Retrieved November 23, 2019, from the MicroStrategy website: www.microstrategy.com/us/resources/introductory-guides/hr-analytics-everything-you-need-to-know

This source defines the role of an HR analyst as someone who collects and studies information related to jobs, issues, and costs that affect their companies (Suttle, 2019).

Suttle, R. (2019, March 6). What Is the role of an HR analyst? Retrieved November 23, 2019, from the Chron.com website: https://smallbusiness.chron.com/role-hr-analyst-34501.html

Authority

Serving as a reminder to managers, challenges to authority will occur, but it is important for managers to exercise emotional intelligence rather than being quick to react. This source provides two reasons as to why an employee may challenge your authority (Tanner, 2019).

Tanner, R. (2019, May 26). Two reasons why employees challenge your authority. Retrieved November 22, 2019, from the Management Is a Journey website: https://managementisajourney.com/two-reasons-why-employees-challenge-your-authority/

Big picture

This blog provides five tips to help people see the big picture and why it's important. These five tips include sharing the big picture regularly, giving details and then adding the context, asking others what they see, connecting the big picture to their work, and connecting the big picture to meaning (Eikenberry, 2015).

Eikenberry, K. (2015). Helping people see the big picture (and why it is so important). Retrieved November 23, 2019, from https://blog.kevineikenberry.com/leadership-supervisory-skills/helping-people-see-the-big-picture-and-why-it-is-so-important/

This article suggests five strategies to get out of the weeds and think about the big picture. These five strategies include allocating time to think, getting a buddy, picking specific goals, identifying actionable first steps, and generating ideas (Rosenstein, 2014).

Rosenstein, J. (2014, September 25). 5 strategies for big-picture thinking. *Fast Company*. Retrieved from www.fastcompany.com/3036143/5-strategies-for-big-picture-thinking

Bullying

The following is a federal government website managed by the U.S. Department of Health and Human Services. It provides resources such as connections to a training center, laws and policies, and tools to prevent bullying (U.S. Department of Health and Human Services, n.d.).

U.S. Department of Health and Human Services. (n.d.). StopBullying.gov. Retrieved November 23, 2019, from StopBullying.gov website: www.stopbullying.gov/

This article provides statistics about workplace bullying (Agarwal, 2018).

Agarwal, P. (2018, July 29). Here is why we need to talk about bullying in the workplace. Retrieved November 23, 2019, from the Forbes website: www.forbes.com/sites/pragyaagarwaleurope/2018/07/29/workplace-bullying-here-is-why-we-need-to-talk-about-bullying-in-the-workplace/#7f5095933259

The following is an article about who the workplace bullies are, what bullying costs the organization, how to stop it, and ways to focus on problem solving to reduce it (Comaford, 2016).

Comaford, C. (2016, August 27). 75% of workers are affected by bullying: Here's what to do about it. Retrieved November 23, 2019, from the Forbes website: www.forbes.com/sites/christinecomaford/2016/08/27/the-enormous-toll-workplace-bullying-takes-on-your-bottom-line/#5ef2bf2d5595

The first and only U.S. organization dedicated to the eradication of workplace bullying provides help on how to deal with workplace bullying when it occurs (Namie & Namie, 2019).

Namie, G., & Namie, R. (2019). Being bullied. Retrieved November 23, 2019, from www.workplacebullying.org/individuals/problem/being-bullied/

Chain of command

A strategy should be in place for when an employee fails to follow the chain of command (Lohrey, 2017).

Lohrey, J. (2017, September 26). How to handle an employee who ignores the chain of command. Retrieved November 22, 2019, from the Bizfluent website: https://bizfluent.com/info-12174725-handle-employee-ignores-chain-command.html

Change

The following is a *Forbes* article that acknowledges the frustration that comes with change and provides five tips on how to manage inevitable change in the workplace (Alton, 2017b).

Alton, L. (2017b, July 26). 5 powerful ways to confront change in the workplace. *Forbes*. Retrieved from www.forbes.com/sites/larryalton/2017/07/26/5-powerful-ways-to-confront-change-in-the-workplace/#b128218290d8

Multiple strategies on how to effectively manage and improve collaboration in the midst of organizational transition and change are addressed in this article (Covi, 2016).

Covi, I. (2016, April 22). Coping with change in the workplace. Retrieved November 24, 2019, from Business Know-How website: www.businessknowhow.com/manage/leadwithin.htm

Coaching

This article defines what coaching is while identifying what it is not, why it's important, when it occurs, and key characteristics of a successful coach (Coaching Skills, 2019).

Coaching Skills. (2019). What is coaching in the workplace? Retrieved November 24, 2019, from the Coaching Skills website: https://coach4growth.com/coaching-skills/what-is-coaching-in-the-workplace

Feedback

The following is a *Harvard Business Review* article that discusses reasons for disconnect in problematic feedback and strategies to improve feedback as a manager (Phoel, 2009).

Phoel, C. M. (2009, April 27). Feedback that works. *Harvard Business Review*. Retrieved from https://hbr.org/2009/04/feedback-that-works

Gossip

Understand when gossip crosses the line from innocuous conversation to something so potentially hurtful or liable that companies are within their rights to forbid it (Wilkie, 2018).

Wilkie, D. (2018, April 11). Workplace gossip: What crosses the line? Retrieved March 15, 2019, from SHRM website: www.shrm.org/resourcesandtools/hr-topics/employee-relations/pages/office-gossip-policies.aspx

This article talks about the danger of workplace gossip, ways to get out of the "gossip pipeline," what an employer can do to minimize gossip, and things to consider when the gossip is about you (Careerstone Group, n.d.).

Careerstone Group. (n.d.). The danger of workplace gossip. Retrieved November 27, 2019, from Careerstone Group website: https://careerstonegroup.com/blog/105/The-Danger-of-Workplace-Gossip

Incivility

An article designed to bring awareness to incivility by understanding why it happens and how to address it (Texas A&M, 2017).

Texas A&M. (2017, October 31). Workplace incivility: The silent epidemic. Retrieved November 27, 2019, from the Science Daily website: www.sciencedaily.com/releases/2017/10/171031120606.htm

This article identifies five common types of toxic employees and what to do about them (Chaffold, 2017).

Chaffold, J. (2017, August 29). Are toxic employees ruining your workplace? Retrieved November 27, 2019, from the Insperity website: www.insperity.com/blog/toxic-employee-types/

Meetings

In addition to discussing the high costs of a meeting, this article provides ten tips on how to conduct effective and productive meetings (Godefroy, n.d.).

Godefroy, R. (n.d.). 10 ways to conduct effective meetings in the workplace. Retrieved November 27, 2019, from motivational speaker Rene Godefroy's website: www.renegodefroy.com/how-to-conduct-effective-meetings-in-the-workplace/

Organizational politics

Life would be simpler if working was just about getting the job done, but organizational politics complicate the workday. When it comes to getting ahead in business, playing the political game and playing it well can make a big difference in who makes the big leagues and who doesn't (Cameron, 2019).

Cameron, S. (2019, January 22). What are organizational politics? Retrieved November 29, 2019, from the Bizfluent website: https://bizfluent.com/info-8151721-organizational-politics.html

Organizational structure

This web article looks at the four different types of organizational structures (Alton, 2017a).

Alton, L. (2017a, July 9). 4 common types of organizational structures. Retrieved November 29, 2019, from All Business: Your small business advantage website: www.allbusiness.com/4-common-types-organizational-structures-103745-1.html

Perfectionism

This article examines the two types of perfectionism: the healthy kind and the unhealthy kind (Madden, 2011).

Madden, K. (2011, October 6). Perfectionists in the workplace. Retrieved November 29, 2019, from CNN website: www.cnn.com/2011/10/03/living/perfection-cb/index.html

Performance appraisal

This guide provides support to writing and conducting a performance appraisal (Juneja, n.d.).

Juneja, P. (n.d.). Performance appraisal. Retrieved November 29, 2019, from the Management Study Guide website: www.managementstudyguide.com/performance-appraisal.htm

Rapport

This is a web page by Indeed's career guide that discusses why building rapport is important and tips on how to build rapport during networking events, interviews, and in the workplace (Indeed, n.d.).

Indeed. (n.d.). Building rapport: Tips and examples. Retrieved November 29, 2019, from Indeed.com website: www.indeed.com/career-advice/starting-new-job/building-rapport

Recruiting

The following is a list of recruiting trends that you should consider implementing come 2020 (Zojceska, 2018).

Zojceska, A. (2018, September 24). 15 new recruiting trends you should implement in 2020. Retrieved November 29, 2019, from the blog website: www.talentlyft.com/en/blog/article/87/15-new-recruiting-trends-you-should-implement-in-2020

This article is a statistics-based look at recruitment from a candidate's perspective (Built In, n.d.).

Built In. (n.d.). Recruiting: A complete guide to recruiting in 2019. Retrieved November 29, 2019, from the Built In website: https://builtin.com/recruiting

Respect

A compelling read on the influence a manager has on employees in the context of respect (Kant, 2006).

Kant, I. (2006, August 17). Respect in the workplace. Retrieved November 29, 2019, from the Creditworthy News website: www.creditworthy.com/3jm/articles/cw81706.html

Trust

A worldwide survey showed that 75% of people see their employer as their most trusted institution. The article discusses six ways to capitalize on that opportunity and further build trust by leading with actions (Grossman, 2019).

Grossman, D. (2019, May 6). Trust in the workplace: 6 steps to building trust with employees. Retrieved November 30, 2019, from the Your Thought Partner website: www.yourthoughtpartner.com/blog/bid/59619/leaders-follow-these-6-steps-to-build-trust-with-employees-improve-how-you-re-perceived

Workaholism

This author provides an overview of workaholism and the different types of workaholics that exist allows readers to reflect on their own habits or those of others and decide if further action should be taken (Killinger, 1997).

Killinger, B. (1997). *Workaholics: The respectable addicts* (1st ed.). Canada: Firefly Books.

This article provides a comprehensive breakdown of the causes of workaholism and why it is ineffective (M. Clark, 2018).

Clark, M. (2018, February 20). These are the four drivers of workaholism. Retrieved November 30, 2019, from the Fast Company website: www.fastcompany.com/40531406/there-are-four-types-of-workaholic-and-none-of-them-work

Based on a recent study, this reading offers a unique list of symptoms to diagnose workaholism in yourself and others (Stillman, 2014).

Stillman, J. (2014, August 28). The 7 signs of workaholism. Retrieved November 30, 2019, from Inc.com website: www.inc.com/jessica-stillman/the-7-signs-of-workaholism.html

Part 6

Taking corrective actions

How to use this part

This part examines some of the various ways that a manager can take corrective actions through the use of progressive discipline, understanding when to deliver a verbal warning, a written warning, or a suspension. This portion will also look at conducting investigations and delivering feedback.

Key terms

The key terms found in the cases in this section are listed here. Their definitions can be found on pages xiv–xvii.

Anger
Coaching
Defensiveness
Discipline
Feedback
Rapport

Choosing the right level of discipline

Main subjects
Coaching, discipline

Who's who
- Shakia Andrews, Executive Housekeeper
- Blake Cassara, Houseman
- Betty Chu, Human Resources Manager
- Yvonne Clark, Director of Sales and Marketing
- Wesley Edwards, Room Service Manager
- Kelsey Garber, PBX Operator
- Henry Hermann, Houseman
- Robert Kunz, General Manager
- Cassidy Mei, Sales Coordinator
- Katherine Norton, Director of Human Resources
- Louise Rausch, Director of Finance
- Kalinda Stenton, PBX Manager

Think point

A common practice for managers to follow when addressing the poor performance of an employee is progressive discipline. In this way, a minor offense has a minor consequence; however, they can build up on each other and lead up to and include termination. Managers must be prepared to be able to respond to a wide range of disciplinary issues.

Taking corrective actions

"When dealing with an employee problem," explained Katherine during the last management outing, "progressive discipline requires you to follow these steps: coaching, verbal warning, written warning, suspension, and finally termination. The trick is to figure out when coaching is the right response and when more serious discipline is in order."

Managers from various departments were asked to write down a few recent disciplinary issues. During the coffee break, Katherine and Betty quickly reviewed the situations and asked some managers to present their stories to the entire team as managerial dilemmas.

Here are the situations the human resources team selected.

a "What's fairest way to discipline these two employees?" asked Shakia. "In housekeeping, I caught two housemen, Henry and Blake, trying on guest shoes together in the shoeshine area. Henry hasn't needed to be disciplined before, but Blake was reprimanded recently for sitting on the bed in an occupied room. Should Blake's discipline be more severe than Henry's?"

b "In accounting," continued Mike, "the night auditor once used the wrong formula on the daily revenue report and sent Louise the document with unrealistic, inflated average daily revenue figures."

c "In PBX, we had a policy breach case," remembered Kalinda. "A new employee, Kelsey, was listening to her iPod while answering the calls. Customers were complaining that they heard loud music and were distracted while talking to the operator. Kelsey forgot to review the operations manual, even though it was included in her orientation package."

d "A few years back, the room service assistant manager shared with one of our servers all the details of a discrimination investigation concerning the room service order taker," added Wesley.

e "I told Cassidy, our sales coordinator," said Yvonne, "that I needed a competitive analysis ready by Thursday. On Thursday, at 6:30 PM, Cassidy placed the document in my mailbox. At that time, I had already left for the day, and I was en route to the regional sales conference, starting on Friday. This analysis was part of my morning presentation. Since Cassidy didn't bring the report to my attention before the end of the shift and did not follow up with an email to me, I definitely wanted to sit down with her. I was wondering if discipline was warranted," asked Yvonne.

"Typically, our progressive discipline system entitles employees to three written warnings in a 12-month period before suspension. We try to stick to this guideline, but, to be honest with you, occasionally, I decide to 'give the guy one more chance' after a final warning. That's the reason I like the flexibility of progressive discipline," Mr. Kunz added to the discussion.

1   What are the advantages of progressive discipline?

2   Help the managers choose the right response.

3   How do you evaluate Mr. Kunz's practice?

The case is based on the principles and situations described in the following:

Mader-Clark, M., & Guerin, L. (2007). *The progressive discipline handbook*. Berkeley, CA: Nolo.

Emily's letters

Case type: application case

Main subjects
Anger, coaching, discipline, feedback

Who's who
• Eddy Bucks, Restaurant Server
• Betty Chu, Human Resources Manager
• Emily Perkins, Lounge and Bar Manager
• Bonifacio da Silva, Restaurant Server

Think point

Supervisors and managers should both be trained on the proper procedure an organization will take with regards to progressive discipline. Understanding that proper documentation is critical in this process is important.

This holiday morning, Emily was working on two different disciplinary warning letters. Earlier, she went down to human resources, where she was surprised to find Betty decorating the corridor. She graciously showed her the employee files and gave her a copy of the employee handbook. "Please make sure that to you send me a copy of the letters, so that I can place them in their files," Betty asked her. "And don't forget the fireworks and concert on the banks of the Bedford River tonight," added Betty as she was leaving the office.

Taking corrective actions

Emily looked confident and satisfied as she glanced at the documents on her desk. Recently, she had attended a training seminar where they were provided with a checklist on how to document disciplinary actions. As the lounge seemed to be quiet, she decided to sit down briefly with the two employees, first with Eddy and then with Bonifacio.

1   What are the advantages of proper documentation?

2   What are the dangers of over-documenting?

3   Based on the two memos, analyze Emily's documentation technique. What mistakes is she making?

4   Please correct the memos accordingly.

5   Assume that Bonifacio responds angrily to the discipline. How do you think Emily should deal with him?

Exhibits

- Disciplinary letters.
- Employees' incident summaries.
- Royal Hotel – employee handbook (excerpts).
- Documentation rules – checklist.

Letter 1

MEMORANDUM

Date: July 4, 2018
From: Emily Perkins
To: Eddy Bucks
Subject: punctuality

Eddy, this letter will document our conversation on June 20, 2018, which raised my concern about your recent punctuality record. Over the last 18 months, you have been repeatedly tardy.

Unfortunately, now you were late again. When I asked you if everything was all right and if there was any specific reason as to why you were late, you answered, "I was running late because I had trouble starting my car." Eddy, we both know that this just baloney. It is a common courtesy to your coworkers for you to show up for work on time. Please remember that employees who are always tardy put an extra burden on their co-workers.

After your previous tardiness, I spoke with you and warned you that it cannot happen again. I later took my two weeks' vacation, and your next tardy arrival was noticed but apparently not documented by the new assistant manager. When I returned to see that the problem had persisted, I was simply shocked.

Previous actions have been taken when you were found drinking soda in front of guests on January 2, 2018, and your name tag was missing on February 2, 2018. Certainly, these other policy violations and your recent tardiness have made me go to the next level of disciplinary action.

This letter is to serve as a formal write-up. A copy of this document will be forwarded to the general manager. Eddy, your punctuality should be improved. As you know, Mother Emily is always here to come up with a great schedule for everybody. We all make mistakes; the reason for this letter is not to scare you or threaten you. However, if this occurs again, you will be disciplined again.

Sincerely,
Emily Perkins

_____
EMPLOYEE'S SIGNATURE

I have read and fully understand this notice.

(Note: Your signature is not required if you disagree with the contents of this document.)

Letter 2

MEMORANDUM

Date: July 4, 2018
From: Emily Perkins
To: Bonifacio da Silva
Subject: suspension

The subject of this letter is to inform you of your gross misconduct yesterday.

As discussed, you left the floor without informing your fellow servers or a manager that you needed to step away.

Upon your return, you were questioned as to your whereabouts, and you informed me that you were needed at the concierge desk. Later, you engaged in an argument with a colleague, and you started harassing him.

Bonifacio, you can't just leave the restaurant without talking to anyone. Furthermore, harassing others is completely against company policy and will not be tolerated. In response to your actions, many of our guests were dissatisfied. This was the second time something like this has come up. I personally addressed this issue with you earlier and clearly notified you that if it were to happen again, you would surely be suspended.

As a result of your actions, you will be suspended without pay effective tomorrow, Saturday, July 5, 2018.

Once again, you are expected to comply with our customer service standards. In order to ensure this does not happen again, I highly recommend that you attend a customer service training seminar.

Your length of service with the Royal Hotel indicates you are valuable to the company. I trust that you will benefit from this experience and make the necessary adjustments. However, if it happens again, you will be suspended for three days.

Sincerely,
Emily Perkins

_____
EMPLOYEE'S SIGNATURE

Your signature means only that you have been advised of the contents of this warning. It does not signify that you agree with its contents.

Incident summary 1 – Eddy's file

Date	Incident	Action
January 14, 2017	Tardy	Coaching discussion (Documentation of conversation attached)
January 28, 2017	Tardy	Verbal warning (attached)
January 2, 2018	Drinking soda in front of guests	Coaching discussion (Documentation of conversation attached)
February 2, 2018	Name tag missing	Verbal warning (attached)
February 15, 2018	Tardy	Coaching discussion (Documentation of conversation attached)
February 20, 2018	Tardy	Verbal warning (attached)

Incident summary 2 – Bonifacio's file

Date	Incident	Action
August 18, 2017	Grooming issue	Coaching discussion (Documentation of conversation attached)
August 19, 2017	Grooming issue	Verbal warning (attached)
September 25, 2017	Grooming issue	Written warning (attached)
September 27, 2017	Grooming issue	One day suspension (attached)
May 20, 2018	Left floor without authorization	Written warning (attached)

Royal Hotel – employee handbook (excerpts)

Attendance and punctuality

- Attendance is a key factor in your job performance. Punctuality and regular attendance are expected of all employees.
- If you are absent for any reason, you must notify your supervisor as far in advance as possible.
- If you are unable to report on time, contact your supervisor directly three hours before your scheduled shift.
- If you are unable to contact your supervisor directly, please contact human resources or security. Do not leave a message with other employees.
- Employees who have excessive absenteeism or tardiness from work, even with acceptable excuses, are subject to discipline.
- Excessive absences or tardiness will be grounds for discipline up to and including termination.
- Any employee who does not report to work or call in to his or her supervisor or human resources for three consecutive working days is considered to have voluntarily resigned without notice.

Standards of conduct

The Royal Hotel has adopted a progressive discipline policy to identify and address employee- and employment-related problems. Preceding termination, the following progressive discipline actions will be performed given the nature of the offense (serious offenses, such as physical or sexual assault or theft will have zero tolerance): verbal warnings, written warnings, suspensions, and termination. While the Royal Hotel will generally take disciplinary action in a progressive manner, it reserves the right, in its sole discretion, to decide whether and what disciplinary action will be taken in a given situation. No disciplinary action may be used against an employee for an offense that is more than 12 months old.

Documentation rules – checklist

1 Introduction
2 Nature of problem
2/a Supporting details (if appropriate)
3 Rules/policies that have been violated
3/a Negative impact on the organization (if appropriate)
4 History of past coaching or corrective actions
5 Disciplinary action
6 Goals and expectations
6/a Training or special direction (if appropriate)
6/b Follow-up/feedback (if appropriate)
7 Positive statement
8 Consequences
9 Employee section

The case is based on the principles and situations described in the following:

Falcone, P. (2000). A blueprint for progressive discipline and terminations. *HR Magazine*, 77(8), 3–5.

Roper, B. (n.d.). *A step-by-step guide to performance documents*. Retrieved September 19, 2017, from Mott Community College Web Site www.mcc.edu/hr_protected/pdf/articles_performance_documents.pdf

Toby's silence

Main subjects
Coaching, defensiveness, discipline, feedback, rapport

Who's who
• Toby Kenney, Purchasing Receiving Clerk
• Paul Bello, Purchasing Manager
• Pascal Gateau, Executive Chef

Think point

When investigating a situation that could lead to progressive disciplinary action on the employee's behalf, it is wise to follow a policy and practice of integrating the employees. Employees can have a variety of different reactions to potentially being accused of something; they might agree and show remorse, they might become defensive and become argumentative, or they may simply go into a silent mode. Consider how you might handle this situation.

Taking corrective actions

Chef Gateau angrily called Paul in purchasing early in the afternoon. He had ordered 40 pounds of product from "Western Quality Meats."

However, when the butcher opened the box, he only found 30 pounds of the product. The chef needed special imported steaks for a corporate event that night. "I already took care of this; the chef of the Promenade hotel will help me out at this time," said the chef. "You know, Paul, it's not the first time this has happened. Please, take some action," the chef finished.

Receiving clerks were required to weigh all meat, fish, and poultry delivered to the Royal Hotel. Paul asked Toby, the receiving clerk, to come to his office.

"What is it about?" asked Toby.

"Please sit down, Toby," answered Paul. "The chef called. Ten pounds of steak is apparently missing from the special order. I am sure you know that it is important that the Royal Hotel only pays for products that have been delivered," Paul continued.

Toby folded his arms around his chest firmly and bit his lips.

"Do you realize that the chef did not have enough steak to prepare a special menu for tonight?" Paul asked him.

Toby responded with stony silence.

"I expect a response. Actually, if you don't answer this minute, I will have to presume that you did not weigh the meat," added Paul.

Toby did not say anything – instead, he gazed down at his lap, appearing not to hear the discussion.

1   What could be the reasons behind an employee's silence during a disciplinary meeting?

2   How should managers generally deal with silent employees?

3   How would you evaluate Paul's last statement?

4   It seems that Toby does not care about the discussion. What are Paul's options?

The case is based on the principles and situations described in the following:

Mader-Clark, M., & Guerin, L. (2007). *The progressive discipline handbook* (pp. 186–191). Berkeley, CA: Nolo.

Investigation

Main subjects
Bullying, discipline, incivility

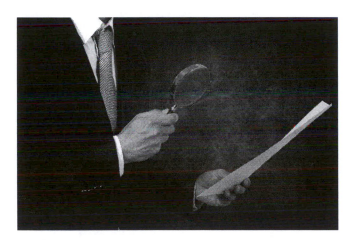

Who's who
• Wesley Edwards, Room Service Manager
• Eric Santos, Room Service Server
• Paul Lopez, Room Service Server
• Christina Barette, Room Service Order Taker

Think point

Investigating requires the individual conducting the investigation to remain neutral and free of bias. This is much easier said than done. The process will include communicating with witnesses and obtaining written statements. At the conclusion, a decision must be rendered. A timely investigation is critical for operations.

Taking corrective actions

Wesley looked up from his work to see a visibly upset Eric standing in his doorway. Eric explained to him that he and Paul had gotten into an argument and that Paul had ended it saying that they would "settle it after work."

Wesley immediately started an investigation, which involved getting a statement from Eric, Paul, and a witness, Christina. This is what he discovered:

According to Eric

- Eric was upset that Paul did not complete his side work and told him that he should.
- Paul immediately started yelling at Eric and then proceeded to follow him into the walk-in cooler, where he told him that they would "settle this after work."

According to Paul

- Eric is always bossing him around. He was going to complete his side work but didn't have a chance to yet. When Eric reminded him, he did snap at him that he would complete it.
- Paul went into the walk-in cooler at the same time as Eric because he had to get something out of it, not because he was following Eric. Once in the cooler, Eric started yelling at him and waving his hands aggressively in Paul's face.

According to Christina

- Eric yelled at Paul that he needed to complete his side work. Paul yelled back at Eric that he would get to it later. Both Paul and Eric went into the walk-in cooler. Christina was not aware of what happened in the cooler because she couldn't hear or see anything, but they both came out looking very angry.

1 What are important things to keep in mind when completing an investigation?

2 Based on what Wesley knows, what should he do now?

Make an exception

Main subjects
Credibility, discipline, unions

Who's who
• Matthew Knorr, Director of Food and Beverage
• Emily Perkins, Lounge and Bar Manager
• Charlotte Carpantier, Bartender

Think point

It is good business practice to have an attendance policy that is clear and easy for the managers and the employees to follow. It is important to document and discipline employees in a timely fashion. One of the aspects to a rule is the ability to break or bend the rule. If you make the exception for one person, are you prepared to make the exception for all employees? Consider the consequences to your decision.

Taking corrective actions

One afternoon, Emily approached Matthew with a concern. "Matthew, I have some sad news. Charlotte's dog, Puck, passed away last night. She's very upset and has called off for her shift tonight. Based on our attendance policy, this would be a verbal warning for her, but it doesn't feel right. What should I do?"

Matthew had to think about it. Everyone knew how much Puck meant to Charlotte. She treated her dog like a child, and pictures of Puck in various holiday costumes were often seen hanging on bulletin boards in the back of the house of the Royal Hotel.

Note: the Royal Hotel attendance policy states that if an associate reaches four call-offs in a 12-month period, he or she will receive a verbal warning.

1 How should Matthew evaluate this situation?

2 What are the consequences of making an exception?

3 What are the consequences of not making an exception?

4 How would this be different if the Royal Hotel were a union property?

> ## Part summary
>
> This section covered the aspect of progressive discipline as a form of holding employees accountable for doing their job. The cases here look at the various types of problems that might be found in an operation. Managers should consider their own personal biases that might exist when investigating. The importance of documentation was also explored.

Additional reading

Books

Anger

This book presents a cost and benefit analysis of anger in the workplace to make the argument that anger can be a positive and productive emotion that can produce valuable data, as well as considerable motivation when managed effectively (Gibson & Tulgan, 2010).

Gibson, D., & Tulgan, B. (2010). *Managing anger in the workplace.* Amazon Digital Services LLC.

This short ebook will give you the strategies to recognize warnings and center yourself to prevent frustrations from influencing how you act (McKinstry, 2016).

McKinstry, J. (2016). *Defuse for HR: Successfully tackling frustration and anger in HR.* Briggs Publishing.

Discipline

Covering every aspect of discipline, this comprehensive book discusses discipline at work by utilizing three decades of research on industrial discipline and case laws on discipline (Ramasamy, 2006).

Ramasamy, G. (2006). *Discipline at work: A guide for managers* (2nd ed.). Retrieved from www.amazon.com/Discipline-at-Work-Guide-Managers/dp/9834048718

Journals

Anger

This article states that ignoring anger and anxiety in the workplace has exacerbated the problem. Human emotions are a free resource that can be harnessed in ethical ways to enhance job productivity (Wachs & Helge, 2001).

Wachs, J. E., & Helge, D. (2001). Turning workplace anger and anxiety into peak performance: Strategies for enhancing employee health and productivity. *AAOHN Journal*, 49(8), 399–408. https://doi.org/10.1177/216507990104900806

This journal defines what toxin handlers are, who they are, what they do, how they reduce the organizational pain, why they are needed, and strategies to minimize the negative impact on them (Daniel, 2017).

Daniel, T. A. (2017). Managing toxic emotions at work: HR's unique role as the "organizational shock absorber." *Employment Relations Today*, *43*(4), 13–19. https://doi.org/10.1002/ert.21599

Defensiveness

A paper that discusses leader-exchange relationships, performance appraisals, and implications of the findings as they relate to organizations (Becker, Halbesleben, & O'Hair, 2005).

Becker, J. A. H., Halbesleben, J. R. B., & O'Hair, H. D. (2005). Defensive communication and burnout in the workplace: The mediating role of leader – member exchange. *Communication Research Reports*, *22*(2), 143–150. https://doi.org/10.1080/00036810500130653

Discipline

The following journal article compares and contrasts two discipline types known as progressive and positive to further discuss the roles of management, unions, and employees as well as discipline pitfalls (Guffey & Helms, 2001).

Guffey, C. J., & Helms, M. M. (2001). Effective employee Discipline: A case of the internal revenue service. *Public Personnel Management*, *30*(1), 111–127. https://doi.org/10.1177/009102600103000110

Rapport

This study examines rapport in a customer-employee relationship (Gremler & Gwinner, 2000).

Gremler, D. D., & Gwinner, K. P. (2000). Customer-employee rapport in service relationships. *Journal of Service Research*, *3*(1), 82–104. https://doi.org/10.1177/109467050031006

The following journal article places emphasis on small talk and its key role in building relationships through business communication (Pullin, 2010).

Pullin, P. (2010). Small talk, rapport, and international communicative competence: Lessons to learn from BELF. *The Journal of Business Communication (1973)*, *47*(4), 455–476. https://doi.org/10.1177/0021943610377307

Web links

Anger

This source provides six tips for how to prepare for, deal with, and respond to anger in the workplace; creating a professional culture; setting expectations and training employees; response training; confrontation of inappropriate and threatening behavior; documenting incidents; and having a zero-tolerance policy (Lotich, 2018).

Lotich, P. (2018, April 11). 6 tips for dealing with anger in the workplace. Retrieved November 23, 2019, from The Thriving Small Business website: https://thethrivingsmallbusiness.com/anger-in-the-workplace/

This source helps you to understand the specific characteristics of anger that are important when it comes to managing negative emotions in the workplace (Great-West Life Centre for Mental Health in the Workplace, n.d.).

Great-West Life Centre for Mental Health in the Workplace. (n.d.). Understanding anger in the workplace. Retrieved November 23, 2019, from Workplace Strategies for Mental Health website: www.workplacestrategiesformentalhealth.com/mmhm/pdf/articles/Understanding_Anger_in_the_Workplace.pdf

This source discusses what topics to discuss and types of method to apply when thinking to provide anger management training. Specifically, there are three approaches to anger management training: one-day workshops, small-group facilitations, and one-on-one therapy sessions (Tyler, 2010).

Tyler, K. (2010, April 1). Helping employees cool it. Retrieved November 23, 2019, from SHRM website: www.shrm.org/h r-today/news/hr-magazine/pages/0410agenda_train.aspx

Coaching

The following is a blog article that identifies the importance of coaching in the workplace and provides tips on how leaders can develop their skills and competencies (Cacioppe, 2012).

Cacioppe, R. (2012, August). Why coaching in the workplace? Retrieved November 24, 2019, from The Integral Business Leadership Group website: www.businessintegral.com/what-is-coaching/

Defensiveness

This book is about how to avoid verbal confrontation and utilize non-defensive communication techniques to avoid power struggles (Ellison, 1998).

Ellison, S. (1998). *Don't be so defensive: Taking the war out of our words with powerful non-defensive communication* (1st ed.). Retrieved from www.amazon.com/Dont-Be-Defensive-Non-Defensive-Communication/dp/0836235940

Discipline

To initiate a positive, systemic change to the discipline system in place at an organization, this article recommends four actions to take to create a positive system (Pennington, 2018).

Pennington, R. (2018, September 18). Viewpoint: Employee discipline for the new workplace. Retrieved November 27, 2019, from www.shrm.org/resourcesandtools/hr-topics/employee-relations/pages/viewpoint-employee-discipline-for-the-new-workplace.aspx

Steps to a progressive discipline system are demonstrated in the following article, along with a discussion on the content of progressive discipline policy (Heathfield, 2019).

Heathfield, S. M. (2019, June 25). Progressive discipline in the workplace and how it works. Retrieved November 27, 2019, from The Balance Careers website: www.thebalancecareers.com/what-progressive-discipline-1918092

Feedback

Based on research and experience at the Center for Creative Leadership (CCL), this article summarizes positive and negative ideas about feedback that the authors agree and disagree with (Chappelow & McCauley, 2019).

Chappelow, C., & McCauley, C. (2019, May 13). What good feedback really looks like. *Harvard Business Review*. Retrieved from https://hbr.org/2019/05/what-good-feedback-really-looks-like

Rapport

This article identifies eight behaviors and tips on creating a dynamic with rapport by living transparently, giving yourself, following through, putting everything together, strategically choosing words, changing the conversation, making visual connections, and being consistent (Mink, 2017).

Mink, M. (2017, September 20). 8 behaviors that bolster workplace rapport. Retrieved November 29, 2019, from the Investor's Business Daily website: www.investors.com/news/management/leaders-and-success/8-behaviors-that-bolster-workplace-rapport/

Part 7

When employees are challenging your leadership

How to use this part

This section examines the aspects that can impact the leadership standing of a manager. There are seven cases, which examine different ways in which an employee may challenge the leadership of a manager. As new entrants into the workforce, specifically in a supervisory or management role, it is important to be prepared for the potential obstacles where employees restrict you as a manager.

Key terms

The key terms found in the cases in this section are listed here. Their definitions can be found on page xiv–xviii.

Assertiveness	Insubordination
Authority	Job design
Buy-in	Job description
Chain of command	Managing up
Change	Open-door policy
Controlling costs	Organizational politics
Credibility	Organizational structure
Defensiveness	Productivity
Discipline	Respect
Flexibility	Trust
Gossip	

I have plans for tonight

Case type: incident case

Main subjects
Authority, buy-in, controlling costs, discipline, flexibility, insubordination, productivity

Who's who
- Jimmy Britton, Valet Parker
- Carlos Diaz, Guest Services Manager
- Eduardo Sullivan, Valet Parker

Think point

In the hospitality industry, the business in many cases, especially in a hotel, will be an operation that is open 24/7. In order to meet the needs of the business volume, there are times when overtime might be required. One of the many considerations might be in what order overtime opportunities are offered to the staff in a department. In this case, a manager should understand the complexity of overtime and the policy at the specific location.

Employees challenging your leadership

Carlos was very concerned. Jimmy, one of the PM valet parkers, called in sick at 10:00 AM. The Royal Hotel was expected to be fully booked that evening, and Carlos knew that Jimmy needed to be replaced. He contacted all part-time and on-call employees; no one was available.

Carlos paged Eduardo, who had just finished parking a car, and asked him on the phone if he could stay longer. "I am sorry that Jimmy called out, but I have plans for tonight," answered Eduardo.

"It's your turn, Eduardo; others did more overtime this month. The hotel policy says I have to give you three hours' notice for overtime. I'm giving you four. If you don't stay, I will write you up." With this, Carlos ended the conversation.

1   Under what circumstances can a supervisor authorize overtime?

2   Can employers require employees to work overtime?

3   How should overtime be distributed?

4   What should Carlos have done differently?

5   How can you minimize the likelihood of a similar situation from reoccurring?

The tipping issue

Main subjects
Authority, discipline

Who's who
• Emily Perkins, Lounge and Bar Manager
• Laura Daley, Restaurant Server

Think point

In the United States, it is customary that food servers receive a lower hourly wage. The wage is supplemented with the gratuities that are left for the server by the guests. Generally, a tip between 15 and 20% of the bill is what is left for the server; a higher percentage could be indicative of the quality of service delivered by the food server. There can be numerous reasons why a guest does not leave a tip at the conclusion of his or her dining experience. One of the most common reasons is a cultural difference. In many other countries, tipping is not expected; thus, it might inadvertently be neglected.

Employees challenging your leadership

"Sorry, Emily," Laura said, her voice raised. "These are the same people who did not leave a tip after I served them last week. I am not serving them!"

Emily seated the party quickly in another server's section, so that the guests did not notice the incident. The lounge got very busy suddenly, and she could not deal with the issue until the end of her shift. Emily knew that servers are paid a low hourly rate, and they rely on tips. As a former server, she was compassionate with the waitstaff, and she was unsure how to address this with Laura.

1 How would you, as Emily, deal with this situation?

2 What could Emily have done differently in the moment?

3 As a manager, how might you better prepare employees to handle cultural diversity?

That's not my job!

Main subjects

Authority, discipline, insubordination, job design/job description

Who's who
- George Kramer, Restaurant Guest
- Carmen Meadors, Restaurant Server
- Jennifer Ortiz, Restaurant Manager

Think point

When one is working with employees, the understanding of the various duties that are required of an individual can sometimes be left up to interpretation. One of the best ways to identify the various tasks and duties required of each position is to have an up-to-date job description. Even with the best job description, a manager may come across an employee who uses the dreaded phrase, "That's not my job." When this occurs, it can be considered a form of insubordination. Employees who travel down the path of insubordination can find themselves subjected to the consequences of progressive discipline.

Employees challenging your leadership

The last breakfast guest, Mr. Kramer, was leisurely reading a newspaper in the restaurant, and the large clock showed noon when he departed. Once he had left, Jennifer asked Carmen, one of the servers, to quickly remove the silver-plated jam stands from the tables.

Carmen's response was "No." She stated that it was not her job; it was a server assistant's responsibility. At this time, Jennifer asked her again to collect a tray and remove the jam stands from the tables, and Carmen replied again, "No. I'm already stretching the limits of my job description without any compensation."

Jennifer asked her a third time to clear the jam stands, and again, the server reiterated that she would not complete this task. Since the first lunch guests were ready to be seated, Jennifer had to run quickly to the front to give the host person a hand. Carmen walked back to the kitchen to serve fresh bread to the arriving guests. The lunch was busy; the jam stands were sitting on the tables for at least another hour until they were finally removed.

In the meantime, Jennifer decided to have a "heart-to-heart" with Carmen once this busy lunch was over.

1 What constitutes insubordination?

2 Identify potential reasons for employees engaging in insubordinate conduct.

3 When can an employee refuse to obey an order?

4 Is disciplinary action warranted? What should Jennifer have done differently?

5 Why should we suspend employees as a final step of our progressive discipline system?

They can wait!

Main subjects
Authority, discipline, insubordination

Who's who
• Steven Kinzer, Restaurant Server
• Jennifer Ortiz, Restaurant Manager

Think point

One of the unique aspects to delivering service in the hospitality industry is the aspect of service expectations. They are in the eye of the beholder and the eye of the consumer. This is a unique juggling act that the manager must ensure is met on both sides. This example looks at a situation where the guests are not being serviced in a timely manner according to the perception by the manager.

A little bit before noon, Jennifer seated a new guest. She had to seek Steven, the server, out in the back-service pantry to inform him that he had a table. Jennifer noticed that during service, the same guest had to flag Steven twice to get more coffee.

Later, another table expressed its displeasure because it had not been approached by a server. Jennifer went to the back and found Steven reading a newspaper. Jennifer told him to go to the table right away. While Steven closed the newspaper slowly, he responded by saying, "Yeah, yeah. I'm going. I'm going. Just relax. Take a Valium."

1　Would you consider Steven's actions as insubordination?

2　If you were Jennifer, what would you do? How might you discipline Steven?

Barbara is going over my head

Main subjects
Authority, chain of command, credibility, open-door policy, organizational structure, trust

Who's who
- Lori Canelle, Spa Manager
- Dan Mazur, Director of Rooms
- Barbara Turner, Spa Employee

Think point

While guests certainly have the right to express displeasure or identify complaints, it is the staff and management who must get through those concerns and determine how best to handle them. There should be policies and procedures that assist both employees and managers in operating a hotel, or in this case, a swimming pool, appropriately. Another unique aspect to business operations is the concept of an open-door policy. This case examines the impact of having such a policy, where it can appear that chain of command can be broken, thus causing issues among an operating team.

After the Raynsford family left the spa, Barbara approached Lori and expressed her concern about the pool temperature. According to her, the Raynsford kids found the pool too cold.

Barbara suggested that Lori should slightly increase the pool temperature.

"Listen, Barbara," said Lori, "I appreciate your ideas, but according to our standards, the pool temperature should be in the range of 78–80 degrees Fahrenheit."

"Don't worry, Lori," answered Barbara. "I will just go and see Dan; he knows his stuff and will fix this problem." At this point, Barbara left the spa to see the director of rooms.

The Royal Hotel had an open-door policy designed to encourage employees to communicate their concerns or suggestions to their direct supervisors and also to provide them with the option of carrying their problems to senior management without fear of retaliation.

When Lori came back after her two days off, she noticed that engineering slightly adjusted the temperature of the pool.

1   What are some of the potential benefits open-door policies offer?

2   What can be some of the drawbacks and implications of violating the chain of command?

    a   From the employee's perspective.
    b   From the first-line supervisor's perspective.
    c   From an organizational perspective.

3   Determine probable reasons for Dan's actions.

4   How do you think Dan should have dealt with the situation?

I am just not comfortable talking to you!

Main subjects
Authority, discipline, insubordination, open-door policy

Who's who
- Rose Romero, PBX Operator
- Kalinda Stenton, PBX Manager

Think point

This case examines the concept of an open-door policy and the impact it can have when chain of command is bypassed. It is more common in business organizations to adopt an open-door policy allowing open lines of communication. However, this open line of communication can in fact cause additional confusion when the traditional chain of command is not utilized. Having an organizational chart depicting lines of reporting can assist in understanding who an employee reports to in the chain of command. Additionally, allowing for a third-party individual, a person who is not in the direct command of an employee, may be an alternative to create open lines of communication or produce a sense of trust within the organization.

Employees challenging your leadership

As Kalinda came back from her break, she witnessed a serious conduct infraction involving Rose, one of the PBX operators. She immediately asked someone to cover the phone and asked Rose to come with her and discuss the situation in her office.

At this point, Rose looked at her and said, "You know, Kalinda, I am sorry, but I am just not comfortable talking to you."

Kalinda paused for a second and told Rose, "I'm sorry to hear about your discomfort. Who are you comfortable talking to?"

Rose's answer was "I will take care of this. I know my rights, Kalinda."

Rather than insisting that employees stay within chains of command when they have unresolved problems, the Royal Hotel promoted an open-door policy, in which employees were encouraged to talk to any manager they felt comfortable speaking with.

1   Would you consider Rose's actions appropriate? Why? Why not?

2   What could Kalinda have done differently?

3   As a manager representing an organization that has an open-door policy, how would you communicate how the policy works to the current employees?

I don't have time to talk to you

Main subjects
Assertiveness, authority, credibility, defensiveness, discipline, insubordination, respect

Who's who
• Judith Grace, Front Office Manager
• Randy Maguire, Front Desk Agent
• Kristianne Tyler, Regular Hotel Guest

Think point

Guest service agents, or in this case, a front desk agent, are tasked with doing their responsibilities and providing service to the guests in a fast, efficient, and friendly manner. The use of technology, while helpful in expediting the process, can also create delays or slowdowns. Add this to the lines of guests that might be present, and the pressure can mount. The manager must identify appropriate times to address a concern or administer disciplinary action with an employee should a concern or violation of policy happen.

Employees challenging your leadership

As Judith entered the front office area, she noticed that Randy, one of the agents, greeted Ms. Tyler, a regular guest, in an unprofessional and unfriendly manner. She was visibly in a hurry and asked politely if she could go up to her room to make a quick phone call and come back to complete the check-in process in a few minutes. Randy raised his voice and responded by saying, "I am working as fast as I can."

Judith waited until Ms. Tyler had left the front desk before she approached Randy. Judith pulled him to the side and asked him to come to see her in the back office. At this point, Randy raised his voice and told her, "I don't have time to talk to you. . . . I am serving my guests! I was hired to make sure our customers are happy!" and he walked back to the desk to check in the next guest in line.

When the next customer left, Judith attempted to confront Randy again, without any success. She stood in the corner for a few more minutes, feeling brushed off.

1 Would you consider Randy's answer to Judith appropriate? Why? Why not?

2 Determine probable reasons for Randy's behavior with Judith.

3 What could Judith have done differently when she witnessed the situation?

4 Is disciplinary action warranted?

I know my stuff!

Main subjects
Authority, change, credibility, defensiveness, discipline, respect, trust

Who's who
• Wesley Edwards, Room Service Manager
• Adam Warren, Room Service Server

Think point

This case examines a new manager working to understand the job and tasks that exist among the employees in his department. It is wise to learn and understand the roles of all of the employees in a department. Not many managers appreciate this shadowing experience. Compounded with being a new manager may be an age difference; various generations take involvement in different ways. In many locations, one finds that the line-level employees have been employed for years or decades, whereas the manager might be new and young. This case examines the different points of view between the manager and the server.

Employees challenging your leadership

Wesley graduated from a hospitality program three years earlier. He joined the Royal Hotel as a management trainee in F&B. Six months later, he became an assistant manager in the lounge. Recently, he was promoted to room service manager. He was very enthusiastic about this great opportunity and started in his position with a great deal of energy.

This morning, he decided to shadow the servers in order to familiarize himself with the service process. Wesley entered the elevator; greeted Adam, the front server; and offered his help. Adam answered by saying, "You know, Wesley, I know my stuff. I was doing this job before you were born. I don't need any guidance here."

"I hate to tell you this, but I will spend the day with you," responded Wesley, and he pushed the "door-close" button.

1 Determine probable reasons for Adam's behavior.

2 Evaluate Wesley's response in the elevator.

3 If you were in Wesley's position, what would your next step be?

4 What could Wesley have done to prevent this situation from happening?

5 How can a manager be prepared to handle people from various generations in the same workplace?

He couldn't find his office without a map!

Main subjects
Authority, credibility, gossip, managing up, organizational politics

Who's who
• Paul Bello, Purchasing Manager
• Romero Barnes, Assistant Purchasing Manager
• Yuan Yao, Assistant Director of Finance

Think point

Each organization has its own type of organizational politics. However, there is a distinction between politics and inappropriate behavior as it relates to gossip in the workplace. In this situation, think about how the distinction between the two (organization politics vs. gossip) plays into how a manager can address the situation.

Employees challenging your leadership

A few managers from various finance departments began to gather in the cafeteria. Romero, the assistant purchasing manager, was speaking about his serious difficulties with one of the wine suppliers. Someone asked him if Paul had already been involved.

"Paul? You don't honestly think anyone's going to take him seriously? He couldn't find his office without a map!" answered Romero in a sarcastic, belittling tone.

None of them noticed that Paul was in the cafeteria and overheard the entire discussion. As Paul proceeded to the coffee machine, he quickly turned back and saw that Yuan was still smiling.

1   Evaluate Romero's behavior.

2   What advice would you give to Paul?

3   What could have been done differently to prevent this situation from happening?

4   The difference between unacceptable public criticism and acceptable disagreement lies in the setting and the manner of presentation. Explain.

> ## Part summary
>
> This section covered the aspects of leadership that are challenged by the employee. There are various aspects that an employee can challenge a manager on. First, this section examined opportunities where overtime can be authorized. How as a manager can you better plan to prevent the use of overtime? Should that not be possible, then have a fair and consistent system in place to authorize the necessary overtime.
>
> The manner and way an employee addresses a manager when a negative guest situation is occurring can border on insubordination, which could result in disciplinary action. When an employee encounters a guest who causes additional conflict, management should be made aware of the situation in a timely fashion so that potential action can be addressed immediately.
>
> To get a complete scope, this section looked at how an open-door policy impacts communication, leadership, and chain of command. Open-door policies are intended for employees to find an individual they feel comfortable with and trust to connect with. However, sometimes, this sense of openness can cause additional confusion. Examine ways that management can provide a clear and well-defined organizational chart with reporting lines.

Additional reading

Books

Assertiveness

Great leadership must be able to balance being both a good leader and a good follower (Willink & Babin, 2018).

Willink, J., & Babin, L. (2018). *The dichotomy of leadership: Balancing the challenges of extreme ownership to lead and win*. Retrieved from https://play.google.com/store/audiobooks/details/The_Dichotomy_of_Leadership_Balancing_the_Challeng?id=AQAAAEAMijrKJM&hl=en_US

The Assertiveness Workbook provides cognitive behavioral techniques aimed to help readers become more assertive while learning to also be more genuine and open in relationships without fearing attack (Paterson, 2000).

Paterson, R. J. (2000). *The assertiveness workbook: How to express your ideas and stand up for yourself at work and in relationships (A new harbinger self-help workbook)*. California: New Harbinger Publications.

This author draws from his own experiences, research, academic experience, and coaching to deliver effective lessons on how to practice assertiveness every day to gain the respect of others while setting boundaries (King, 2018).

King, P. (2018). *The art of everyday assertiveness: Speak up. Say no. Set boundaries. Take back control*. California: CreateSpace Independent Publishing Platform.

Authority

Jonathan Raymond shares what he has learned over his 20 years of experience as an executive, entrepreneur, team leader, and leadership trainer. Using real-life examples, Jonathan brings his audience through a step-by-step approach in how to transform company culture through great leadership and management of people (Raymond, 2016).

Raymond, J. (2016). *Good authority. How to become the leader your team is waiting for.* Retrieved from http://catalog.2seasagency.com/book/good-authority/

Through his decades of experience in "consulting with corporations and teaching MBA students the nuances of organizational power," Jeffrey Pfeffer aims to help readers understand organizational dynamics but, more specifically, how and why people succeed (Pfeffer, 2010).

Pfeffer, J. (2010). *Power: Why some people have it – and others don't.* Retrieved from www.gsb.stanford.edu/faculty-research/books/power-why-some-people-have-it-others-dont

Buy-in

John Kotter and Lorne Whitehead unveil the key to winning the support of others for the idea you pitch at work, using different strategies and giving practical advice (Kotter & Whitehead, 2010).

Kotter, J. P., & Whitehead, L. A. (2010). *Buy-in: Saving your good idea from getting shot down.* Boston: Harvard Business Press.

Defensiveness

Practical exercises to alter organizational defensive routines (Noonan, 2007).

Noonan, W. R. (2007). *Discussing the undiscussable: A guide to overcoming defensive routines in the workplace* (1st ed.). San Francisco, CA: Jossey-Bass.

Gossip

The following is a business guide to addressing the leading challenge to workplace productivity and employee retention (Chapman, 2009).

Chapman, S. (2009). *No gossip zone: A no-nonsense guide to a healthy, high-performing work environment* (1st ed.). Illinois: Sourcebooks.

Job design

The following book chapter discusses one of the most well-known approaches to job design, called the job characteristics model (JCM), and its five core characteristics (Norris & Porter, 2012) (Garg & Rastogi, 2006).

Norris, S. E., & Porter, T. H. (2012). Job design. In *The Encyclopedia of Human Resource Management* (pp. 288–291). https://doi.org/10.1002/9781118364741.ch53

Garg, P., & Rastogi, R. (2006). New model of job design: Motivating employees' performance. *Journal of Management Development, 25*(6), 572–587. https://doi.org/10.1108/02621710610670137

Managing up

This guidebook shows readers how to advance their career agenda through networking, build relationships that bring targets and deadlines within reach, persuade decision makers to champion their initiatives, collaborate more effectively with colleagues, deal with challenging bosses, and navigate office politics (Harvard Business Review, 2013).

Harvard Business Review. (2013, January 29). HBR guide to managing up and across. Retrieved November 27, 2019, from HBR Store website: https://store.hbr.org/product/hbr-guide-to-managing-up-and-across/11218

This book gives you strategies for developing these all-important connections and building more than rapport; you become able to quickly assess situations and determine which actions will move you forward; you become your own talent manager and your boss's top choice for that new opportunity (Abbajay, 2018).

Abbajay, M. (2018). *Managing up: How to move up, win at work, and succeed with any type of boss* (1st ed.). California: Amazon Digital Services LLC.

This book goes beyond networking, giving real-world strategies and actionable steps that are supplemented by expert advice from a top leadership consultant to help readers manage up and begin building their best future (Sutton, 2017).

Sutton, R. I. (2017). *The asshole survival guide: How to deal with people who treat you like dirt*. Boston, MA: Houghton Mifflin Harcourt.

Overtime

The first comprehensive economic evaluation of the overtime phenomenon, examining theoretical, empirical, and policy aspects of overtime hours and pay (Hart, 2004).

Hart, R. A. (2004). *The economics of overtime working* (1st ed.). New York: Cambridge University Press.

Productivity

This book discusses how to take advantage of nature and its healing powers for it to be a part of the environmental design that influences the physical, mental, and social well-being of people (Clements-Croome, 2017).

Clements-Croome, D. (Ed.). (2017). *Creating the productive workplace: Places to work creatively* (3rd ed.). New York: Routledge.

Respect

Rooted in neuroscience research, this book breaks down how to create positive environments and avoid disrespectful ones to allow employees to perform at their highest levels (Meshanko, 2013).

Meshanko, P. (2013). *The respect effect: Using the science of neuroleadership to inspire a more loyal and productive workplace* (1st ed.). New York: McGraw-Hill Education.

Journals

Assertiveness

This article reviews scholarship to present the problematic consequences of having "too little" or "too much" assertiveness. Relevant mechanisms to the sources of assertive behavior include motivation, expectancy, and self-regulation (Ames, Lee, & Wazlawek, 2017).

Ames, D. (2009). Pushing up to a point: Assertiveness and effectiveness in leadership and interpersonal dynamics. *Research in Organizational Behavior*, 29, 111–133. https://doi.org/10.1016/j.riob.2009.06.010

This article takes on the perspective of assertiveness having an inverted-U-shaped relationship with leadership effectiveness (Ames, 2009).

Ames, D., Lee, A., & Wazlawek, A. (2017). Interpersonal assertiveness: Inside the balancing act. *Social and Personality Psychology Compass, 11*(6). https://doi.org/10.1111/spc3.12317

Authority

Compliance with authority is necessary for the success of any organization's operation. It is still a norm for compliance to exist when an individual is off the clock from work and the incentive of monetary benefits are removed (Karakostas & Zizzo, 2016).

Karakostas, A., & Zizzo, D. J. (2016). Compliance and the power of authority. *Journal of Economic Behavior & Organization, 124*, 67–80. https://doi.org/10.1016/j.jebo.2015.09.016

This article distinguishes four types of authority: capacity-based, ontological, moral, and charismatic (Alasuutari, 2018).

Alasuutari, P. (2018). Authority as epistemic capital. *Journal of Political Power, 11*(2), 165–190. https://doi.org/10.1080/2158379X.2018.1468151

Buy-in

This article demonstrates practical frameworks and tactics for managers to gain traction for their ideas and earn both attention and resources (Ashford & Detert, 2015).

Ashford, S. J., & Detert, J. R. (2015, January 1). Get the boss to buy in. *Harvard Business Review* (January–February 2015). Retrieved from https://hbr.org/2015/01/get-the-boss-to-buy-in

Controlling costs

Managing labor is one of the most important measures to control costs in an organization (Lewis, 2011).

Lewis, M. (2011). How to reduce labor costs in your business. Retrieved November 22, 2019, from www.moneycrashers.com/reduce-labor-costs-business/

Discipline

This study investigated the effects of disciplinary management on employee performance (Anthony, 2017).

Anthony, A. E. (2017). Effects of discipline management on employee performance in an organization: The case of county education office human resource department, Turkana

County. *International Academic Journal of Human Resource and Business Administration*, 2(3), 18.

Flexibility

A report that aims to help organizations better understand workplace flexibility and to support moving flexibility from the organizational margins to the mainstream (SHRM Foundation, n.d.).

SHRM Foundation. (n.d.). Leveraging workplace flexibility for engagement and productivity. *SHRM*, 60.

Insubordination

To better understand insubordination, this article examines the various types and how best to handle the matter (Maingault, Fiester, & Dooley, 2007).

Maingault, A., Fiester, M., & Dooley, R. (2007). Insubordination, adoption leave, confidentiality. *HRMagazine*, *52*(4), 41–42.

Office politics

The differences among organizational politics can be better understood in this article (Jarrett, 2017) or a deeper more extensive look with the entire landscape (Bolander, 2011).

Bolander, J. (2011, February 28). How to deal with organizational politics. Retrieved March 15, 2019, from www.thedailymba.com/2011/02/28/how-to-deal-with-organizational-politics/
Jarrett, M. (2017, April 24). The 4 types of organizational politics. *Harvard Business Review*. Retrieved from https://hbr.org/2017/04/the-4-types-of-organizational-politics

Open-door policy

While open-door policies have a lot of benefits, there are some leaders who believe that such a policy is not wise; this article will help you understand the negative aspects better (Kruse, 2016).

Kruse, K. (2016, April 24). Why successful leaders don't have an open-door policy. Retrieved from www.forbes.com/sites/kevinkruse/2016/04/24/why-successful-leaders-dont-have-an-open-door-policy/#1250c9ec31ef

There can be several benefits for managers to maintain an open-door policy; as a new manager, understanding them can be helpful. This resource assists in giving a better understanding of those benefits (Quast, 2013).

Quast, L. (2013, October 7). New managers: 4 reasons you need an "Open Door" policy. *Forbes*. Retrieved from www.forbes.com/sites/lisaquast/2013/10/07/new-managers-4-reasons-you-need-an-open-door-policy/#1a1b80b37cde

Overtime

Issues with service can be impacted by overtime (Alton, 2017).

Oliva, R., & Sterman, J. D. (2001). Cutting corners and working overtime: Quality erosion in the service industry. *Management Science*, *47*(7), 894–914.

This study highlights the costs and benefits of overtime work as tools for utilizing human capital and reveals the critical contingency of organizational trust that enables firms to attenuate the costs of the overtime level and accentuate its potential benefits (Ko & Choi, 2019).

Ko, Y. J., & Choi, J. N. (2019). Overtime work as the antecedent of employee satisfaction, firm productivity, and innovation. *Journal of Organizational Behavior, 40*(3), 282–295. https://doi.org/10.1002/job.2328

Productivity

This study examines the relationships between work engagement, productivity, and self-reported work-related sedentary behavior (Ishii, Shibata, & Oka, 2018)

Ishii, K., Shibata, A., & Oka, K. (2018). Work engagement, productivity, and self-reported work-related sedentary behavior among Japanese adults: A cross-sectional study. *Journal of Occupational and Environmental Medicine, 60*(4), e173. https://doi.org/10.1097/JOM. 0000000000001270

Trust

This article is a collection of tips and tricks to approach and handle trust building and cases of mistrust in the workplace in a better manner (O'Hara, 2014).

O'Hara, C. (2014, June 27). Proven ways to earn your employees' trust. *Harvard Business Review*. Retrieved from https://hbr.org/2014/06/proven-ways-to-earn-your-employees-trust

Web links

Assertiveness

Assertiveness is the perfect medium between aggression and passivity, representing a quality of leaders who understand creating a win-win scenario for themselves and others they are working with. This article provides examples of situations and what it would look like when taking a passive, aggressive, or assertive approach (Wilding, 2015).

Wilding, M. J. (2015, January 14). How to be more assertive at work (not aggressive). Retrieved November 23, 2019, from The Muse website: www.themuse.com/advice/ how-to-be-more-assertive-at-work-without-being-a-jerk

Training in communication and conflict management can help individuals to change the way they view and think about communication and build confidence to reflect in the workplace as assertive. This article reviews the pitfalls and misunderstandings surrounding the topic of being assertive (P. Russell, 2018).

Russell, P. (2018, June 29). Assertiveness in the workplace. Retrieved November 23, 2019, from the Global Banking & Finance Review website: www.globalbankingandfinance.com/ assertiveness-in-the-workplace/

Authority

This article defines "workplace authority" and discusses topics such as maintaining workplace authority as management, earning it as an employee, the effects of positive workplace authority on profitability, and the negative economic consequences of power abuse (Mueller, 2017).

Mueller, D. (2017, September 26). What is workplace authority? Retrieved November 22, 2019, from the Biz Fluent website: https://bizfluent.com/info-7758942-workplace-authority.html

Authority is a quality by which your employees recognize and respect you as a managerial person of prestige. This article discusses how individuals may establish an attitude of authority in the workplace by displaying their leadership qualities, providing employees with what they need to perform their tasks, keeping customers in front of their employees' minds, acting with consistency, and striving for balance between an overly directive and an overly collaborative environment (Paige, n.d.)

Paige, A. (n.d.). How to establish attitude of authority in the workplace. Retrieved November 22, 2019, from the Chron.com website: https://smallbusiness.chron.com/establish-attitude-authority-workplace-10114.html.

Buy-in

This article discusses ways to establish buy-in among employees, as buy-in helps employee engagement (Lucas, 2019).

Lucas, S. (2019, September 16). How can employee buy-in encourage workplace engagement? Retrieved November 24, 2019, from The Balance Careers website: www.thebalancecareers.com/how-employee-buy-in-can-promote-workplace-engagement-4171745

This article reviews why buy-in should be a top priority when it comes to the introduction of new projects, how to generate it, and what to do after establishing buy-in with your team ("How to get buy in at work," 2019).

How to get buy in at work: A step by step guide. (2019, January 18). Retrieved November 24, 2019, from Lighthouse: A blog about leadership & management advice website: https://getlighthouse.com/blog/get-buy-in-at-work-how-to/

This article discusses the five steps to implementing change and ensuring a smooth transition with employees who are on board and will work hard because they want to (Broder, 2013).

Broder, L. (2013, August 22). Change is good. Now, how to get employees to buy in. *Entrepreneur*. Retrieved from www.entrepreneur.com/article/227920

Chain of command

A chain of command is established so that everyone knows whom they should report to and what responsibilities are expected at their level. A chain of command enforces responsibility and accountability (Kabuye, 2013).

Kabuye, J. (2013, July 1). A chain of command is needed for accountability. Retrieved November 22, 2019, from the New Vision website: www.newvision.co.ug/new_vision/news/1325104/chain-command-accountability

Change

Rather than perceiving change as a negative deficit in a business, this article identifies benefits that come with transition (McQuerrery, 2019).

McQuerrery, L. (2019, February 4). Benefits from change in the workplace. Retrieved November 24, 2019, from the Chron.com website: https://smallbusiness.chron.com/benefits-change-workplace-13255.html

This article provides ten tips on how to positively handle change in the workplace (Schawbel, 2014).

Schawbel, D. (2014, July 2). 10 tips for handling change in the workplace. Retrieved November 24, 2019, from the Quick Base website: www.quickbase.com/blog/10-tips-for-handling-change-in-the-workplace

Controlling costs

Boosting productivity and controlling labor costs are helpful; read these tips (Mittelman, 2019).

Mittelman, J. (2019, January 16). 11 tips for controlling your labor cost and boosting productivity. Retrieved November 22, 2019, from the PC Payroll website: https://pcpayroll.com/control-labor-costs-and-boost-productivity/

With the increase in labor costs in the restaurant industry, this article looks at some opportunities to control costs (Walker, 2017).

Walker, J. (2017, August). 5 ways to reduce labor costs. Retrieved November 22, 2019, from FSR magazine website: www.fsrmagazine.com/expert-takes/5-ways-reduce-labor-costs

Credibility

Because it is imperative that professionals maintain their credibility, this article suggests that this may be accomplished by understanding the team, making sound judgments in the nick of time, making commitments, and having great communication skills (Kukreti, 2016).

Kukreti, A. (2016, February 29). Maintaining your credibility in the workplace. *Experteer Magazine*. Retrieved from https://us.experteer.com/magazine/the-importance-of-maintaining-your-credibility/

This article provides ten ways to boost credibility at work and earn opportunities for growth within the company (Parker, 2018).

Parker, P. (2018, May 25). 10 tips to boost your credibility at work. Retrieved November 24, 2019, from BioSpace website: www.biospace.com/article/10-tips-to-boost-your-credibility-at-work/

This article provides examples of keeping trust, integrity, and accountability and boosting sales to uphold credibility as an employee under the employer company (Ramjee, 2013).

Ramjee, P. (2013). Importance of employee credibility in the workplace. Retrieved November 24, 2019, from the Woman website: https://woman.thenest.com/importance-employee-credibility-workplace-17713.html

The following is a five-minute read that identifies tips to help an individual build credibility in any given situation (M. Russell, 2018).

Russell, M. (2018, July 29). Building credibility in the workplace. Retrieved November 24, 2019, from the Medium website: https://medium.com/swlh/strategic-leadership-building-credibility-in-the-workplace-4b99e125635f

This article states nine ways to build credibility as a leader through respect, trust, loyalty, accountability, focus on goals, words backed by action, expertise, hunger to learn, and honesty (Scarlet, 2019).

Scarlet, A. (2019). 9 easy ways to build credibility as a leader. Retrieved November 24, 2019, from the AllBusiness.com website: www.allbusiness.com/9-easy-ways-build-credibility-leader-19543-1.html

Discipline

The need and purpose for acquiring a progressive discipline policy is explained in this article (Mayhew, n.d.).

Mayhew, R. (n.d.). Purpose of discipline in the workplace. Retrieved November 27, 2019, from the Chron.com website: https://smallbusiness.chron.com/purpose-discipline-workplace-10898.html

This *Forbes* article argues to get rid of content in an employee handbook about work discipline, as it is believed that you can't policy your way to greatness (Ryan, 2015).

Ryan, L. (2015, March 6). The truth about workplace discipline. Retrieved November 27, 2019, from the Forbes website: www.forbes.com/sites/lizryan/2015/03/06/the-truth-about-workplace-discipline/#727e304a7f4a

Gossip

This article identifies the six toxic traits of workplace gossip as being immature, embellished, emotionally violent, seductive, insecure, and parasitic (Campbell, 2015).

Campbell, A. (2015). Word of mouth model of sales. *Economics Letters*, *133*, 45–50. https://doi.org/10.1016/j.econlet.2015.04.019

The following paper utilizes social information theory and social cognitive theory to analyze literature on the topic of gossip and test hypotheses about the antecedents of gossip (Kuo, Chang, Quinton, Lu, & Lee, 2015).

Kuo, C. C., Chang, K., Quinton, S., Lu, C.Y., & Lee, I. (2015). Gossip in the workplace and the implications for HR management: A study of gossip and its relationship to employee cynicism. *The International Journal of Human Resource Management*, *26*(18), 2288–2307. https://doi.org/10.1080/09585192.2014.985329

Insubordination

The Society for Human Resource Managers is an excellent source for information; they indicate what constitutes insubordination (Society for Human Resource Management, 2018).

Society for Human Resource Management. (2018, March 6). Disciplinary issues: What constitutes insubordination? Retrieved March 14, 2019, from www.shrm.org/resourcesandtools/tools-and-samples/hr-qa/pages/cms_020144.aspx

This article defines insubordination in four components, failure to perform, intimidation or harassment, confrontational actions, and abusive language (Leonard, 2018).

Leonard, K. (2018, June 29). What types of behavior indicate insubordination? Retrieved November 27, 2019, from the Chron.com website: https://smallbusiness.chron.com/types-behavior-indicate-insubordination-10370.html

Job description

SHRM members have exclusive access to more than 1,000 job description templates. SHRM also offers a premium job description manager that lets employers create, maintain, and organize job descriptions online without any software downloads (SHRM, 2019).

SHRM. (2019, September 4). Job Descriptions. Retrieved November 27, 2019, from SHRM website: www.shrm.org/resourcesandtools/tools-and-samples/job-descriptions/pages/default.aspx

Managing up

This article gives insight on how individuals can manage up, or build productive relationships with higher-ups, to shape their careers (Shellenbarger, 2018).

Shellenbarger, S. (2018, April 10). The right and wrong way to manage up at the office. *Wall Street Journal*. Retrieved from www.wsj.com/articles/the-right-and-wrong-way-to-manage-up-at-the-office-1523366792

Organizational structure

Organizational structure defines the hierarchy of the organization. It identifies each job, its function, and where it reports to in the organization. This structure is developed to establish how an organization operates and assists an organization in obtaining its goals to allow for future growth (Friend, 2019).

Friend, L. (2019, February 6). What is the meaning of organizational structure? Retrieved November 29, 2019, from the Chron.com website: https://smallbusiness.chron.com/meaning-organizational-structure-3803.html

Overtime

This government website provides resources on overtime in the United States (U.S. Department of Labor, n.d.).

U.S. Department of Labor. (n.d.). Overtime pay – Wage and hour division (WHD). Retrieved November 29, 2019, from the U.S. Department of Labor website: www.dol.gov/whd/overtime_pay.htm

A resource for employees to better understand overtime (Fairy God Boss, n.d.).

Fairy God Boss. (n.d.). What is overtime, and am I eligible for it? Retrieved November 29, 2019, from the Fairy God Boss website: https://fairygodboss.com/career-topics/what-is-overtime-rules-regulations

Productivity

This article reviews guidelines on how a business can increase its workplace productivity (Culp, 2017).

Culp, S. (2017, March 30). How to increase productivity in a workplace. Retrieved November 29, 2019, from Time Doctor website: www.timedoctor.com/blog/workplace-productivity/

This article discusses 11 proven strategies on how to increase employee productivity for an improved culture of engagement (Albright, 2018).

Albright, D. (2018, December 20). 11 strategies to increase productivity in the workplace. Retrieved November 29, 2019, from the Hubstaff Time Tracking Software website: https://blog.hubstaff.com/employee-productivity/

Respect

This article touches on the importance of and training to create mutual respect in the workplace (Reddy, n.d.).

Reddy, C. (n.d.). Why is respect important in the workplace? Retrieved November 29, 2019, from WiseStep website: https://content.wisestep.com/respect-important-workplace/

Trust

With the approach of starting trust building within a smaller unit or department and then propagating it throughout the organization as a whole, this article gives several tips to HR and other managers to build trust in the workplace (Heathfield, 2018).

Heathfield, S. M. (2018, December 17). Top 10 ways to build trust at work. Retrieved November 30, 2019, from The Balance Careers website: www.thebalancecareers.com/top-ways-to-build-trust-at-work-1919402

Part 8

Relationship with your boss

How to use this part

The relationship you have with your boss is, one hopes, a positive one. However, on occasion, there might be situations that would be less than ideal. This part will examine how best to utilize the chain of command and open-door policies to be the most efficient with communication in order to seek the most effective results.

Key terms

The key terms found in the cases in this section are listed here. Their definitions can be found on pages xiv–xviii.

Accepting criticism
Assertiveness
Authority
Big picture
Chain of command
Coaching
Credibility
Delegation
Feedback
Managing up
Micromanagement
Motivation
Open-door policy
Organizational politics
Perfectionism
Promotion
Trust

My way or the highway

Main subjects
Big picture, delegation, hands-on, managing up, micromanagement, perfectionism, trust

Who's who
• Yvonne Clark, Director of Sales and Marketing
• Fiona O'Brien, Public Relations Manager
• Luke O'Brien, Fiona's Husband

Think point

Delegation is a skill that is not easy for everyone to utilize as a management strategy. It can, on occasion, take time to learn how best to delegate and feel confident in the approach. Missed delegation opportunities can be perceived as micromanagement. Extreme levels of oversight can be considered micromanagement, thus not allowing individuals to have control over the work they are expected to complete. When working for a manager who is considered a micromanager, the subordinates might need to consider how to manage up to best get results from the manager, so they are in turn most efficient.

Relationship with your boss

Fiona was desperate. She recently joined the Royal Hotel as the public relations manager. Although she found the job rewarding, after six months in her job, she felt trapped and somewhat betrayed. She remembered her first discussion with her future boss, Yvonne, the director of sales and marketing. "I will do what is necessary to ensure your success. I was the public relations manager upon opening this hotel, and I built everything from scratch. I would like to make your job easier by sharing my experience and knowledge," she explained to Fiona. "But no worries–I'm not a micro," Yvonne added jokingly.

Last night, at home, Luke, Fiona's husband, was gently questioning her about why she was so depressed lately. Finally, Fiona shared with him some of her concerns:

- *Yvonne has very high standards and wants detailed progress reports on her projects twice a day. At the same time, she doesn't delegate any work of real significance to her.*
- *Even low-level decisions (like selecting photos for media requests) must be approved by her.*
- *The other day, Yvonne was home with the flu, and she still called Fiona twice during the day.*
- *Yvonne watches Fiona's every move; last week, she was on the phone with a local reporter when Yvonne showed up, sat down, and listened to what Fiona was saying.* "I just don't feel in control of anything. Does that make sense?" Fiona asked.

1   Identify potential causes for Yvonne's behavior.

2   Highlight some consequences that such situations cause. What is the underlying leadership issue?

3   What do you think Fiona should do about this matter?

4   What advice would you give to Yvonne?

The buffet setup

Main subjects
Authority, chain of command, credibility, managing up, open-door policy, organizational politics

Who's who
• Jeff Gillespie, Assistant Banquet Manager
• Monica Luigi, Guest, On-Site Contact
• Rhiannon Palmer, Convention Services Manager
• Jane Peterson, Hotel Manager
• Thomas Waxer, Banquet Manager

Think point

"Proper preparation prevents poor performance" is a saying that is a wise mantra to have when working in hospitality. Advanced preparation and proper communication are two tactics to utilize to operate efficiently. Consider how best to handle situations, and use the proper channels of communication when working in a department, despite the opportunity to engage in the use of an open-door policy.

Ms. Luigi, the on-site contact, was very disappointed and upset with the dinner setup for her pharmaceutical group. She originally arranged with Rhiannon for two double-sided buffets for the dinner, as the group was on a tight time schedule. Earlier that day, due to the slight decrease in attendee numbers, Thomas, the banquet manager, decided to set up one double-sided buffet for the group, without informing Ms. Luigi in advance. Thomas was the opening manager and left for the day around 3:00 PM. Jeff, the assistant manager, professionally dealt with Ms. Luigi. He profusely apologized and offered free ice cream for the entire group.

After the group left, Jeff picked up the phone; after a moment's hesitation, he dialed the hotel manager's extension and left the following voice mail:

"Hi, Jane, this is Jeff from banquets. This is regarding the in-house pharmaceutical group. Unfortunately, Ms. Luigi was very angry tonight because of the wrong dinner setup. It seems that Thomas did not read the banquet event order properly. By the way, he left early today, so I could not discuss this with him. I know how much revenue this group brings, so I felt it is my responsibility to make sure that you know exactly what's going on. See you tomorrow. Bye."

Rather than insisting that employees stay within chains of command when they have unresolved problems, the Royal Hotel promoted an open-door policy, in which employees were encouraged to talk to any manager they felt comfortable talking to.

1   Why do employees often go above their own boss? Why do others never bypass?

2   What are the pros and cons of allowing employees to talk to any manager at any level about any issue?

3   How do you explain Jeff's behavior?

4   What do you think Jane should do about this matter?

Lipstick on the glass

Case type: issue case

Main subjects
Authority, chain of command, influence, managing up

Who's who
- Margot Cooper, Hotel Guest
- John Ferreira, Chief Steward
- Bruce Koss, Assistant Chief Steward
- Jane Peterson, Hotel Manager

Think point

Inevitably, there will be problems that occur in a business operation that unfortunately may impact the guest experience. It is how those problems are dealt with that can make a turnaround or positive experience for the guest; in addition, it is also how it is handled with the internal guests (the employees) that also matter for proper learning. Consider how managers not specifically in charge of a department can seek to understand a problem better prior to attempting to resolve it individually.

Relationship with your boss

Jane had a few minutes before the start of the morning meeting, so she quickly reviewed the daily guest incident report. "At check-out, Ms. Cooper mentioned that the martini glass with which she was served at the bar last night had lipstick and ugly white spots on it." This glitch made Jane really angry.

"Once again, Stewarding. I really need to talk to those guys in person," Jane said as she was walking down the kitchen corridor.

After a very busy back-to-back shift, Bruce, the new assistant manager, was sitting in the stewarding office, about to do the labor forecast, when Jane entered.

"Standard number one." Jane pointed to the stewarding key expectations posted on the wall. "Stewarding should ensure customers never see a dirty dish. So, what are we doing about this martini glass issue?" Jane smiled.

Bruce was unsure and said he would look into the problem.

"Minerals in hard water can cause white film deposits and ugly spots to build up on glasses in the dishwasher," Jane was lecturing Bruce. "To match the hardness of the water, please increase the amount of detergent by 25%." Jane provided Bruce with specific instructions and went to the morning meeting.

Several hours later, John, the chief steward who worked in the PM shift, noticed that someone had adjusted the amount of detergent used.

"Jane Peterson told me to do it," Bruce said to him.

"What? We can't just change the amount of detergent!" John was fuming. "Bruce, I left you a message yesterday morning in the log book explaining that there is a loss of water pressure because of pump obstruction, and martini glasses needed to be hand-washed until further instruction."

1 How can leaders influence the development and effectiveness of individuals who are not reporting directly to them?

2 Managers often engage in direct one-to-one relationships with supervisors at lower levels of organizations beyond their direct reports. Why?

3 Identify problems Jane's action is causing.

4 What would you recommend John do?

Alison, the credit manager

Main subjects
Influence, motivation, organizational politics, promotion

Who's who
- Piet Brown, Hotel Guest
- Yvonne Clark, Director of Sales and Marketing
- Alison Finley, Credit Manager
- Charlie Jones, Director of Engineering
- Matthew Knorr, Director of Food and Beverage
- Robert Kunz, General Manager
- Sylvain Lucas, Local Party Planner
- Dan Mazur, Director of Rooms
- Katherine Norton, Director of Human Resources
- Jane Peterson, Hotel Manager
- Louise Rausch, Director of Finance
- Yuan Yao, Assistant Director of Finance

Think point

Succession planning is a strategy that many organizations utilize to better identify and prepare employees and supervisors for the next-level position. Consider how you can take information obtained from a 360-degree point of view and use it as a tool to better train and prepare the employee for the next stage in a motivation method.

Louise Rausch was preparing herself for the next succession planning meeting. *They will definitely spend some time on the credit manager*, she thought. Alison recently expressed her interest in becoming the assistant director of finance, if the position should become available.

Executive committee members all had something to say about Alison. Here are some quotes from the meeting minutes:

Louise

Whenever Yuan is asking Alison to work on a project, she emails him back the completed assignments in a timely manner. However, I noticed that she always cc's me on the correspondence.

Katherine

I asked her opinion about the development plan we put together for the finance interns. Alison said that, as a team player, she was not here to criticize management's ideas; she prefers going with flow and making things happen.

Dan

Last week, after the budget meeting, she told me that my presentation on the Rooms Division had inspired her so much that she is now considering a career change. I am wondering if she really wants to stay in finance.

Yvonne

At the same meeting, Alison proudly announced that she managed the returned check from the Brown party. Well, I called Piet Brown personally and asked him to mail us a new check.

Matthew

I asked her to review the direct billing request of Sylvain Lucas, a local party planner. It took her six weeks to determine their eligibility and credit limits. She claimed that it's a complex issue, and she is working hard to get an answer. Is Alison procrastinating?

Charlie

I see her only twice a month. She is systematically late for the safety meeting. Her verbiage is always the same: "Charlie, please forgive me. I know your time is valuable."

Jane

May I make a quick note on Matthew's observation? I am not sure about that. I have a very different experience in terms of her follow-through skills. Last November, I asked her to circulate the invitation to the credit management training workshop. She actually did it very efficiently. I was only curious why she changed the layout of the original document and placed the application form at the very end of the email. I wondered why she included 20 pages of additional background information on credit management before the application form as well, making it almost impossible to find.

Robert

I don't know, guys. I perceive Alison as a warm and supportive individual. She loves my ideas on how to deal with payment problems. Last month, she even circulated a musical card – playing my favorite song – for all managers to sign for my birthday.

1 Evaluate Alison as a manager.

2 What are the pros and cons of praising those with more power?

3 What are the pros and cons of self-promotion tactics in the workplace?

4 Why do workplace politics have a bad connotation? What can management do to change this negative perception?

5 Assume that you are hired by the Royal Hotel as a management-trainee. You will have to attend a four-day management orientation program. What actions would you take to promote yourself and emerge as a potential leader?

The new table pick-up system

Main subjects
Authority, chain of command, coaching, credibility, feedback, managing up, open-door policy, organizational politics

Who's who
- Wesley Edwards, Room Service Manager
- Matthew Knorr, Director of Food and Beverage
- Danielle Rosenthal, Room Service Assistant Manager

Think point

Businesses intentionally design an organizational chart that will identify the reporting lines from associates to supervisors to management. This is designed to be clear and easy to follow for the employees, so that they know whom they are to report to. One aspect of confusion can lie in also having an open-door policy. Such a policy allows for the employee to come to whomever they feel most comfortable with to discuss issues of concern. While the intent is to open the lines of communication, the lines of reporting can thereby be ignored or overlooked and cause additional concern or unnecessary drama in a specific department. Consider the impact of such organizational design.

After a busy breakfast service, Danielle, the assistant manager, approached Wesley. "Listen, Wes, as you know, I have been working in various hotels and know something about room service. To be honest, every hotel has a hard time coming up with an efficient table retrieval technique. I think the new table pick-up system you implemented here is great. We are receiving fewer complaints, and dirty trays have basically disappeared from the corridors."

"I truly appreciate your feedback, Danielle. We all need to work together and consistently stick to this new procedure," answered Wesley. "By the way, as you suggested, we will be placing a computer in front of the service elevator in order to track the status of retrievals," he added.

Later, on the same day, the following conversation occurred between Danielle and Matthew:

Danielle:	Do you have a moment for a poor middle manager?
Matthew:	(laughing) Sure, come on in.
Danielle:	What I really like here at the Royal is that we can talk to any manager we feel comfortable talking to.
Matthew:	(smiling) Of course, we are proud of our open-door policy. What can I do for you?
Danielle:	I think you should know what's happening in room service.
Matthew:	(still smiling) Should I?
Danielle:	It's about Wesley. He changed the table retrieval system, and I am worried that it will negatively affect the level of service.
Matthew:	(unsure) Yeah, I don't think our pick-up system was the most efficient one . . .
Danielle:	This new system is wrong and highly distracting for servers, but you know, Matthew, this is not the main issue. Wesley doesn't involve us in anything; he just doesn't appreciate ideas, which is, in my mind, the opposite of how a Royal manager should behave. He is lacking people skills, and the morale is down in room service.
Matthew:	(hesitating) Have you discussed your concern with Wesley?
Danielle:	I was not comfortable doing it . . . and I thought it's work related so I came to see you . . .
Matthew:	(somewhat annoyed) Your feedback is important; thank you for sharing it. I really thought that this new procedure was working well. It seems that we have to go back to the old system. Regarding Wesley, I guess you want me to serve as a referee between you and him.
Danielle:	(uncertain) I guess, yes.

Matthew always wanted to deal with issues in the right way. At the same time, as Danielle was walking out from his office, he felt slightly confused and had a couple of questions on his mind.

1 Should managers pay attention to what others say about them when they are not present?

2 What is the major issue facing Matthew?

3 What motivation might Danielle have behind her action?

4 What mistakes is Matthew making, if any? How would you have handled the situation if you had been in Matthew's place?

5 How can managers diminish the chances of being the object of manipulation?

6 How can exit interviews help HR to pick up on signs of negative office politics?

The missing cancellation clause

Main subjects

Accepting criticism, assertiveness, defensiveness, feedback, managing up

Who's who
• Yvonne Clark, Director of Sales and Marketing
• Rhiannon Palmer, Convention Services Manager

Think point

Defensiveness can easily be a mechanism to use if you feel like you are being personally attacked when receiving criticism. Instead, consider how you can listen objectively and then take a moment to examine the situation so you can respond appropriately.

This morning, Yvonne came back from the morning meeting with a piece of returned mail in her hand. The following conversation occurred between her and Rhiannon:

Yvonne: Rhiannon, this isn't the first group contract your people have sent out without the cancellation clause. If you don't start getting it right fast, there will be trouble.

Rhiannon: Me? That's a joke. If only sales wouldn't make so many errors. They should have gotten it right in the first place.

Yvonne: Your errors aren't just sales-related. You leave sales to me and worry about your own area.

Rhiannon: I'd worry a lot less about convention services if HR could hire more competent staff members.

Yvonne: You get the same people as everyone else. Have you ever thought of training them? No, too busy moaning. By the way, I created for you a new coordinator position, and you're still complaining!

Rhiannon: I know . . . it's just that . . . well, there's not really enough time to train the new coordinator.

Yvonne: Well, that's for you to manage.

Rhiannon: I know. I'm sorry. . . . We try our best, but . . . well . . . there's just so much pressure at the moment.

Yvonne: We're all under pressure, Rhiannon. That's no excuse. What I want to know is what you are going to do about it because if you don't get it sorted out, I will.

1 Highlight some of the benefits of being criticized.

2 What key mistakes is Rhiannon making?

3 An assertive person expresses his or her thoughts, feelings, and needs directly, while considering the rights and feelings of others. Describe assertive techniques on how Rhiannon should have answered initially and how she should have addressed the following issues:

• There are errors in the contract; some of them are originated by sales.
• There is new coordinator in convention services.
• Finding solutions.

The case is based on the principles and situations described in the following:

Gillen, T. (1992). *Assertiveness for managers* (pp. 107–117). Brookfield, VT: Gower.

> ### Part summary
>
> This section covered a variety of relationships that could be found between an employee and his or her boss. Chain of command, open-door policies, and managing up are strategies that can be utilized to further develop a department.

Additional reading

Books

Accepting criticism

How to turn criticism into an educating, energizing experience using real-life examples for both accepting and giving criticism (Weisinger, 2007).

Weisinger, H. (2007). The power of positive criticism (1st ed.). New York: HarperCollins: AMACOM.

Dr. John L. Lund discusses steps we can take when giving and receiving criticism to lead ourselves and others toward positive change without offending others (Lund, 2004).

Lund, J. L. (2004). Without offense: The art of giving and receiving criticism (1st ed.). Utah: Covenant Communications.

Delegation

This book discusses ten ways to boost self-confidence, essential tasks of team leaders, the benefits of delegation, guidelines for successful delegation, delegating mistakes, and one's inner fortitude to successfully delegate tasks to others (Malone, 2015).

Malone, C. C. (2015). The art of delegation: Maximize your time, leverage others, and instantly increase profits. Amazon Digital Services LLC.

Micromanagement

This author presents a specific, detailed definition of micromanagement; illustrates examples; shares how to eliminate your micromanaging behaviors; and tells you what to do if you have a micromanaging manager (Chambers, 2004).

Chambers, H. E. (2004). My way or the highway: The micromanagement survival guide (1st ed.). San Francisco, CA: Berrett-Koehler Publishers.

This book reveals strategies for working with a micromanager and how not to be one (Geddis, 2015).

Geddis, R. L. (2015). Moving from Micromanagement to Masterful Leadership: It's a Control Thing (1st ed.). Rhonda L. Geddis, LLC.

Organizational politics

The following is a definitive guide to working with – and surviving – bullies, creeps, jerks, tyrants, tormentors, despots, backstabbers, egomaniacs, and all the other assholes who do their best to destroy you at work. "What an asshole!" In this groundbreaking book, Stanford University professor Robert I. Sutton builds on his acclaimed *Harvard Business Review* article to show you the best ways to deal with assholes and why they can be so destructive to your company (R. I. Sutton, 2010).

Sutton, R. I. (2010). The no asshole rule: Building a civilized workplace and surviving one that isn't. New York: Business Plus.

Perfectionism

This book offers an optimal way of thinking about failure and success – and the very way we live. The author provides exercises for self-reflection, meditations, and "time-ins" to help you rediscover what you really want out of life (Ben-Shahar, 2009).

Ben-Shahar, T. (2009). Pursuit of perfect: Stop chasing perfection and find your path to lasting happiness! (1st ed.). United Kingdom: McGraw-Hill.

Promotion

This book reveals the secret to minimizing the chances of being overlooked for future promotions and learning how to increase the chances of advancing in HR (Collins & Quinn, 2019).

Collins, A., & Quinn, A. (2019). She stole my HR promotion: An unforgettable story about not getting promoted in human resources & THE NUMBER ONE SUCCESS SECRET for advancing your HR career faster and easier than you thought . . .! (1st ed.). Success in HR Publishing.

Journals

Accepting criticism

This source dives into the topic of teaching the social skill of accepting criticism to adults with developmental disabilities (Eckert, 2000).

Eckert, S. P. (2000). Teaching the social skill of accepting criticism to adults with developmental disabilities. Education and Training in Mental Retardation and Developmental Disabilities, 35(1), 16–24. Retrieved from JSTOR.

This study evaluates the social validation of behaviors, such as following instructions, accepting criticism, and negotiating to resolve conflicts (Quinn, Sherman, Sheldon, Quinn, & Harchik, 1992).

Quinn, J., Sherman, J. A., Sheldon, J. B., Quinn, L. M., & Harchik, A. E. (1992). Social validation of component behaviors of following instructions, accepting criticism, and negotiating. Journal of Applied Behavior Analysis, 25(2), 401–413. https://doi.org/10.1901/jaba.1992.25-401

This source teaches the social skill of accepting criticism with grace and appreciation to adults. More specifically, the source teaches the audience to rethink their first reaction, how to turn negatives into positives, thanking the critic, learning from the criticism, and how to be the better person (Babauta, 2007).

Babauta, L. (2007, July 27). How to accept criticism with grace and appreciation: Zen habits. Retrieved November 23, 2019, from Zen Habits website: https://zenhabits.net/how-to-accept-criticism-with-grace-and-appreciation/

This source provides a six-step process to dealing with the confrontation of criticism from a manager or peer. These six steps include stopping your first reaction, remembering the benefit of feedback, listening for understanding, saying thank you, asking questions to deconstruct the feedback, and requesting time to follow up (Lindsay, 2017).

Lindsay, N. (2017, September 29). How smart people respond to constructive criticism. Retrieved November 23, 2019, from The Muse website: www.themuse.com/advice/taking-constructive-criticism-like-a-champ

Three points to calm and motivate include suggesting a look into the future when the current issue can be seen as a temporary patch, reminding clients of past troubles and how they were able to overcome through endurance, and talking about exciting new projects that the company has ahead of them (R. Sutton, 2019).

Sutton, R. (2019, June 19). Imaginary time travel as a leadership tool. MIT Sloan Management Review. Retrieved from https://sloanreview.mit.edu/article/imaginary-time-travel-as-a-leadership-tool/

Authority

This article examines the association between job authority and the exposure to interpersonal conflict in the workplace and potential gender and age contingencies in that association (Schieman & Reid, 2008).

Schieman, S., & Reid, S. (2008). Job authority and interpersonal conflict in the workplace. Work and Occupations, 35(3), 296–326. https://doi.org/10.1177/0730888408322448

In this article, Eisenhauer touches upon the psychological component of authority, suggesting that "you can use the principle of authority to boost employee morale and, more importantly, build trust through seven authority activators. These seven authority activators include aesthetics, early engagement, top-down mentality, walk your talk, make your employees visible, support career development, and model positive traits (Eisenhauer, n.d.).

Eisenhauer, T. (n.d.). How to use the persuasion principle of "authority" at work. Retrieved November 22, 2019, from https://axerosolutions.com/blogs/timeisenhauer/pulse/837/how-to-use-the-persuasion-principle-of-authority-at-work

Credibility

Integrity and trust carry great significance at the corporate level in creating a great work culture (Shahid, 2013).

Shahid, A. (2013). Integrity & trust: The defining principles of great workplaces. Journal of Management Research, 5(4), 64–75. https://doi.org/10.5296/jmr.v5i4.3739

Delegation

A study and analysis that delegation promotes feedback-seeking behavior by psychologically empowering subordinates (Zhang et al., 2017).

Zhang, X., Qian, J., Wang, B., Jin, Z., Wang, J., & Wang, Y. (2017). Leaders' behaviors matter: The role of delegation in promoting employees' feedback-seeking behavior. Frontiers in Psychology, 8, 920. https://doi.org/10.3389/fpsyg.2017.00920

Micromanagement

Rather than viewing micromanagement as a complete negative, this article reviews how micromanagement can be appropriately used as an effective management tool if one knows when and when not to get involved (Delgado, Strauss, & Ortega, 2015).

Delgado, O., Strauss, E. M., & Ortega, M. A. (2015). Micromanagement: When to avoid it and how to use it effectively. American Journal of Health-System Pharmacy, 72(10), 772–776. https://doi.org/10.2146/ajhp140125

Organizational politics

The article presents a basis for an understanding of organizational politics and provides various approaches to decreasing its presence and generally negative effects on the organization (Schneider, 2016).

Schneider, R. C. (2016). Understanding and managing organizational politics. Kinesiology, Sport Studies and Physical Education Presentations and Papers, 14. Bangkok-Thailand.: Digital Commons @Brockport.

Perfectionism

This article examines how to manage a direct report who has high standards and a fine attention to detail (Gallo, 2011).

Gallo, A. (2011, October 19). How to manage a perfectionist. Harvard Business Review. Retrieved from https://hbr.org/2011/10/how-to-manage-a-perfectionist

Web links

Big picture

Utilizing the stonecutter short story to demonstrate the value of thinking positively and seeing the bigger picture, this blog post touches upon important leadership qualities by building a shared vision (Higson & Sturgess, 2007).

Higson, P., & Sturgess, A. (2007). Leadership quality: Seeing the bigger picture. Retrieved November 23, 2019, from The Happy Manager website: http://the-happy-manager.com/articles/leadership-quality/

This article suggests considering that diversity isn't the same as affirmative action since there are no laws that require diversity programs. Methods to promote diversity programs include developing a diversity mission statement, showing profiles of managers and employees from a variety of backgrounds, having mentoring programs, creating affinity groups, showcasing suppliers whose owners come from a variety of backgrounds, creating community outreach programs, and showcasing community diversity organizations or activities that the company sponsors (Carsen, 2017).

Carsen, J. (2017, November 3). Understanding the big picture of workplace diversity. Retrieved November 23, 2019, from the HR Daily Advisor website: https://hrdailyadvisor.blr.com/2017/11/03/understanding-big-picture-workplace-diversity/

Big picture thinking allows leaders to act proactively rather than reactively. This article reviews having a definite strategy and the ability to think in perspective to see the big picture (Joseph, 2018).

Joseph, I. (2018, February 1). As a leader, how do you think "big picture"? Retrieved November 23, 2019, from the Leaderonomics.com website: https://leaderonomics.com/ leadership/leaders-and-big-picture-thinking

Chain of command

The Turnaround King, Marcus Lemonis, host of *The Profit* has insight on the reasons for chain of command in this article along with some video clips (Dill, 2017).

Dill, K. (2017, July 25). Cautionary tale shows why you need a clear chain of command at your workplace. Retrieved November 22, 2019, from CNBC website: www.cnbc.com/2017/07/24/ cautionary-tale-shows-why-you-need-a-chain-of-command-at-your-work.html

Coaching

There is a growing need to coach employees in the workplace, and this article explains exactly why it produces results, what coaching methods to use, and how to make it a habit to enjoy the results of greater employee engagement and job satisfaction (Ainomugisha, 2018).

Ainomugisha, G. (2018, January 10). Best practice guide to coaching employees in the workplace. Retrieved November 24, 2019, from The 6Q Blog website: https://inside.6q.io/ coaching-employees-in-the-workplace/

Credibility

This *Forbes* article identifies the three ways to build credibility at work by removing filler words and not saying "sorry," knowing when to speak up, and getting your point across as a collective idea rather than as one person's (Prossack, 2018).

Prossack, A. (2018, April 23). 3 ways to build credibility at work. Forbes. Retrieved From www.forbes.com/sites/ashiraprossack1/2018/04/23/3-ways-to-build-credibility-at-work/ #15e82caa49fe

Forbes establishes nine steps to follow to build and maintain professional credibility (Jacobs, 2011).

Jacobs, D. L. (2011, November 22). Boost your credibility at work. *Forbes*. Retrieved From www.forbes.com/sites/deborahljacobs/2011/11/22/how-to-boost-your-credibility-at-work/ #2eba41af7eb7

This article identifies four ways to build credibility at work by being good at what you do, seeking feedback, ensuring integrity, and being likable (The Resource Connection, 2018).

The Resource Connection. (2018, September 19). How to build your credibility at work. Retrieved November 24, 2019, from The Resource Connection website: www.resource-connection.com/2018/09/19/how-to-build-your-credibility-at-work/

Delegation

Readers are given six guided steps to follow in order to successfully and effectively delegate tasks (Randall, 2013).

Randall, M. (2013, March 6). 6 steps for more effective delegation. Fast Company. Retrieved from www.fastcompany.com/3006643/6-steps-more-effective-delegation

Feedback

Critiquing weak performance is a job nobody likes, but by taking a more open approach, you can be a better boss – and get a lot more from your team (Manzoni, 2002).

Manzoni, J.-F. (2002, September 1). A better way to deliver bad news. Harvard Business Review (September 2002). Retrieved from https://hbr.org/2002/09/a-better-way-to-deliver-bad-news

Micromanagement

This article identifies ten signs of micromanagement and provides advice on how to deal with micromanagers (Webster & Webster, 2012).

Webster, V., & Webster, M. (2012, November 12). 10 signs of micromanagement – Strategies for dealing with micromanagers. Retrieved November 27, 2019, from the Leadership Thoughts website: www.leadershipthoughts.com/10-signs-of-micromanagement/

This *Forbes* article presents a positive perspective on micromanagement and identifies seven reasons why micromanagers can be great for teams and companies (Angelovska, 2018).

Angelovska, N. (2018, November 5). 7 reasons why micromanagers are good for teams and companies. Retrieved November 27, 2019, from the Forbes website: www.forbes.com/sites/ninaangelovska/2018/11/05/why-you-should-add-micromanagement-as-a-skill-in-your-job-application/#5b64db8a68bc

Motivation

This *Forbes* article presents statistics surrounding employee motivation and addresses what Millennial and Generation Z employees want (Comaford, 2018).

Comaford, C. (2018, January 20). Why leaders need to embrace employee motivation. *Forbes*. Retrieved from www.forbes.com/sites/christinecomaford/2018/01/20/why-leaders-need-to-embrace-employee-motivation/#1ba883127257

Open-door policy

An examination of the divide over the open-door policy (Gray, 2010).

Gray, K. (2010, June 9). Look inside "open-door" policies. Retrieved November 27, 2019, from the SHRM website: www.shrm.org/resourcesandtools/hr-topics/employee-relations/pages/opendoorpolicies.aspx

The following is a simple sample policy as a guide to include in an employee handbook about the open-door policy (Heathfield, 2019a).

Heathfield, S. M. (2019a, February 19). What does having an open door policy at work mean for employees? Retrieved March 15, 2019, from The Balance Careers website: www.thebalancecareers.com/open-door-policy-1918203

Organizational politics

This web article talks about the various terrains to organizational politics (Wroblewski, 2018).

Wroblewski, M. T. (2018, November 14). The impact of power and politics in organizational productivity. Retrieved November 29, 2019, from the Chron.com Website: https://smallbusiness.chron.com/impact-power-politics-organizational-productivity-35942.html

Perfectionism

Results show that performance and perfectionism are not related to each other – perfectionists are not better or worse performers than others (McClear, 2019).

McClear, S. (2019, January 4). It's a fact: Your perfectionism isn't helping your performance at work. Retrieved November 29, 2019, from the Ladders: Business News & Career Advice website: www.theladders.com/career-advice/its-a-fact-your-perfectionism-isnt-helping-your-performance-at-work

Promotion

This article reviews the difference between promotion versus lateral moves, promotion dilemmas, the idea that not all employees want a promotion, and examples of promotion in the workplace (Heathfield, 2019b).

Heathfield, S. M. (2019b, July 21). How an employee promotion recognizes their contribution to the firm. Retrieved November 29, 2019, from The Balance Careers website: www.thebalancecareers.com/a-promotion-rewards-an-employee-for-work-contributions-1918231

Trust

This article provides a link to a podcast interview with leading trust authority Charles H. Green that touches on the evolution of trust from a simple handshake to hefty legal documents, the impact of technology on trust, the trust equation, the motives of Millennials, and much more (Morgan, 2014).

Morgan, J. (2014, September 11). Trust in the workplace: What happened to it, and how do we get it back? Retrieved from www.forbes.com/sites/jacobmorgan/2014/09/11/trust-in-the-workplace-what-happened-to-it-and-how-do-we-get-it-back/#2c8831787030

This article opens a conversation on the importance of trust in the workplace and more so what mistrust can do. It provides a useful acronym and thorough understanding of actions to take (Manning, 2018).

Manning, B. A. (2018, May 16). 5 steps for building trust in the workplace. Retrieved November 30, 2019, from www.td.org/insights/5-steps-for-building-trust-in-the-workplace

Part 9

Managing a diverse workforce

How to use this part

This part of the book examines opportunities where diversity and inclusion should be carefully considered. The hospitality industry is well known for being an industry whereby diversity is the norm in all operations. Seek to identify the ways that management can be more inclusive. Start at the beginning with a job description, and conclude with training.

Key terms

The key terms found in the cases in this section are listed here. Their definitions can be found on pages xiv–xvii.

Bias
Coaching
Discrimination
Diversity
Feedback
Harassment
Insubordination
Job design
Job description
Prejudice
Promotion
Recruiting
Religion
Respect
Stereotypes

Why diversity matters

Main subjects
Discrimination, diversity

Who's who
• Betty Chu, Human
Resources Manager
• John Ferreira, Chief Steward

Think point

The hospitality industry is well known for employing diverse candidates. Title VI of the Civil Rights Act of 1964 prevents discrimination of protected classes. In turn, many companies seek to employ a more diverse workforce by having an affirmative action plan, a way to increase the volume of candidates in the recruitment pool who come from the underrepresented classes. Diversity committees are becoming more frequently utilized to review various methods to better integrate diversity in the workplace.

Managing a diverse workforce

Betty has recently joined the Royal Hotel as the new assistant director of human resources. As part of her yearly action plan, she has decided to set up a diversity committee. She invited some department heads and members of protected classes to join the first meeting next week. This morning, Betty received the following email from John, the chief steward.

Email

Hello Betty,

Thanks for inviting me to join the diversity committee of the hotel.

Let me share some of my thoughts with you regarding this new committee.

Personally, I feel that the steps that need to be taken by minority workers are their own responsibility to take on. In this country, it is illegal to discriminate based on race. Minority workers have the same opportunities as any other American workers, and the resources to learn English are readily available to everyone. It is up to the minority workers to take the initial step in recognizing that the English language is a necessary skill to be learned.

I have no worries that the minority workers (whom I respect as equally capable people) who want to become managers will indeed be successful here at the Royal Hotel.

I will stop by this afternoon to discuss this further.

Regards,
John

1   Some people believe that we should treat all employees equally regardless of their personal characteristics. Do you agree? Explain.

2   Some organizations require that members of protected classes sit on their diversity committee. What are the dangers of this practice?

3   What suggestions would you offer to Betty to set up the committee?

4   It has become common for companies to develop recruitment and selection programs that focus on percentage or number of minorities hired.

5   What are the risks of implementing such programs?

The levels of exclusion

Main subjects
Bias, discrimination, diversity, prejudice, stereotypes

Who's who
• Betty Chu, Human
Resources Manager

Think point

Unfortunately, discrimination in the workplace can happen rather easily. Individuals tend to stereotype people and have a pre-determined sense of prejudice and even an inherent sense of bias toward others. Consider how you can create an environment that is more inclusive with the diversity that exists in the world.

Managing a diverse workforce

The Royal's diversity committee was committed to systematically spotting hidden biases across the hotel. "We may avoid or exclude someone because of a belief that people from that group are inferior in some way. The problem is that if you bring together a group of Royal managers and say, 'OK, we're going to do antidiscrimination training – who has a prejudice?' my sense is nobody will raise their hand because people just aren't going to define themselves as a racist," said Betty.

"When someone is accused of discrimination, they take great offense," added another manager. "By the way, guys, do we know what the difference between stereotype, prejudice, and discrimination is?" wondered one of the members on the committee.

To move forward, the committee decided that the members would listen and take note of suspicious comments about and incidents with Latinos for a month. According to the meeting minutes, "Based on the findings and to help employees face their biases, at a future committee meeting, we will work out an action plan."

Here is the list of the statements and situations committee members collected during the month:

Cafeteria

1 Are you looking for burritos, Dominga?

F&B

2 Hispanics like spicy foods.
3 I don't like Latinos, like Francisco; they are taking our front-of-house jobs.
4 Jose is the chef? I'll have to talk loud and slow to make sure he is able to understand me.
5 We shouldn't let Santos in charge of the register; he might steal.
6 I don't think Enrique, the busboy, should be the new server; customers will think we can't afford American staff.

Rooms Division

7 Guest service employees referred to Carlos as "that Mexican guy," when he is from Guatemala.
8 I avoid immigrants like Soledad from housekeeping; they are illegal.
9 Luiz has been in the laundry longer than other white employees but gets paid less.
10 Esteban was not invited to the employees' Fourth of July party after work because they did not consider him to be American.

Engineering

11 Where is Cruz, the plumber? They have a "mañana" attitude.
12 Manuel must have only gotten the electrician job because they need to fulfill a quota.
13 Consuelo was not picked for a special renovation task because he couldn't speak English well.

Spa

14 Latino men are macho.
15 I wouldn't invite Jorge to play golf; they have low income.

Sales

16   I'll write this email myself; his grammar is probably bad.

Royal Hotel job fair

17   They don't mind working for lower-paying jobs.
18   They can't speak English well.
19   Ramona can be placed in a housekeeping position; this is where most Latinos are.
20   Let's place Ines in a less-visible position.

1   What is the difference between stereotyping, prejudice, and discrimination?

2   How can hidden biases hurt our business?

3   Review the statements and situations, and identify each as an example of stereotyping, prejudice, or discrimination.

4   How would you advise an employee who feels that his or her minority status is a stumbling block at work?

The case is based on the principles and situations described in the following:

Babcock, P. (2006). Detecting hidden bias. *HR Magazine*, *51*(2), 50–55.
Carr-Ruffino, N. (2005). *Making diversity work*. Upper Saddle River, NJ: Pearson Prentice Hall.

Please hire him; he is like me!

Main subjects
Discrimination, diversity, recruiting/selection

Who's who
• Fred Poitier, Banquet Server
• Thomas Waxer, Banquet Manager

Think point

A referral program that incorporates a bonus for length of service can serve as a motivator for present employees to recommend individuals who have a similar work ethic. Examine the impacts that such a program might have when diversity in the workplace exists.

Thomas, the banquet manager, was looking at the list of open positions on the wall and sighed heavily. *Business is picking up; they will most definitely need additional servers*, he thought to himself. Thomas was thinking about going down to HR to see if there were any new applicants when the phone rang. It was Fred Poitier, one of the most experienced banquet servers.

"Hi, Thomas. Is this referral bonus thing still going on? I would like to recommend my old buddy from back home. He just moved to the States, and he is looking for a job. He is very nice, and he could do the job," Fred told him.

"That's great, Fred!" Thomas replied enthusiastically. "Why don't you just ask your friend to give me a call tomorrow?"

Most of the banquet servers at the Royal Hotel were of Haitian origin. They were all hardworking; hiring another employee with the same background seemed to be a logical decision.

1   Should the manager just go ahead and interview the candidate? Why? Why not?

2   What are some of the pros and cons of using employee referrals?

3   How can employers avoid racial discrimination when recruiting and hiring?

4   How can HR departments further minimize the likelihood of the "like-me bias" during the interview process?

English only

Main subjects
Discrimination, diversity

Who's who
• Katherine Norton, Director of Human Resources
• Emily Perkins, Lounge and Bar Manager

Think point

The United States is known for being a melting pot of various languages, as individuals come from various countries. One of the preferences we have is to seek to hire individuals with the ability to be multi-lingual. However, there are occasions where the native language of individuals is not English. Consider how best to be inclusive in an environment when English is expected to be the common language in the business.

> ## Voice mail
>
> "Hi, Katherine. This is Emily. We have an issue here at the lounge. As you know, most of our employees are Hispanic, and they tend to talk to each other in Spanish, although they are fluent in English. It really bothers me, and I believe guests find this offensive too.
>
> "Is it OK with you guys in HR if I establish an English-only policy? I would love to start it on Monday. Thanks, Katherine."

> 1. Can the Royal Hotel enforce a policy that requires all employees to speak English at all times?
>
> 2. What advice would you give to Katherine?
>
> 3. How can the Royal Hotel help employees who speak different languages work in harmony?

Can I have another boss please?

Main subjects
Coaching, discrimination, diversity

Who's who
• Shakia Andrews, Executive Housekeeper
• Patu Manga, Houseman
• Katherine Norton, Director of Human Resources
• Thomas Waxer, Banquet Manager

Think point

The customs that individuals from countries other than the United States come with can sometimes be very different. While these customs might be important or a way of life in another country, in the U.S., they can be seen as discrimination. Consider how a manager can embrace the diversity that exists in the operation and coach employees to avoid discrimination.

Shakia, the executive housekeeper, was rather happy today. Finally, she was able to fill all the open positions. Last week, she hired Patu, a male employee, for the houseman position. Patu originally was also interested in an open banquet position, but he agreed with Thomas, the banquet manager, that housekeeping was the priority.

Patu has recently emigrated from an African country and seemed to be very happy in his new job. This afternoon, Shakia received an email from the HR director notifying her that Patu was complaining that he was not comfortable being a subordinate to a female boss.

As Shakia was walking down to HR, she was wondering how to handle the situation.

1   What actions could Shakia take before her meeting with Patu?

2   How would you address the situation with Patu?

3   What, if any, reasonable accommodation could be made that would enable Patu to successfully perform his job?

Can I have another server please?

Main subject
Discrimination, diversity

Who's who
• Mary Kim, Room Service Order Taker
• Johnny Moerschell, Assistant Room Service Manager
• Louis Nichols, Room Service Server
• Peter Fischer, Room Service Server
• Marc Watkins, Hotel VIP Guest

Think point

Our society, in some ways, has become more accepting of individuals who have a different way of representing themselves. The work environment is more commonly found to have people who are gay, lesbian, bisexual, or transgender. However, not everyone in the world is accepting of such individuals; discrimination can easily occur. In a service environment, consider how managers are expected to make accommodations of requests by paying guests that create an official discriminatory situation.

Mary, the room service order taker, took her dinner break, and Johnny, the assistant manager, covered for her. Just before the end of Mary's break, Mr. Watkins called from the Royal Suite to place his dinner order.

After Johnny repeated his order, Mr. Watkins added, "One more thing! May I request that I don't have Jenny as a server? I'm not comfortable with her/him/it/whatever."

"I beg your pardon?" exclaimed Johnny.

"You know, I have nothing against transgender people," replied Mr. Watkins. "But I just feel more comfortable talking with a straight person. By the way, I don't want to have Peter either; he spilled the coffee twice already on my laptop."

At this point, another line rang, and according to the Royal Hotel's high standards, Johnny placed Mr. Watkins on hold.

Mr. Watkins was a top VIP at the Royal. He had already spent thousands of dollars at the hotel and recently booked a major conference for next year.

Most servers were busy delivering orders, and only Jenny, a transgender employee, was present, waiting for the next order. Johnny also noticed Mary as she was walking back from the cafeteria.

1   Should Johnny accommodate Mr. Watkins first request?

2   How about Peter?

3   Assume that Mr. Watkins requests a male therapist in the Royal Spa? Would you accommodate that request?

The cake order

Main subject
Harassment

Who's who
• Rusty Fitzgerald, Pastry Chef
• Lucy Moores, Rusty's Friend

Think point

Sexual harassment comes in two forms: quid pro quo or hostile work environment. It is prudent that businesses adopt an official sexual harassment policy and communicate and train the employees on the policy. Part of this training will be how to handle situations when one feels as though one is being sexually harassed. Not only can harassment occur in the workplace by those employed by the business, but it can also occur outside of the business, through the vendors or guests of the organization. Consider how best to handle situations in all of these areas.

Rusty, the pastry chef, was exhausted. She had been without an assistant pastry chef for four months, and still, there were no potential candidates to interview. "Let's see what's going on next week," she said to herself.

The Royal Hotel would be hosting a major VIP conference for CruiseDream, an International Cruise Line company. On Friday evening, a dinner dance would conclude the event. *The usual stuff*, she thought. The company requested a huge strawberry shortcake with a custom decoration. According to the banquet event order, the details of the cake design would be directly emailed to pastry. When she opened the email, she could not believe her eyes. The attached photo showed a bare-breasted mermaid but sculpted with unrealistic-sized breasts. Rusty was shocked and opened her drawer containing training documents and handouts she had received at orientation. She remembered that the Royal Hotel had pledged to create a "harassment-free" environment and that the hotel protected its employees from harassment caused by nonemployees. Then she called Lucy, her best friend, who worked at a local law firm as a secretary. She could not understand all the words Lucy used but later remembered one term: *hostile environment*.

The next day, she filed a complaint at the State Commission against Discrimination.

1   Hospitality organizations in general are especially vulnerable to incidents of sexual harassing behaviors. Why?

2   A hostile environment is created when sexual behaviors have the purpose or effect of unreasonably interfering with an individual's work performance or creating an intimidating, hostile, or offensive work environment. From the information presented in this case, can this situation be considered harassment? Why or why not?

3   What steps can an employer take to avoid potential liability?

I am not your slave!

Main subjects
Diversity, feedback, harassment, respect, stereotypes

Who's who
• John Jones, Restaurant Assistant Manager
• Ben Cotten, Server Assistant

Think point

Restaurant operations can be an all-hands-on deck experience. The meal crunch can be compounded when weather and being short-staffed are also incorporated. In an environment that is rather diverse with employees, it is important to consider how best to communicate expectations with employees.

It was a rainy and chilly night, and most guests at the Royal Hotel decided to stay in and have dinner at the hotel restaurant. John, the assistant manager, was in charge of the restaurant that night. They were completely booked. To make matters worse, at 5:00 PM the food runner called out.

Instead of assigning someone to run the food, they agreed during the pre-meal meeting that everyone would run their own food and that the chef would page John if there was a problem.

John did his best. He was everywhere to ensure that the restaurant ran smoothly.

The pager went off at 7:00 PM. The chef was nervous, as the food plated for two large tables was sitting on the kitchen counter. John looked around, and Ben, one of the server assistants, seemed to be available. "Ben! Come! Let's run the food!" shouted Johnny.

Ben came over and said, "You know, John, I am not your slave! No one should speak to us like that! By the way, I am busy with bread service," said Ben as he left.

John finally found another employee to run the food and was wondering what he did wrong. "Is it something to do with that fact the Ben is African American and I am white?"

1   What are the typical stereotypes about African Americans?

2   What are the key values that are associated with the African American community? What major issues are important to African Americans?

3   John is clearly caught in a difficult situation. Where should he begin?

4   What would you suggest happen when they meet to discuss the issue?

5   When speaking with employees, how can we ensure that everyone feels a sense of equality?

Name calling

Main subjects
Diversity, harassment

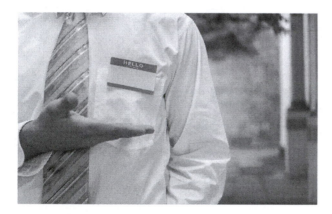

Who's who
• Lori Canelle, Spa Manager
• Mahmoud Hassani, Spa
Employee
• Caitlin Smith, Hotel Guest

Think point

Considering the fact that our industry employs a vast and diverse community of people, it will be expected that employees from other countries will have names that are difficult to pronounce. Determine how best you can embrace this diversity and respect the individuals, while being able to properly serve clients.

"Hey, Mike, how are you?" asked Lori, the spa manager.

"I am doing fine, but you know, my name is not Mike. I am Mahmoud, and I would really like to be called by my name," replied Mahmoud.

"I know," Lori said and smiled. "I just have a hard time pronouncing your name. Also think about our clientele. Using a name like Mike will increase your chance to be noticed and be recommended as employee of the month. Anyway, did you offer a drink to Mrs. Smith? She just finished her aerobics class," said Lori.

1   Would you consider calling the employee Mike racially derogatory?

2   From the information presented in this case, can this situation be considered harassment? Why or why not?

3   What can the Royal Hotel do to minimize the possibility of this type of harassment?

A strong accent

Case type: issue case

Main subjects
Coaching, discrimination, diversity, promotion

Who's who
• Carlos Diaz, Guest
Services Manager
• Attila Kuncze, Houseman

Think point

When job descriptions are designed, they should be made to clearly express what the needs of the position are in order to be effective. The job specification can identify the expectations of the individual. In many positions, English, as both the spoken and written language, can be required. Consider how best to handle an employee where the English language is not his or her native or primary language and how a manager can better prepare line-level employees for promotion opportunities.

Attila was knocking on the office door of Carlos, the guest services manager.

"How is everything in housekeeping, Attila?" asked Carlos.

"Good! I heard that you are looking for a concierge. I am really interested in this position," replied Attila.

"Honestly, I think your verbal communication skills would hinder your ability to perform well behind the concierge desk," answered Carlos.

"I know I have an accent, but I haven't had any problems in the past," said Attila, a native Hungarian.

"You may not realize it, but you are extremely difficult to understand," pointed out Carlos.

"Have customers complained about my accent?" asked Attila.

"Your heavy accent would make it a little difficult for our English-speaking customers to understand. I really think you should take an English course and work on your enunciation," said Carlos. This concluded the discussion.

1   Can you refuse a job or promotion to someone who doesn't speak English well enough to do the job properly?

2   What advice might you have for the hotel?

The empty conference room

Main subjects
Diversity, religion

Who's who
• Rhiannon Palmer,
Convention Services Manager
• Fred Poitier, Banquet Server

Think point

With diversity in the workplace comes the opportunity for the religious preferences of the employees to come into action. Consider whether the organization needs to have any policies on religion in the workplace. Use of hotel space, for employees' personal use, is a policy that should be examined. In order to be non-discriminatory, consider what, if any restrictions, should be adopted.

Phone call

"Good afternoon, Convention Services, Rhiannon speaking, how may I assist you?"

"Hi, Rhiannon, this is Fred, the banquet server."

"What can I do for you, Fred?" asked Rhiannon.

"We have received the event schedule for next month, and I see that the second week is rather slow," answered Fred.

"Yes, that's right," answered Rhiannon.

"I am wondering if we could use one of the conference rooms to hold a prayer group. Six of us in banquets belong to the same church. Of course, we would pay all the costs," added Fred.

"Carpet cleaning is scheduled for that week," replied Rhiannon hesitantly. "Can I call you back?" she asked, ending the conversation.

1   How would you advise Rhiannon? Should the hotel allow this conference room usage?

2   During lunch break, Fred engages another employee in a polite discussion of why his faith should be embraced. The other employee disagrees with Fred's exhortation but does not ask that the conversation stop. Should the Royal Hotel restrict such speech?

Special skills

Main subjects
Discipline, diversity, insubordination, job design/job description

Who's who
• Luis Vargas, PBX Operator
• Kalinda Stenton, PBX Manager

Think point

A business should consider the needs for various positions and identify those clearly in a job description and job specification. Typically, the job description will also include a phrase similar to "other duties as identified by the manager." One such skill might be the ability to be multi-lingual. It might be wise to determine the best method to identify the team members and the languages that they are able to communicate with to best serve guests. In this way, you will not make assumptions and offend staff members. Consider how best to handle this type of scenario.

"Luis, could you please do me a favor?" asked Kalinda, the PBX manager.

"Sure, what is that?" Luis smiled.

"There is a guest from Mexico in the business center who needs someone to translate some brief documents. He doesn't understand English at all. He's waiting for you. No worries; I'll cover you!"

"I'm not sure, Kalinda," replied Luis. "I was born in Colombia, and I came here at the age of four. When my friends talked to me in Spanish, I replied to them in English. My parents chose to raise me in an English-only household. I made efforts to learn Spanish through classes in middle school, but my vocabulary is really limited."

"Your Spanish is obviously way better than mine. We can only achieve our goals if we work as a team," Kalinda insisted.

"I prefer focusing on my own duties," Luis answered. "I don't feel comfortable about this assignment. I'm a switchboard operator, and being an interpreter or translator is not included in my job description."

"Do you realize that the failure to follow reasonable and lawful instructions is considered insubordination?" Kalinda said angrily. "Please go home. You're suspended for two days!"

1   Is disciplinary action warranted? Why, or why not?

2   How could problems of this nature be avoided in the future?

The case is based on the principles and situations described in the following:

Alexander Hamilton Institute. (2000). *The employee problem solver* (Accent discrimination, pp. 1–9). Ramsey, NJ: Alexander Hamilton Institute.

People like Yuan

Case type: issue case

Main subjects
Discrimination, diversity, stereotypes

Who's who
- Charlie Jones, Director of Engineering
- Robert Kunz, General Manager
- William Ming, IT Manager
- Katherine Norton, Director of Human Resources
- Louise Rausch, Director of Finance
- Yuan Yao, Assistant Director of Finance

Think point

On occasion, the stereotypes of certain ethnicities can create an inherit bias or be seen as discrimination. Consider how best to ensure that language used in the workplace doesn't allow for the viewpoint of stereotypes to impact the efficiency of the business.

"We need to provide a continuous flow of talented candidates to meet the Royal's management needs. The executive committee's role is to identify high-potential employees capable of rapid advancement to positions of higher responsibilities," Robert Kunz reminded everybody after the lunch break at the yearly succession planning meeting. "Who is next?" he asked.

"Yuan, from finance." Katherine, the HR director, helped him out.

"How is he doing?" asked Robert as he turned to the others.

"He has been tracking our expenses in an organized manner, and as you know, he was instrumental in guiding William in the implementation of our new computer system. You know, they are great at crunching numbers!" said Louise, his boss.

"Yuan is always so polite and patient with me; it's a pleasure doing business with him," Charlie, from engineering, said and smiled. "It's good to have people like Yuan in finance."

"OK, let's move on," Robert said.

1   What are the typical stereotypes about Asian Americans?

2   How can positive stereotypes negatively affect Asian Americans' upward mobility?

3   How can organizations help Asian Americans to overcome cultural traits that are more pronounced within the Asian community?

> ### Part summary
>
> This section covered the various aspects that are inherent in a business where diverse individuals are employed. Seek to identify ways to be more inclusive. Start with the job description to identify the needs of the jobs, and carry that through to the job specification to identify the skills of the individual desired for the position. Proper training of managers can assist in ensuring that discrimination in the workplace based on ethnicity is avoided and a more inclusive culture is embraced.

Additional reading

Books

Bias

Helen Turnbull asserts that companies hire people for their unique differences to create diversity in the workplace, yet they teach them directly and indirectly what they have to do to fit into the corporate culture (Turnbull, 2016).

Turnbull, H. (2016). *The illusion of inclusion: Global inclusion, unconscious bias, and the bottom line*. New York: Business Expert Press.

This book provides ways to motivate real change while defeating biases (Thiederman, 2015).

Thiederman, S. (2015). *3 keys to defeating unconscious bias: Watch, think, act*. Woburn, Massachusetts: Cross-Cultural Communications.

This author reveals the secret to avoiding drama in the workplace; understand the causes, effects, and solutions to problems such as sexual harassment, unconscious bias, and ethics lapses to inspire a healthy culture and work environment (Perez, 2019).

Perez, P. (2019). *The drama-free workplace: How you can prevent unconscious bias, sexual harassment, ethics lapses, and inspire a healthy culture*. New Jersey: Wiley.

The authors' readers reflect upon their stories and experiences to unveil the hidden bias that exists within our conscience. The goal of this book is to help others become more self-aware to be the solution rather than the problem (Jana & Freeman, 2016).

Jana, T., & Freeman, M. (2016). *Overcoming bias: Building authentic relationships across differences* (1st ed.). San Francisco, CA: Berrett-Koehler Publishers.

Discrimination

With the purpose of providing a deep understanding of the historical background and the long-term impact on the development of employment discrimination law, important cases are addressed in this book (Friedman, 2005).

Friedman, J. (2005). *Employment discrimination stories* (1 edition). New York: Foundation Press.

Diversity

The following is an award-winning book packed with research, statistics, policy, and case examples to support the argument that inclusion is the key to unlocking the potential for a multicultural workforce; it provides a practical four-stage intervention to create an inclusive workplace (Barak, 2016).

Barak, M. E. M. (2016). *Managing diversity: Toward a globally inclusive workplace.* Thousand Oaks, CA: SAGE Publications.

Harassment

The following is a book for managers who are responsible for addressing and preventing workplace discrimination and harassment to find guidance on various topics, such as what harassment is, how to stop it, and how to conduct training on it (England, 2012).

England, D. C. (2012). *The essential guide to handling workplace harassment & discrimination* (2nd ed.). Berkeley, CA: NOLO.

Job Specification

This book is designed to help readers understand job analysis, job description, job specification, and job evaluation to decide when to use it and evaluate whether compensation of employees is appropriate (U.S. Small Business Administration. Office of Management Assistance, 1980).

U.S. Small Business Administration. Office of Management Assistance. (1980). *Job analysis, job specifications, and job descriptions* (Vol. 1020). Illinois: U.S. Small Business Administration, Office of Management Assistance.

Prejudice

This book presents tips, case studies, and the "Ten Commandments of Implement Change" to overcome prejudice at work (Parekh & Bell, 2015).

Parekh, R., & Bell, C. (2015). *Overcome prejudice at work.* Boston: Rosetta Books.

The following is a book chapter that examines how prejudice, discrimination, and racism can influence health (National Research Council (US) Panel on Race, Ethnicity, and Health in Later Life, 2004).

National Research Council (US) Panel on Race, Ethnicity, and Health in Later Life. (2004). Prejudice and discrimination. In R. A. Bulatao & N. B. Anderson (Eds.), *Understanding Racial and Ethnic Differences in Health in Late Life: A Research Agenda.* (Vol. 7). Washington, DC: National Academies Press (US).

Respect

The following article presents ten "laws" to create a work environment that fosters respect for employees and timeless stories and principles to give clear understanding of said "laws" (Taiwao, 2009).

Taiwao, N. (2009). *The top ten laws of respect in the workplace: A professional guide.* Longwood, FL: Xulon Press.

Stereotypes

Oracle Organizational Developer writes a blueprint for managing people and their inherent interpersonal dynamics rather than the labels that precede them specifically in terms of generational stereotypes (Kriegel, 2016).

Kriegel, J. (2016). *Unfairly labeled: How your workplace can benefit from ditching generational stereotypes* (1st ed.). Hoboken, New Jersey: Wiley.

Journals

Bias

Gender stereotypes have impeded women's advancement in the workplace. This paper discusses both the descriptive and prescriptive gender stereotypes and negative performance expectations that form as a result of them (Heilman, 2012).

Heilman, M. E. (2012). Gender stereotypes and workplace bias. *Research in Organizational Behavior, 32,* 113–135. https://doi.org/10.1016/j.riob.2012.11.003

This study concludes that older employees receive more severe recommendations for poor performance than younger counterparts (Rupp, Vodanovich, & Crede, 2006).

Rupp, D. E., Vodanovich, S. J., & Crede, M. (2006). Age bias in the workplace: The impact of ageism and causal attributions. *Journal of Applied Social Psychology, 36*(6), 1337–1364. https://doi.org/0.1111/j.0021-9029.2006.00062.x

This article provides recommendations of things to consider when applying work policies to minimize racial and gender bias (Bielby, 2000).

Bielby, W. T. (2000). Minimizing workplace gender and racial bias. *Contemporary Sociology, 29*(1), 120–129. https://doi.org/10.2307/2654937

Discrimination

Understand the ways to identify discrimination at work (Pager & Western, 2012).

Pager, D., & Western, B. (2012). Identifying discrimination at work: The use of field experiments. *Journal of Social Issues, 68*(2), 221–237.

A variety of different workplace discrimination types exist; this article assists in understanding them (Fuhs, 2018).

Fuhs, B. (2018, March 12). 11 types of workplace discrimination employers should be aware of. Retrieved November 23, 2019, from the Rocket Lawyer website: www.rocketlawyer. com/blog/11-types-of-workplace-discrimination-employers-should-be-aware-of-925296

Harassment

The perception of employees and their attitude toward sexual harassment are measured in the restaurant industry in addition to guidance on what policies to implement (Weber, Coats, Agrusa, Tanner, & Meche, 2008).

Weber, J., Coats, W., Agrusa, J., Tanner, J., & Meche, M. (2008). Sexual harassment in the hospitality industry: Perceptions of restaurant employees. *Journal of Human Resources in Hospitality & Tourism, 1*(1), 75–93. https://doi.org/10.1300/J171v01n01_06

Prejudice

This article discusses workplace discrimination (Fleischer, 2018; Hedegaard & Tyran, 2018).

Fleischer, C. (2018, June 29). Putting a price on prejudice. *American Economic Journal: Applied Economics*.

Hedegaard, M. S., & Tyran, J.-R. (2018). The price of prejudice. *American Economic Journal: Applied Economics*, *10*(1), 40–63. https://doi.org/10.1257/app.20150241

Promotion

This study examines the impact of practiced promotion systems, such as up-or-out systems, absolute merit-based systems, relative merit-based systems, and seniority-based systems to understand organizational promotion systems from a contingency perspective (Phelan & Lin, 2000).

Phelan, S., & Lin, Z. (2000). Promotion systems and organizational performance: A contingency model. *Computational and Mathematical Organization Theory*, *7*, 207–232. https://doi.org/10.1023/A:1011986519310

Religion

This article proposes a new organizational framework that addresses the shortcomings of existing ones in relation to human, religious, legal, and organizational dynamics (Miller & Ewest, 2015).

Miller, D. W., & Ewest, T. (2015). A new framework for analyzing organizational workplace religion and spirituality. *Journal of Management, Spirituality & Religion*, *12*(4), 305–328. https://doi.org/10.1080/14766086.2015.1054864

This study found that when employees perceive religious discrimination in their organization, their commitment and engagement are affected (Messarra, 2014).

Messarra, L. C. (2014). Religious diversity at work: The perceptual effects of religious discrimination on employee engagement and commitment. *Contemporary Management Research*, *10*, 1. https://doi.org/10.7903/cmr.12018

Stereotypes

A look at how language can subtly encourage stereotyping in the workplace and strategies to make employees and management more aware (Gassam, 2019).

Gassam, J. (2019, March 15). Are you reinforcing gender stereotypes in the workplace? *Forbes*. Retrieved from www.forbes.com/sites/janicegassam/2019/03/15/are-you-reinforcing-gender-stereotypes-in-the-workplace/#1e76be3169bb

This organizational behavior study tests how descriptive and prescriptive gender stereotypes manifest in the workplace and impede women's career advancement (Heilman, 2012).

Heilman, M. E. (2012). Gender stereotypes and workplace bias. *Research in Organizational Behavior*, *32*, 113–135. https://doi.org/10.1016/j.riob.2012.11.003

The following is a 20-year study on the processes, situational cues, and strategies to reduce stereotype threat in an organization (Walton, Murphy, & Ryan, 2015).

Walton, G. M., Murphy, M. C., & Ryan, A. M. (2015). Stereotype threat in organizations: Implications for equity and performance. *Annual Review of Organizational Psychology and Organizational Behavior*, 2(1), 523–550. https://doi.org/10.1146/annurev-orgpsych-032414-111322

Web links

Bias

This article reviews how bias impacts the workplace, what unconscious bias is, and what it looks like. In addition, the author provides a five-step guided process to mitigate bias; steps include setting expectations while gathering feedback, encouraging active participation, building bias awareness, reducing opportunities for bias through structure, and setting measurable goals that inspire fairer processes and decision-making (Sabel, 2018).

Sabel, J.-M. (2018, April 23). 5 steps to reduce bias in the workplace. Retrieved November 23, 2019, from HireVue website: www.hirevue.com/blog/5-steps-to-mitigating-bias-in-the-workplace

This article reviews the negative impact that a manager's unconscious bias can have on employees. Discussion topics include who needs to receive a raise, how you decide who gets the promotions, and most important, how to fix your unconscious bias (Heathfield, 2019).

Heathfield, S. M. (2019, February 19). What does having an open door policy at work mean for employees? Retrieved March 15, 2019, from The Balance Careers website: www.thebalancecareers.com/open-door-policy-1918203

Coaching

This article addresses six keys to building a successful coaching relationship through trust, empathy, honesty, guidance, respect, and integrity (Liska, 2019).

Liska, C. (2019, September 23). Six keys to building a successful coaching relationship. Retrieved November 24, 2019, from the Human Resources Today website: www.humanresourcestoday.com/books/coaching/?open-article-id=11605964&article-title=six-keys-to-building-a-successful-coaching-relationship&blog-domain=coachcert.com&blog-title=center-for-coaching

Diversity

This article includes four steps to make workplace diversity a reality (Meir, 2018).

Meir, S. (2018, August 22). Why workplace diversity is so important, and why it's so hard to achieve. Retrieved November 27, 2019, from the Forbes website: www.forbes.com/sites/rsmdiscovery/2018/08/22/why-workplace-diversity-is-so-important-and-why-its-so-hard-to-achieve/#7a163b0c3096

The benefits of workplace diversity are having a variety of different perspectives, increased creativity, higher innovation, faster problem-solving, better decision-making, increased profits, higher employee engagement, reduced turnover, better company reputation, and improved hiring results (Martic, 2018).

Martic, K. (2018, December 19). Top 10 benefits of diversity in the workplace. Retrieved November 27, 2019, from the blog website: www.talentlyft.com/en/blog/article/244/top-10-benefits-of-diversity-in-the-workplace-infographic-included

Feedback

Giving feedback, particularly constructive feedback, is often a stressful task. As counterintuitive as it may seem, giving feedback to a top performer can be even tougher. Top performers may not have obvious development needs, and in identifying those needs, you can sometimes feel like you're being nitpicky or over-demanding (Gallo, 2009).

Gallo, A. (2009, December 3). Giving a high performer productive feedback. *Harvard Business Review*. Retrieved from https://hbr.org/2009/12/giving-a-high-performer-produc

Insubordination

This article discusses what insubordination in the workplace is, its general elements, and five examples of it (Chris, 2015).

Chris, J. (2015, August 5). Define insubordination in the workplace. Retrieved November 27, 2019, from Joseph Chris Partners website: www.josephchris.com/define-insubordination-in-the-workplace

This article identifies nine ways to discipline insubordination in the workplace and what you need (Thibodeaux, 2017).

Thibodeaux, W. (2017, April 8). How to discipline insubordination in the workplace. Retrieved November 27, 2019, from the Chron.com website: https://smallbusiness.chron.com/discipline-insubordination-workplace-17408.html

Job description

Indeed.com provides information on how to write a job description for employers by addressing job title, job summary, responsibility and duties, and qualifications and skills and giving examples for specific occupations (Indeed, n.d.).

Indeed. (n.d.). How to write a job description. Retrieved November 27, 2019, from Indeed.com website: www.indeed.com/hire/how-to-write-a-job-description

Job specification

This article identifies practical applications of job descriptions and components of a job specification (What Is Human Resource?, n.d.).

What Is Human Resource? (n.d.). Job descriptions and job specifications. Retrieved November 27, 2019, from www.whatishumanresource.com/job-descriptions-and-job-specifications

Prejudice

This article reviews discrimination in its history, different forms, pertinent laws, remedies, and preventative solutions (Huebsch, n.d.).

Huebsch, R. (n.d.). Discrimination and prejudice in the workplace. Retrieved November 29, 2019, from the Chron.com website: https://smallbusiness.chron.com/discrimination-prejudice-workplace-4876.html

This *Forbes* article discusses emerging evidence that showcases prejudice in qualitatively different forms and recommends that it must be managed in different ways from the traditional image (Morris & Fiske, 2009).

Morris, M., & Fiske, S. (2009, November 12). The new face of workplace discrimination. Retrieved November 29, 2019, from the Forbes website: www.forbes.com/2009/11/12/discrimination-workplace-prejudice-leadership-managing-bias.html#33726c6b1b75

This *Forbes* article discusses how our unconscious biases impact the way we view others and identifies five surprising facts about prejudice at work (Swart, 2018).

Swart, T. (2018, May 21). 5 facts about prejudice at work. Retrieved November 29, 2019, from the Forbes website: www.forbes.com/sites/taraswart/2018/05/21/prejudice-at-work/#63eb020011c1

Promotion

This article looks at the impacts and preparation for when an internal employee is overlooked for a promotion (Tyler, 2007).

Tyler, K. (2007, August 1). Helping employees step up. *SHRM*. Retrieved from www.shrm.org/hr-today/news/hr-magazine/pages/0807tyler.aspx

Recruiting

Entrepreneur provides a library of articles on all aspects of the recruiting process (Monarch, n.d.).

Monarch, J. (n.d.). 3 hiring challenges leaders must overcome to build a successful team. *Entrepreneur*, *Recruiting News & Topics*. Retrieved from www.entrepreneur.com/topic/recruiting

Religion

A FAQ page created by the U.S. Equal Employment Opportunity Commission on workplace religious accommodation (U.S. Equal Employment Opportunity Commission, n.d.).

U.S. Equal Employment Opportunity Commission. (n.d.). What you should know about workplace religious accommodation. Retrieved November 29, 2019, from the U.S. Equal Employment Opportunity Commission website: www.eeoc.gov/eeoc/newsroom/wysk/workplace_religious_accommodation.cfm

The following article contains the suggested religious accommodations made by a top-tier employment law and business litigation attorney (Walker, n.d.).

Walker, J. O. (n.d.). Understanding religion in the workplace. Retrieved November 29, 2019, from the Business website: www.business.com/articles/religion-in-the-workplace/

Stereotypes

The following article presents an overview of stereotyping examples, their impact, and how to build a more diverse workplace (Leonard, 2018).

Leonard, K. (2018, November 5). How does stereotyping affect the workplace environment? Retrieved November 29, 2019, from the Chron.com website: https://smallbusiness.chron.com/stereotyping-affect-workplace-environment-78286.html

This article provides a look at the three major types of stereotypes that exist in workforces (McCoy, n.d.).

McCoy, W. (n.d.). Types of stereotypes in the workplace. Retrieved November 29, 2019, from the Woman: The Nest website: https://woman.thenest.com/types-stereotypes-workplace-12495.html

Index